COURAGEOUS CONVERSATION TESTIMONIALS

"Aotearoa New Zealand, and especially Auckland, is becoming increasingly diverse. Our learner population reflects that diversity, including Māori, Pacific, and over 100 other ethnic groups. We are striving to create an environment that enables equity of success for all. That involves learning how to engage with these learners on their terms and confronting how people of different racial backgrounds understand and interact with each other. *Courageous Conversations* provides vital insights that guide our journey."

Rick Ede, Chief Executive
Unitec Institute of Technology
Auckland, NZ

"*Courageous Conversations About Race* has guided our cultural transformation at Portland Public Schools toward becoming a more racially aware and culturally responsive institution—from our classroom instruction to our business and hiring practices. This protocol not only provides a way in to difficult conversations, it gives each of us the tools to see, own, and act upon our role in perpetuating the status quo and understanding the urgency to reframe the paradigm for the success of all students."

Carole Smith, Superintendent
Portland Public Schools
Portland, OR

"*Courageous Conversations About Race* came across my desk at a time that I had almost given up on engaging in discussions of race and equity. I was exhausted from countless painful and unproductive conversations on this sensitive topic. I quickly learned why so many people choose not to engage in these conversations—because it is hard. This book not only inspires educators and system-level leaders to courageously address what we have all become comfortable with ignoring, but also gives us concrete tools for productively entering a conversation about race."

Veronica Benavides, Doctoral Candidate
Education Leadership, Harvard University
Cambridge, MA

"In a nation that too often eschews either real dialogue or courage when it comes to issues like race and inequality, and particularly in regard to education, Glenn Singleton has demonstrated over many years just how important fearlessness can be in transforming schools and communities into places where justice is possible. The Courageous Conversation approach to enhancing equity is invaluable to the struggle for a more fair-minded and truly just America."

Tim Wise, Antiracism Educator and Author
White Like Me: Reflections on Race From a Privileged Son

"The 'so what' and 'what now' options this guide presents for self and institutional learning are clear. The 'so what' describes the necessary work in addressing the under education of 'children of color' and the 'mis-education' of white students and many current educators. The 'what now' is framed by the important message that 'this is not easy work' and it is fraught with the unaddressed dangers for those who undertake to do it. It is those dangers that allow racism to persist in our country."

Randall Lindsey, Emeritus Professor
California State University
Los Angeles, CA

"Glenn E. Singleton has provided yet another powerful and still relevant book in this useful revision. If you are serious about engaging in exercises that can truly interrogate race and unearth privilege for the purpose of obtaining equity in our schools, read this book. Indeed, this book inspired me to do my own racial autobiography, and also inspired my principalship students to start the journey to become more racially aware leaders who can skillfully lead courageous conversations. Since then they have taken action through practice, often using this volume, to make impactful changes to eradicate inequities in their schools in meaningful, life-altering ways."

Mark Anthony Gooden, PhD
M. K. Hage Centennial Professorship in Education Fellow
Director of the Principalship Program, Associate Professor
The University of Texas at Austin
Associate Editor, *Urban Education*

"The Courageous Conversations About Race (CCAR) protocol has provided significant depth to my diversity and inclusion practice at the University of Western Australia (UWA). Since the inception of our work in 2008, CCAR has provided a robust and comprehensive framework to embed cultural competence across all facets of university life. CCAR is now a regular feature on the annual UWA staff development calendar and this programming is now being emulated in fifteen universities across Australia and New Zealand."

Malcolm Fialho, Associate Director, Equity and Diversity
University of Western Australia
Perth, Australia

"The protocols of Courageous Conversation have changed my life as a leader, an educator, and fellow citizen of our forever-changing world. As a white woman, I have deepened not only my racial consciousness but also my ability to engage, both personally and professionally, in richer and truer capacities. I once heard Cornell West say that the heart of a strong, liberal education rests within the ability 'to be prepared for the conversation and to be prepared to be changed by it.' Courageous Conversations have allowed me that sort of preparation."

Ellanor N. Brizendine, Head of School
The Spence School
New York, NY

"The work Glenn is doing through *Courageous Conversations About Race* will stir you intellectually and move your personal beliefs beyond what you knew possible. This is the first approach I've seen that moves everyone along on their journey based on where they are personally first. The application of Glenn's work goes beyond education and into many sectors of our society and industries. I am excited to see how his work can impact the advertising industry. Writing mission statements and policies and coming up with programs are all boxes many companies check. That part is too easy. And I think many companies will admit to feeling stuck. Glenn's approach takes true courage to get real about one major obstacle which is the belief system I have that may block my perspectives on diversity. Cheers to Glenn for challenging the conversation!"

Keesha Jean-Baptiste, Director of Human Resources
Wieden+Kennedy
Portland, OR

TESTIMONIALS FOR THE FIRST EDITION OF *COURAGEOUS CONVERSATIONS ABOUT RACE*

"The beauty of this volume is that it is designed to help lay people—teachers, administrators, parents, community leaders, and even university professors—begin to engage in the emotionally and psychically difficult conversations about race. Glenn Singleton and Curtis Linton have offered us an important book that provides us with empirical data and well-constructed exercises to help us think through the ways that race affects our lives and our professional practices. My sincere desire is that after you have had an opportunity to read this volume you will, indeed, engage in some courageous conversations about race."

Gloria Ladson-Billings, Professor
University of Wisconsin-Madison
Author, *The Dreamkeepers*

"Challenges educators to talk in honest and open ways about race, and provides various tools to stimulate and inform the conversation. Singleton and Linton remind us that the achievement gap will not be eliminated until we learn to talk about race in ways that build bridges of understanding that lead to effective action."

Dennis Sparks, Emeritus Executive Director
Learning Forward

"Given the sensitive issues of race in our nation, schools and school leaders need tools that can illuminate the concerns, guide the discussions, and generate momentum for growth and change. This book provides the tools and resources needed to move from open dialogue to meaningful action that can make excellence and equity in schools a reality."

Monte C. Moses, Former Superintendent
Cherry Creek School District
Greenwood Village, CO

"Talking about race and its effect on academic achievement remains one of the most elusive conversations today. In their new book, Singleton and Linton help educators understand and engage in the discourse around race that affects the success of any curriculum, instructional methodology, or program implementation. The book's exercises and prompts assists school and district leadership teams in articulating those innate behaviors, beliefs, and attitudes that impair our ability to be effective in closing the racial achievement gap. I am encouraged to know that educators will be empowered and supported as we develop our personal capacity to address one of the most crucial elements of our society: the education of our children."

Yvette M. Irving, Principal
Del Roble Elementary School
San José, CA

"This is an important book that challenges one to think critically about the effects of race and student achievement. It is an invitation to sustain a strong desire for fairness and equity for all children."

SMSG Newsletter

"In an era when America seems content to sweep candid talk of race under the rug, Courageous Conversations About Race recognizes that denial isn't a prescription for interracial tolerance and social progress. The authors provide thoughtful educators with innovative instructional tools to successfully navigate the most robustly diverse nation on earth."

Hugh B. Price, Former President and CEO
National Urban League

"Singleton and Linton challenge educators to move beyond recognizing the existence of a racial achievement gap and to develop strategies to eliminate it."

Curriculum Connections, Fall 2006
School Library Journal

SECOND EDITION

COURAGEOUS CONVERSATIONS ABOUT RACE

This book is dedicated to Mom, Nana, and Granny . . . the three phenomenal women, courageous inspirations, and guiding forces lining my purpose to achieve racial equity.

SECOND EDITION

COURAGEOUS CONVERSATIONS ABOUT RACE

A **Field Guide** for Achieving Equity in Schools

GLENN E. SINGLETON

Foreword by Gloria Ladson-Billings

CORWIN
A SAGE Company

FOR INFORMATION:

Corwin
A SAGE Company
2455 Teller Road
Thousand Oaks, California 91320
(800) 233-9936
www.corwin.com

SAGE Publications Ltd.
1 Oliver's Yard
55 City Road
London EC1Y 1SP
United Kingdom

SAGE Publications India Pvt. Ltd.
B 1/I 1 Mohan Cooperative Industrial Area
Mathura Road, New Delhi 110 044
India

SAGE Publications Asia-Pacific Pte. Ltd.
3 Church Street
#10-04 Samsung Hub
Singapore 049483

Acquisitions Editor: Dan Alpert
Associate Editor: Kimberly Greenberg
Editorial Assistant: Cesar Reyes
Production Editor: Cassandra Margaret Seibel
Copy Editor: Cate Huisman
Typesetter: C&M Digitals (P) Ltd.
Proofreader: Susan Schon
Indexer: Jean Casalegno
Cover Designer: Rose Storey
Senior Manager, Multimedia Product
Development: Barbara De Hart
Marketing Manager: Stephanie Trkay

Printed in the United States of America.

A catalog record of this book is available from the Library of Congress.

ISBN 978-1-4833-8374-3

This book is printed on acid-free paper.

SUSTAINABLE FORESTRY INITIATIVE
Certified Chain of Custody
Promoting Sustainable Forestry
www.sfiprogram.org
SFI-01268
SFI label applies to text stock

19 20 21 12 11

Contents

To access the video clips, please visit www.corwin.com/CCAR
or scan the QR codes located throughout the book. To read a
QR code, you must have a smartphone or tablet with a camera.
We recommend that you download a QR code reader app that is
made specifically for your phone or tablet brand.

Foreword

In the decade since the publication of the first edition of *Courageous Conversations About Race* much has happened in our country—some wonderfully progressive things have transpired, and some horribly regressive things took place. We saw the election and reelection of the nation's first African American president. That in itself was something many of us thought we would never witness. Attendant to the election of Barack Obama came the appointment of the first African American attorney general and the appointment of the first Latina to the Supreme Court. In 2014, the Academy of Motion Picture Arts and Sciences (i.e., the Oscars) gave its Best Picture award to a film titled *Twelve Years a Slave,* which was the dramatization of the life of Solomon Northrup, a free Black man who was kidnapped and sold into slavery. The film's director was Steve McQueen, a Black man from the United Kingdom.

Clearly, the nation was changing. However, at the same time we saw amazing change and forward movement, we also witnessed some terrible setbacks. Two young African American males—Trayvon Martin and Jordan Davis—were shot and killed for what could only be described as "being Black." Martin had a confrontation with a neighborhood watch participant, who shot the 17-year-old for "looking suspicious." Martin's assailant, George Zimmerman, was acquitted of the murder because of Florida's "stand your ground" statute that permits citizens to defend themselves if they feel threatened.

Jordan Davis sat in an SUV with his friends. As the boys sat in a service station with their radio blasting, Michael Davis Dunn asked them to turn down their music and then inexplicably fired shots into the vehicle and drove off. Although Dunn was convicted of attempting to murder the other three passengers in the car, he was not convicted of Jordan Davis's murder.

As I write this foreword, we are in the aftermath of another devastating death of an unarmed Black male youth—Mike Brown of Ferguson, Missouri. This particular death at the hands of a police officer has had a chilling effect on the Black community, and it has sparked protests, rioting, and looting in that metropolitan St. Louis community. Black parents are once again asking themselves what, if anything, they can do to keep their children safe.

Each of these events sent chills through African American communities across the nation and forced us to question the value of Black life in the United States. On some level people could argue that these events are unhappy coincidences that do not represent anything systemic about race in America. The shooters are not connected in any way, and the outcome of each case may be quite different from the others. They can be read as separate and distinct unfortunate incidents. However, even a cursory look at some of the large data sets that speak to the differences in life chances between Black and White people demonstrate how separate and unequal the nation remains around race. US Census Bureau data show that the median household income in 2012 was $57,009 for Whites and $33,321 for Blacks. Average household wealth in 2010 was $631,530 for Whites and $98,305 for Blacks. The percentage of the populace in poverty in 2011 was 9.8% for Whites and 27.5% for Blacks. The percentage of children in poverty for that same year was 12.5% for Whites and 37.4% for Blacks. The United States has more people incarcerated than any other highly technological nation. About 2.3 million people are in jail or prison, and more than 1 million of them are African Americans. It is interesting that the United States does not have a rising crime rate. It has a rising incarceration rate, because it has decided to arrest people for things it formerly sent them to treatment for.

I cite the data for these larger systemic issues because we are hearing from both sides of the ideological spectrum that we have "already dealt with race." From the right we hear that we are a "colorblind" society. From the left we learn we are a "postracial" society. I contend that both perspectives are incorrect. We are deeply divided by race, and race remains the topic around which we still cannot have open, honest, courageous conversations. This book, the second edition of *Courageous Conversations About Race,* is an important beginning place for those who will first admit that we are "not yet done" with race and, second, commit to engaging in forthright, honest talk with people who have had very different experiences around race.

For those who believe that there is nothing more to be said about race or who feel we are suffering from "racial fatigue," I remind you that this is not a concept that those who are victimized by racism constructed. It is one that was ascribed to us. We entered the society "raced." We come to school "raced." We apply for jobs "raced." We enter the market place "raced." We can never leave our race at home or on a shelf. So because we are plagued by the social construct, we have to find ways to live our lives and participate in society with one aspect of our identity that seems to enter the room before we do.

Americans are great believers in talking as a way toward solutions. People with psychological and emotional challenges recognize the value of talk therapy. Couples with relationship struggles understand the value in counseling that opens up the lines of communication to improve their relationships. Our entire government structure—executive, legislative, and judicial branches—depends heavily on people talking. Our executive enters into "talks" with other world leaders. Our Congressional representatives talk through the legislative process to enact laws. Our judges make decisions as they listen to legal advocates talk through their positions on cases. Most contracts come as a result of people talking about what the terms should be. However, whenever someone suggests talking about race, often we are told, "We wouldn't have these problems if we would just stop talking about race!" Nothing could be further from the truth.

Courageous Conversations About Race (2nd ed.) is our opportunity to enlarge and enrich the conversation, particularly among educators. I believe that most educators do have the best interests of students at heart. I believe that most educators want their students to be successful, both for their students' futures and for their own sense of accomplishment and satisfaction. But, I also believe that most educators do not know enough about how race and culture impact everyone's lives—the students, their parents, the community, and the educators. Lacking that understanding typically leads to a series of missteps that result in a lack of trust and ability to work together. Having the courageous and yes, hard conversations is where we begin.

We begin by challenging our own assumptions about who is a "good" student, a "good" parent, or a "good" teacher. We ask ourselves, what are the inherent biases that we enter schools and classrooms with? Have we ever asked (or thought):

- This work will be too hard for my [insert race] students.
- These parents just don't care.
- These children can't control themselves.
- These families don't value education.
- These children need discipline/structure.
- These children lack exposure/experiences.
- These children are not "ready" for school.

The above statements are but a few that I have encountered over the years. They are generally grounded in anecdotal experiences, not evidentiary knowledge. Scholars like Luis Moll have documented "funds of knowledge" in communities of color that educators know little or nothing about. The statements above reflect negative experiences and/or hearsay that become instantiated in the lore of the school. The data are clear that low- and working-class families start with aspirations for their children that are similar to those of middle-class families. It is only after they come face to face with lowered expectations from school personnel, substandard schools, limited resources, and the realities of racism that they adjust those aspirations down.

Another thing that Courageous Conversation will help educators do is become more observant of the ways that race and racism are operating in their schools. Engaging in these tough conversations will help educators to see inequity at work, as in some of the following examples:

- Gifted and Talented Education (GATE) and AP classes composed solely of White and Asian students
- Special education classrooms where Black students are overrepresented
- School orchestras with no Black, Brown, or Indigenous students
- Suspension and expulsion data showing that a disproportionate number of Black, Brown, and Indigenous students are suspended or expelled
- Remedial classrooms with high proportions of Black, Brown, and Indigenous students
- Honors classes with low proportions of Black, Brown, and Indigenous students

These examples should provoke important questions about how these programmatic racial inequities have emerged and what school personnel are doing to maintain them. Participating in Courageous Conversation helps make us more cognizant of the perspectives of others and helps us develop "informed empathy" rather than sympathy toward our students, their families, and their communities. Ultimately, Courageous Conversation helps us to be better educated, and that is exactly what every educator should want. *Courageous Conversations About Race* (2nd ed.) is a perfect place to begin.

Gloria Ladson-Billings
Kellner Family Chair in Urban Education
University of Wisconsin–Madison

Acknowledgments

I would like to acknowledge the following for their generous assistance, support, and dedicated efforts in helping all students succeed:

Chapel Hill-Carrboro City Schools
Cherry Creek Schools
St. Paul Public Schools
Pacific Educational Group, Inc.
Oak Grove School District
San José State University, Urban High School Leadership Program

School Improvement Network

Jamie Almazán
Michelle Bierman
J. Brooks
Courtlandt Butts
David Davidson
Malcolm Fialho
Gabriel Gima
Nettie Collins-Hart
Rev Hillstrom
Andrea Johnson
Leidene King
Melissa Krull
J. Lagoo
Chris Lim

Curtis Linton
Maria Martinez
Graig Meyer
Pamela Noli
Neil G. Pedersen
Janet L. Perkins
Patrick Sánchez
Valeria Silva
Wendell "EJ" Singleton
Jackie Thompson
Pablo Vega
Luis Versalles
Frederique Wynberg
UnSuk Zucker

The contributions of the following reviewers are gratefully acknowledged:

Stephen Bergen
Principal
Lab School for Creative Learning
Ft. Collins, CO

Dr. Karen Hayes
Assistant Professor
Department of Educational Administration and Supervision
University of Nebraska
Omaha, NE

Elizabeth J. Lolli
Superintendent
Barberton City School District
Barberton, OH

Franklin CampbellJones
Associate Professor of Education Leadership
Rowan University
Glassboro, NJ

About the Author

Glenn E. Singleton is the president of Pacific Educational Group, Inc. (PEG). In 1992, he founded PEG to address systemic educational inequity by providing support to school systems in meeting the needs of underserved students of color. As chief executive officer, Singleton introduces PEG's Framework for Systemic Racial Equity Transformation to preK–12 district administrators and higher education executive leadership throughout the United States of America and various countries around the world.

Singleton and his team design comprehensive racial equity support for partner school districts and institutions of higher education. PEG helps educators heighten their awareness of institutional racism and develop effective strategies for eliminating systemic racial achievement disparities. In 1995, Singleton developed Beyond Diversity, a nationally recognized professional learning series aimed at helping educators identify and examine the powerful intersection of race and schooling. Beyond Diversity introduces the Courageous Conversation protocol and provides the foundation for all PEG-led programs.

Singleton appears on radio and television and has authored two books and written numerous articles on the topics of racial equity, institutional racism, leadership, and staff development for national journals, magazines, and newspapers. He served on the conference planning committee for Learning Forward (formerly National Staff Development Council) and annually produces the National Summit for Courageous Conversation. He is the 2003 recipient of the Eugene T. Carothers Human Relations Award for outstanding service in the fields of human rights and human relations. In 2009, Singleton was elected to serve as a commissioner on the California State Board of Education African American Commission.

Singleton was an adjunct professor of educational leadership at San José State University from 2004 to 2012. He has worked with teachers and administrators in various countries throughout Africa and has lectured at universities throughout the United States, Australia, and New Zealand. He is founder and member of the board of advisors of Foundation for a College Education of East

Video

About the Author:
Glenn E. Singleton
www.corwin.com/
CCAR

Palo Alto, California. Singleton earned his master's degree from the Graduate School of Education at Stanford University and his bachelor's degree from the University of Pennsylvania. A member of Phi Beta Sigma Fraternity, Incorporated, Singleton is a native of Baltimore, Maryland, and currently resides in San Francisco, California.

Introduction

Race matters. Race matters in part because of the long history of racial minorities being denied access to the political process. . . . Race also matters because of persistent racial inequality in society—inequality that cannot be ignored and that has produced stark socioeconomic disparities. . . . This refusal to accept the stark reality that race matters is regrettable. The way to stop discrimination on the basis of race is to speak openly and candidly on the subject of race, and to apply the Constitution with eyes open to the unfortunate effects of centuries of racial discrimination. . . . As members of the judiciary tasked with intervening to carry out the guarantee of equal protection, we ought not sit back and wish away, rather than confront, the racial inequality that exists in our society.

—Hon. Sonya Sotomayor, Supreme Court Justice (2014)

I decided to dedicate the first edition of *Courageous Conversations About Race* to Wendell "EJ" Singleton, the youngest member of my extended family. Then, I spoke of how my family lovingly sent a precocious, inquisitive boy off to school for the first time. EJ started school with pride and joy, but—like so many young African American boys—he was greeted by a system that did not expect much from him and had already determined much for him. In two short years of formal schooling, EJ had been labeled a failure, special needs, at risk, and ADD. History suggests that EJ will find it virtually impossible to shake loose from these deficit descriptors. Nearly a decade later, as I sit down to revise *Courageous Conversations About Race,* EJ, now a senior in the Baltimore public school system, is poised to graduate after a long and perilous journey through institutions determined to make him an unfortunate statistic.

Then and now, my reasons for writing this book remain the same. EJ and the many Black, Brown, Southeast Asian, and Indigenous children who will continue to attend US public schools deserve qualified and skilled teachers who love them instead of fear them. These students deserve competent instructors who understand, value, and affirm their colorful African American, Latino, Indigenous, Asian, and other cultures. They are owed a procession of teachers and administrators who will be skilled in drawing out their innate brilliance, curiosity, and creativity.

Roughly 40 years ago, also in the Baltimore public school system, Mrs. Hall, Mrs. Sandifer, and Mrs. Thomas, to name only a few, effectively taught me in the way my cousin EJ deserved to be instructed. Why is it, then, that EJ's professional educators, more often than not, proved to be incapable of meeting his academic, social, and emotional needs?

For 14 years, my family has worried about EJ's spirit as he traveled the mean streets of Baltimore into the meaner hallways of his public schools. The daily affirmations EJ recites became a weak defense against a system that predetermined him to be incapable of achieving at a high level. Rather than point out all that is wrong with our schools and the adults who inhabit them, however, this book has been written to support educators and assist them in meeting the needs of EJ and the thousands of other students of color and indigenous students like him.

■ ■ ■

Given the increasing number of young Black males growing up in Baltimore, Chicago, Sanford, Jacksonville, and Ferguson who have not lived to see their high school graduation day, I feel the greatest sense of relief that EJ is alive, and also my family is relieved that he is finally done with a traumatic, protracted episode in compulsory schooling. Thus the untimely and unexplainable killings of Trayvon Martin, Jordan Davis, and Michael Brown, as Dr. Ladson-Billings so eloquently explains in her foreword, reveal America's most despicable racial circumstance and perhaps the boldest indication that our society is not advancing toward an end to racial injustice. In this wealthy, technologically advanced, highly educated nation, more and more of our darkest children are dying on the streets, literally. Still, this uncontested reality polarizes adults along racial lines, not as we attempt to discover meaningful solutions to these brutal slaughters, but in our racially balkanized expression of beliefs and determinations regarding the cause of these senseless deaths. I am fed up with this aspiring beacon of the free world being positioned in an interracial holding pattern, in which our highest leaders across the various sectors practice, as Dr. Barbara Sizemore wrote, "walking in circles." This book is my contribution toward breaking that cycle of cross-racial silence, ignorance, mistrust, judgment, and assassination.

MORE WALKING IN CIRCLES: AFFIRMATIVE ACTION

Back in 2003 when Curtis Linton and I began writing the first edition of *Courageous Conversations About Race,* the US Supreme Court had just ruled on its latest challenge to the use of affirmative action in university admissions processes. *Grutter v. Bollinger* involved a racial discrimination claim by Barbara Grutter, a White female applicant who was denied admission to the University of Michigan Law School. The court ruled that race could be considered in the admissions process when other factors were being evaluated, and that such consideration did not amount to the kind of racial quota system that was determined to be unconstitutional under the 1978 *Regents of the University of California v. Bakke.*

Persistent legal attacks on Affirmative Action, espousing the belief that such policies award preferential treatment to students of color, fail to acknowledge and calculate the benefit White students receive from university systems steeped in residual racism. By this I mean institutions in which the faculty composition, perspective, teaching method, and culture are decidedly and overwhelmingly White. Nearly a decade later as I revise *Courageous Conversations About Race,* the most threatened federal policy in our nation continues to be Affirmative Action. And while we can celebrate our first Latina Supreme Court Justice, the Honorable Sonya Sotomayor, being confirmed to the bench, her lone voice does not ring loud and strong enough to roll back the tide or calm the resistance of those intent on abolishing the only regulatory process that successfully challenges systemic racism and offers remedy to the resulting centuries of federal government sponsored and perpetuated racial inequality.

On June 24, 2013, the Supreme Court decided on the case of *Fisher v. University of Texas,* in which two female high school students argued that they had been unfairly denied admission to the university's entering freshman class because they were White. Ms. Fisher's case is the latest claim that follows the growing and predictable assaults on the use of Affirmative Action in higher education, often by White females, who may be failing to recognize the importance of racially diverse perspective and experience in the nation's undergraduate, graduate, and professional schools. Without a vigorous Affirmative Action mandate, not only would people of color (and women) possibly not be serving as justices on the highest court in the land, but more personally, I definitely would not be in a position to write this book today.

But despite the indisputably positive impact of affirmative action, persons of color who persist through to graduation more than pay the fullest price each day in the academy, as we stare down predictably low institutional expectations, isolation from family and peers, and racial humiliation. Simply put, race matters, and racism is alive and well in 2014 just as it was in 2006 when the first edition of *Courageous Conversations About Race* was published. And as Justice Sotomayor states, "The only way to stop discrimination based on race is to talk openly and candidly on the subject of race. . . . We ought not sit back and wish away, rather than confront, the racial inequality that exists in our society."

THE BACKDROP FOR COURAGEOUS CONVERSATION

A consequence of federal legislation such as the No Child Left Behind Act, and more recently, Race to the Top and Common Core State Standards, has been a heighted awareness among educators and the general public of the statistical gaps in achievement between White students and most students of color and indigenous students. I believe that a primary and essential way of addressing these gaps is to create a culture and provide structures that encourage ALL educators to discuss race openly, honestly, and as safely as possible in the school environment.

Contrary to popular assumption, this is an issue of concern not only to educators and families who are people of color or indigenous but to all; the welfare of all students—no matter what their race—depends on *all of us* succeeding at this conversation.

This is a book about race and, specifically, talking about race. In schools, as well as in other agencies and institutions, race plays a primary role in sustaining if not widening the omnipresent achievement gaps. But educators have not been willing to enter into discussion about this extraordinarily complex and emotionally charged topic. Thus collectively, we as educators have also not become very skillful at talking about race, and therefore we have failed to develop the requisite capacity to examine and address the impact of race on learning—neither our own learning nor that of our students. I write this book to provide a protocol and strategy—Courageous Conversation—that educators can use to engage, sustain, and deepen the conversation about race in their schools.

With so much written in the area of achievement disparity, the last thing the field needs is another book pointing out the obvious—that we have not quite figured out how to educate all children well. What I offer, instead, is a detailed, thoughtful, ongoing, and influential strategy for having conversations about race that advances our understanding of how and why the racial achievement gap persists in most schools, across all economic levels, and among native speakers of English and English learners alike. It is precisely because few educators have explicitly and unapologetically investigated the taboo intersection of race and achievement that I offer this book. My rationale is quite simple: We will never eliminate racial achievement disparities unless we have conversations about race.

I have been keenly aware of my own racial identity as a Black American since I was in the seventh grade, but growing up White, my former coauthor, Curtis Linton, was unaware of his equally powerful racial identity until he began working with me while producing and writing a program for *The Video Journal of Education* entitled "Closing the Achievement Gap." I coauthored the first edition of *Courageous Conversations About Race* with Curtis Linton, because I believed that many readers might better relate to the racial narrative and experience of a White person. While I still believe this to be true, I also want readers to consider that much of the slow racial progress in the United States is precisely due to White people's inability and/or unwillingness to listen to and learn from people of color and indigenous people about that which afflicts and affects us on a daily basis. Curtis discovered in our writing journey that another challenge for many White people, educators included, is their overall lack of trust in people of color and especially in our ability to honestly share our truths about race. After he made this discovery, Curtis developed a more expansive, less distorted personal racial consciousness. Simply because he chose to start believing me, as a Black man, and my narratives depicting race and racism in my life, he was able to understand, in a more profound way, how race impacts his life and, more recently, the lives of his two adopted children of color.

■ ■ ■

This conundrum of White disbelief, as well as the almost universal challenge many of us face when trying to learn from racially marginalized people, is one reason I have continued to advance some critical insights of Curtis Linton in this second edition. Although Curtis didn't actively participate in this revision, his story of an evolving racial consciousness was meaningful to many readers of the first edition. Another reason I will continue to introduce Curtis's voice is because he has visited hundreds of the most effective schools and school systems across North America, documenting on video their effective practices and creating training resources that help to duplicate those successes elsewhere.

Purposely in this latest edition of *Courageous Conversations About Race,* I am also insisting that all readers, White, indigenous, and of color, develop greater proficiency in learning from a Black person. Today, Curtis and I continue to use this very important skill and awareness to guide us in our mutual racial discoveries as well as in our racial equity leadership development. Within this context, we work closely to come to a better understanding of our own separate and interdependent racial experiences. While Curtis continues to view his personal and professional work through a lens of racial equity, his focus has not been specifically on developing and advancing Courageous Conversation.

Since publication of the first edition of *Courageous Conversations About Race,* I have guided thousands of educators all over the world in examining themselves racially, and I have helped leaders develop the culture and structure necessary to eliminate racial achievement disparities. I have guided my talented and skilled team at Pacific Educational Group (PEG) to focus exclusively on discovering ways to perfect this method for talking about race and to determine how it gets incorporated as a framework in systems of education and beyond. Today, PEG develops and leads Courageous Conversation communities of practice throughout the preK–12 and higher education sectors in the United States and Canada as well as in universities across Australia and New Zealand.

■　■　■

To provide some background information about my work, I introduced Courageous Conversation in a two-day seminar entitled Beyond Diversity, which I developed and first facilitated in 1995. Nearly two decades later, hundreds of people continue to enroll in the Beyond Diversity seminar each week, be it in its traditional, face-to-face format or through the more recently produced online platform. For many in a room or online, it is the first time they have ever been encouraged to openly and honestly discuss race with someone of a skin color different than their own. At the seminar's conclusion, the facilitator offers participants some concluding thoughts to answer some predictable yet unspoken queries. Many White people, emotionally moved by what they have heard, ask, "So what do I do now?" "How can I stop being racist?" "How can you forgive me for having been racist?" "How can I fix this?" My answer in 1995 and now, almost 20 years later, is still quite simple and still viewed as profound: "Just believe me."

Just believe me—is that all? Believe me when I say that I experience racial profiling almost daily. Believe me when I say that my White neighbors treat me differently or more accurately, "deficitly." Believe that I am a victim of lowered expectations, that I am accused of succeeding *only* because of affirmative action, and that I actually have a lifetime of accumulated racist and racially discriminatory experiences.

Courageous Conversation, as a strategy, begins with the premise that initially, educational leaders collectively view themselves and the schooling enterprise to be inherently non-racist. In fact, their tightly held beliefs and understandings regarding the significance of race make it difficult for teachers to comprehend, examine, and rectify the very ways in which race dramatically impacts achievement.

Unfortunately, the racial situation in schools only mirrors what takes place in the larger society. John Dewey suggested that schools must be the engine of social transformation. In this second edition of *Courageous Conversations About Race*, I have set out to redefine the educational context and then provide the content and process for educators to grapple personally with race as a critical sociopolitical construct. In our work with a variety of schools, districts, universities, agencies, and regional programs, my team at PEG and I have found that Courageous Conversation effectively enables leaders to develop and operate from a transformed racial philosophy that guides their policy analysis, institutional restructuring, and programmatic reform. Such exceptional racial equity work, beginning with Courageous Conversation, in education systems will certainly have a dramatic and positive impact on the broader society and our larger world.

As educators engage in, sustain, and deepen interracial dialogue about race with each other and with students and their families, systems then can truly support all children in achieving at higher levels. As schools work toward equity, they will narrow the gaps between the highest- and lowest-performing groups and eliminate the racial predictability regarding which groups achieve in the highest- and lowest-performing categories.

A DECADE OF LEARNING: THE NEW EDITION OF *COURAGEOUS CONVERSATIONS ABOUT RACE*

Courageous Conversations About Race is divided into three parts reflecting the three essential characteristics of racial equity leadership: *passion, practice,* and *persistence.* In the first part, "Passion," the book begins by exploring the landscape of educational reform and exposing the issue of race as a most devastating phenomenon impacting the lives and learning of all children. I urge my readers to maintain an unwavering focus on race, rather than income level or other variables of difference that may be more comfortable topics of discussion. The next series of chapters, "Practice," takes the reader on a step-by-step journey into the race conversation, providing the language, markers, tools, and insights necessary to begin and stay in the dialogue. Finally, in "Persistence," educators will learn about the leadership that is necessary to eliminate racial achievement gaps.

This book provides a foundation for those educational leaders at the system and school level who are willing and ready to begin or accelerate their journey toward educational equity and excellence for all children. This includes superintendents, board members, district administrators, principals, teacher leaders, and members of the broader community. It is designed to assist in facilitating effective dialogue about the racial issues that impact student achievement. As you progress through each chapter, you will be prompted to reflect on your learning and, in particular, your own racial experience. At the end of each chapter, you will find implementation activities that you can use with your colleagues to lead them in discussing the impact of race in the classroom. If you are a leader at the school or district level, this book will guide you in engaging your staff in a conversation about race as a first step in eliminating racial achievement disparities.

As you address the prompts and complete the exercises I have carefully embedded in each chapter, you will feel a surge in your own will, skill, knowledge, and capacity to lead others through the same journey. Although I urge you to avoid involving others too soon in your own developmental process, I realize and predict that at some point you will not be able to resist ushering your friends, family, and colleagues into a Courageous Conversation. I have witnessed this process unfold for thousands of educators over the past two decades.

Closing the teaching and learning gap requires that teachers think about their craft differently. As EJ graduates from high school, his teachers, both past and future, certainly have their work cut out for them, as many of them need to envision and practice pedagogy in ways that they have never seen or experienced before. But a teacher's faith in undiscovered potential, along with an unwavering belief that our families really do want the best schooling for our children, can sustain them in this work.

I am writing a second edition of this book in the hope that our readers embrace what I view as a moral imperative to arrive at a deeper understanding of race and racism. I suspect most educators already believe that racism is morally wrong. The challenge for us is to advance our shared moral position into a realizable and comprehensive foundation for challenging systemic racism each day, whenever and wherever it appears. Our students deserve nothing less.

Given the magnitude of race as a topic and the long history of racial achievement disparities, no one book can solve this educational problem and address the broader societal issues that underlie it. What this book can do is get us pointed in the right direction by engaging, sustaining, and deepening the conversation about race, racial identity development, and systemic racism. In contrast to the first edition of *Courageous Conversations About Race*, the book you now hold offers more than a decade of developed insight from working around the world with educators, community members, students, and families at differing levels of will, skill, knowledge, and capacity to talk about race. From this inspiring work, I have been able to craft new ways in which Courageous Conversation practitioners and facilitators can bolster our courage, enhance our skills, and accelerate our achievement of results. The second edition offers more focused and relevant voices from a diverse group of racial equity leaders in the form of racial autobiographies and through links to online videos accessible through QR codes. Finally, this book introduces the reader to St. Paul Public Schools, a Minnesota school system that has, for more than four years, stayed on track with Courageous Conversation and consistently implemented the Systemic Racial Equity Transformation Framework with fidelity. More than ever, it is my hope and belief that thoroughly immersing yourself in this text and practicing Courageous Conversations will create the lasting foundation on which magnificent new relationships between teacher and student are built and higher achievement is gained.

To my ancestors and elders who have provided the historic foundation on which my contemporary understanding and insights about race are built, I thank you. I also recognize that without the patience, practice, and persistence of our partner districts and other educational leaders throughout this nation and around the world, I could have never discovered the deep and lasting impact of Courageous Conversation in today's schools. My most sincere acknowledgment of the many who have contributed greatly to this book is seen in my efforts to capture their work and words in a thoughtful and thorough way. Writing about these transformative dialogues represents my hardest work yet. But the greatest learning also occurs as we engage, sustain, and deepen the interracial conversation about race in schools and districts. Through this transformative work, student success will increase, racial achievement disparities will disappear, and you will personally be impacted as you deepen your discovery about the impact of race in your life. And now, it is time for you to join me on this journey to a new possibility!

ONE

Breaking the Silence

Ushering in Courageous Conversation About Race

Of all the civil rights for which the world has struggled and fought for 5,000 years, the right to learn is undoubtedly the most fundamental. We must insist upon this to give our children the fairness of a start which will equip them with such an array of facts and such an attitude toward truth that they can have a real chance to judge what the world is and what its greater minds have thought it might be!

—W. E. B. DuBois (1949/1970, pp. 230–231)

What is a child's right to learn? This is a fundamental question that we pose to you, the reader of this book. Our assumption is that most educators enter the profession believing that *every* child has a right to learn, whatever the child's race, culture, or economic class.

In reaction to the preceding quote, Linda Darling-Hammond (1997) asks, "How [can we] reinvent the system of US public education so that it ensures a right to learn for all its students, who will enter a world in which a failure to learn is fast becoming an insurmountable defeat?" (p. 2). There is no time left for educators in the United States to let this question linger.

Of particular interest to me is the topic of race and its role in the education of this country's children. I believe that race—and thus racism, in both individual and institutionalized forms, whether acknowledged or unacknowledged—plays a primary role in students' struggle to achieve at high levels. I am writing this book with hopes that the reader shares my moral understanding of this issue and is willing to engage with me to come to a deeper understanding of race and racism. Most educators inherently believe that racism is morally wrong. The challenge is to advance that moral position into real, comprehensive, cognitive, and intellectual foundations of understanding that will allow us to challenge racism in our everyday personal interactions and professional practices.

THE RACIAL ACHIEVEMENT GAP AND OTHER SYSTEMIC RACIAL DISPARITIES

Video

The Racial
Achievement Gap
*www.corwin.com/
CCAR*

The significant achievement gap that exists between Black, Brown, and Indigenous students and their White and some Asian counterparts became more publicized than ever due to the federal No Child Left Behind Act of 2001. This is indeed a *racial* achievement gap, because the variance in performance exists between students of different skin colors. To begin addressing this *racial* gap—intentionally, explicitly, and comprehensively—is the purpose of this book.

With all of the recent attention given the achievement gap, which has been thoroughly investigated and evidenced by the Education Trust (2013a, 2013b), Ruth Johnson (2002), Belinda Williams (2007), and countless other esteemed colleagues in the field, I am not asking *if* the achievement gap exists. My intention is to move educators beyond acknowledging the reality of the racial gap toward developing a strategy for eliminating it. I want to illuminate a primary reason the gap persists and propose a strategy for its elimination. My primary and essential question to you is as follows:

> To what degree do you and your system have the will, skill, knowledge, and capacity to understand and address issues of race as they relate to existing racial achievement disparities?

Based on our experience, few classrooms, fewer whole schools, and far fewer entire school districts can offer up educators who are truly willing and prepared to address the racial achievement gap head-on. Considering that the racial composition of our student population is rapidly changing, how will educators who are the racial inverse of the emerging student population arrive at a new and necessary level of cultural proficiency and instructional effectiveness? Whereas the number of students of color continues to increase dramatically, the number of teachers of color is actually dropping. Data from KidsCount (2014) indicate that more than 73% of all children in our most populous state, California, are non-White, and hence the majority of public school students in California may be assumed to be non-White also. More recently, demographic studies determine 2014 to be the last year in which White students represent a statistical majority in US public schools. Thus, there is a dramatic need to build interracial knowledge and understanding so that the adults in schools comprehend the needs of their children.

Essential Questions

Related to the aforementioned systemic preparedness question are three essential questions, adapted from *Understanding by Design* by Grant Wiggins and Jay McTighe (1998, p. 179), that all educators need to address in their work in school:

1. What is it that students should know and be able to do?

2. How will we know when students know it and are able to do it?

3. What do we do when we discover that students don't know it and are not yet able to do it?

In this book, I take these questions further by framing them in terms of the personal and professional inquiry and action educators must consider as they address the racial achievement gap:

1. What is it that educators should know and be able to do to narrow the racial achievement gap?

2. How will educators know when they are experiencing success in their efforts to narrow the racial achievement gap?

3. What do educators do as they discover what they don't yet know and are not yet able to do to eliminate the racial achievement gap?

If they don't ask these questions, educators are left searching—knowing there is a problem but not knowing what to do about it.

External Factors

Frustrated by the racial achievement gap's existence, educators often blame social, economic, or political factors external to the school and unrelated to the quality of curriculum and instruction. I have found this kind of blaming to be insufficient at best and destructive at worst when trying to address racial achievement disparities. Families send their children off to school each day, and it is the educators' responsibility to greet students with the highest-quality, most rigorous academic instruction and emotional support possible.

In his article "The Canary in the Mine," Mano Singham (1998) disputes common and simplistic explanations that educators invoke to explain the persistence of the racial achievement gap. Among these are

The "liberal interpretation," which claims that "educational disparities are caused by socioeconomic disparities" (Singham, 1998, p. 10). However, as has been well documented elsewhere and will be evidenced later in this book, racial achievement gaps exist even among students within the same socioeconomic levels. In other words, poverty alone cannot explain the gap. Specifically, if this poverty explanation were valid, most students at similar family income levels would be performing at nearly the same level in school. In our work, we have discovered that poor White students, on average, outperform poor Black students, and this pattern persists at the middle and upper income levels as well. Even more alarming are data that indicate poor White students may outperform middle-income Black and Brown students.

The "conservative" or "sociopathological model," which says that because the civil rights movement removed legal barriers to Black advancement, "various social pathologies within the Black community (lumped under the euphemism 'Black culture') must be at fault" (Singham, 1998, p. 10). Thus, supporters of this model "tend to lecture Black Communities constantly about the need for a wholesale spiritual awakening to traditional virtues and the work ethic" (Singham, 1998, p. 10). The problem, however, with this approach is that the White critics are—in essence—asking the Black community to just "act White." As Singham (1998) continues, "Given the behavior of Whites during the time of slavery, to ask Blacks to regard Whites as role models for virtuousness seems presumptuous, to put it mildly" (p. 10).

The "genetic model" is the third view put forth to explain the achievement gap. For example, Herrnstein and Murray's (1994) *The Bell Curve* concludes that "educational disparity is a fact of nature, the result of long-term evolutionary selection that has resulted in Blacks' simply not having the genetic smarts to compete equally with Whites" (according to Singham, 1998, p. 10). Singham strongly refutes this view. Furthermore, this argument has been thoroughly debunked by extensive research, such as that presented by Kati Haycock (Education Trust, 2009).

Educational Responsibility

To move beyond these refutable and hotly debated explanations and arrive at a deeper and more useful understanding of the racial achievement gap, educators need to stop placing blame on the places and people beyond their control. By doing this, they will avoid faulting children for who they are and what their background is. I advocate a new strategy, because it encourages educators to engage in difficult self-assessment and to take responsibility for what they can control: the quality of their relationships with colleagues, students, and their families, both in the classroom and throughout the school community. My message seems to be one that many reputable educators previously have offered with little apparent success. We must consider why the following critical counternarratives to that of blaming children of color and their families for the poor quality schooling they receive continue to fall on deaf ears.

According to Linda Darling-Hammond (2010),

Both segregation of schools and inequality in funding have increased in many states over the past two decades, leaving a growing share of

African-American and Hispanic students in highly segregated apartheid schools that lack qualified teachers; up-to-date textbooks and materials; libraries, science labs and computers; and safe, adequate facilities.

Clearly we need more than a new set of national goals to mobilize a dramatically more successful educational system. We also need more than pilot projects, demonstrations, innovations and other partial solutions. We need to take the education of poor children as seriously as we take the education of the rich, and we need to create systems that routinely guarantee all the elements of educational investment to all children.

To meet twenty-first-century demands, the United States needs to move beyond a collection of disparate and shifting reform initiatives to a thoughtful, well-organized and well-supported set of policies that will enable young people to thrive in the new world they are entering. We must also finally make good on the American promise to make education available to all on equal terms, so that every member of this society can realize a productive life and contribute to the greater welfare. (pp. 1–2)

Three decades earlier, Tomas A. Arciniega (1977) put it this way:

Public education has successfully shifted the blame for the failure of schools to meet the needs of minority students on to the shoulders of the clients they purport to serve. They have pulled off the perfect crime, for they can never be held accountable, since the reason for failure in school is said to be the fault of poor homes, cultural handicaps, linguistic deficiencies, and deprived neighborhoods. The fact that schools are geared primarily to serve monolingual, White, middle-class and Anglo clients is never questioned. (p. 123)

I, too, believe that the racial achievement gap exists and persists because fundamentally schools are not designed to educate students of color and indigenous students, and educators continue to lack the will, skill, knowledge, and capacity to affirm racial diversity. Consequently, educators need to begin a deep and thorough examination of their beliefs and practices in order to "re-create" schools so that they become places where all students do succeed.

Change is tough—any change! Thus, another primary challenge to addressing racial achievement disparities is that school systems struggle with change. If school systems truly care about *all* children, then why have they not been more willing to address the racial achievement gaps? How can educators in good conscience allow a racial achievement gap to persist? Are they unaware of some of the inherent racial inequities or racial biases in the system? Or are they perhaps conscious of the inequities but unwilling to address them? It certainly seems easier not to deal with the hard work of change, because it requires educators to be innovative in their search for a new solution and courageous in the face of those resistors who wish to at least maintain and perhaps even perpetuate the status quo.

Janice E. Hale (2004) recently wrote, "It is hypocritical to talk about 'equal opportunity' when the system ensures never-ending advantages for upper-income White students" (p. 34). The disparity is easy to see; what remains invisible is a focused and concerted effort to adequately and successfully address the racial achievement gap.

THREE CRITICAL FACTORS

Through my fieldwork and research, I have defined three critical factors necessary for school systems to eliminate the racial achievement gap: passion, practice, and persistence. Without a focus on developing and nurturing these critical factors, a system quickly disengages from an intentional desire to change how students are taught and supported in their learning. The three factors for closing the racial achievement gap can be described as follows.

Passion

Passion is defined as the level of connectedness educators bring to racial equity work and to district, school, or classroom equity transformation. One's passion must be strong enough to overwhelm institutional inertia, resistance to change, and resilience in maintaining the status quo. Furthermore, passion is required to confront these challenges, because our society as a whole—despite what may be said—continuously proves unwilling to support schools financially or politically to the degree that is needed to bring about deep and lasting change. But passion is insufficient if it is not translated into transformed beliefs about one's own intraracial and interracial relationships and practices; these beliefs in turn prompt improved teaching and learning for every child, in every school, every day.

Practice

Practice refers to the essential individual and institutional actions taken to effectively educate every student to his or her full potential. Substantial knowledge exists, in the form of research-based practices, about what works in the classroom for students of color and indigenous students. Educators need to develop and engage this knowledge and these practices. Because the most effective practices are infrequently amplified, the racial achievement gap might legitimately be seen as a teaching gap, even a racial teaching practice gap. Specifically, achievement disparities among White, Black, Brown, Southeast Asian, and Indigenous student groups can be defined as much by teachers' inability to recall and engage effective strategies as it is by students' inability to master the standards. Again, my work in schools provides evidence that many educators have an insufficient repertoire of instructional practices as well as lack the cultural proficiency to effectively teach students of color and indigenous students.

Persistence

Persistence involves time and energy. Persistence calls for each of us to exercise a rare and seemingly oxymoronic combination of patience and urgency. Rarely do we dedicate sufficient time to addressing the racial achievement gap. Persistence at the institutional level is the willingness of a school system to stick with it despite slow results, political pressure, new ideas, and systemic inertia or resistance to change. A persistent school system institutionalizes real school change with effective leadership, classroom implementation, and community partnerships. Individual educators who are persistent remain focused on equity and eliminating the racial achievement gap regardless of which direction the educational reform wind is blowing.

THE COURAGEOUS CONVERSATION STRATEGY AND PROTOCOL

These three critical factors provide a philosophical context within which we will introduce to you Courageous Conversation, a strategy and protocol for addressing the various impacts of race on student achievement. Engaging the Courageous Conversation strategy begins with a deep-seated *passion* to address a multitude of race matters, personally and professionally, both inside and outside of the education arena. The protocol begins with a commitment to embrace the Four Agreements of Courageous Conversation that ensure openness, honesty, and relative safety. Beyond this, the protocol invites educators to *practice* the Six Conditions of Courageous Conversation, which provide a road map for participating in and facilitating interracial dialogue about race. The Courageous Conversation Compass, the third protocol feature, informs educators of where they and other participants are located in the dialogue. Finally, as a leader for racial equity, you will exercise *persistence* in exploring the strategic role of Courageous Conversation in systemic racial equity transformation, which creates the lasting structures within which to achieve equity in your classroom, school, or school system.

Organization of This Book

Courageous Conversations About Race is divided into three parts, reflecting the three critical factors for systemic transformation and also the three characteristics of racial equity leadership: passion, practice, and persistence. Part I, "Passion: An Essential Characteristic of Racial Equity Leadership," explores the landscape of educational reform and exposes the issue of race as a phenomenon that affects the lives and learning of all children. In these chapters, we help the reader to focus on race in lieu of the traditional topics—such as poverty, language, and learning disabilities—that have long occupied educators' attention and have resulted in only unsatisfactory incremental systemic changes.

Part II, "Practice: The Foundation of Racial Equity Leadership," takes the reader on a step-by-step journey into the race conversation, providing the language, markers, tools, and insights necessary to begin and stay in the dialogue.

Finally, in Part III, "Persistence: The Key to Racial Equity Leadership," educators learn about the characteristics of leadership that are necessary to eliminate racial achievement gaps. Part III provides specific strategies for teachers, schools, and districts to use in the implementation of systemic racial equity transformation, including organizational ideas that help teachers develop better ways to teach and help school leaders to embrace the communities they serve. The book concludes with a description of the work of St. Paul Public Schools (Minnesota) and its success as well as its challenges implementing Courageous Conversation systemwide.

I have included in each chapter prompts and exercises designed to help readers personally reflect on what they've learned. Use these questions to guide deeper examination of your own attitudes, beliefs, and actions. You might also ask a trusted friend or colleague to join you in conversations that help you reflect on your own thoughts and feelings. These interactions are critical in helping you to deepen your understanding of race, its impact on students, and your own abilities to engage in racial equity leadership.

Likewise, at the end of each chapter are implementation exercises for focused school- and systemwide professional learning. These will guide you and your colleagues in the immediate and effective application of the Courageous Conversation protocol. Follow the guidelines to conduct safer and more productive dialogues and activities. I encourage you to keep a journal as you make your way through the book, as well as provide a Courageous Conversation Journal for each friend or colleague who joins you in the activities, so that they, too, can reflect back on their learning, growth, and challenges.

This book provides a foundation for those educational leaders at the system and school level who are willing and ready to begin or accelerate their journey toward educational equity and excellence for all children. This includes superintendents, board members, district administrators, principals, team and teacher leaders, and engaged members of the community. It is designed to assist in facilitating effective dialogue about the racial issues that impact student achievement. The key requirement of the Courageous Conversation strategy, however, is that the reader commit to learning and practicing using the protocol. Only through mastering the Courageous Conversation protocol can we effectively confront interpersonal and institutional racism whenever and wherever it is present.

Language of Race

The language that I use in this book to define and discuss racial matters is the language that I have discovered to be most effective in my work with thousands of educators in this country and other parts of the world. I believe my language of choice will help you gain access to and find your voice in Courageous Conversations about race. Because language is at the heart of culture, it is essential both that we establish a common language around race, and at the same time remain open to understanding how our varied racial experiences shape our own vocabulary and comfort with the conversation in general as well as with specific word choice.

The language surrounding racial issues has remained elusive precisely because constructive and courageous conversations about race occur infrequently in North American and other Western cultures. To address race, the language of race must become concrete so that school leaders can effectively guide the conversations that will assist them in eliminating racial achievement disparities.

As you enter into this conversation, please accept this necessary degree of ambiguity regarding my use of language that defines and describes race. Working through the Six Conditions of Courageous Conversation in Part II, you will come to understand why I often refer to people's skin color rather than to their culture or ethnicity. Furthermore, I capitalize racial descriptors such as White, Black, Brown, and Indigenous. This is to acknowledge and place racial identity on a par with ethnic identity, such as Asian American and African American. Conversely, when referring to groups, I will not typically capitalize when I reference people of color or indigenous people. Pay attention to when you experience personal dissonance with my chosen terminology, and take time to clarify what the words mean to you. Willingly use racial terms in your own conversations as a way of thoughtfully examining race and its impact. Do not allow another person's challenge to your particular racial word choice to become reason for you to grow timid or even silent. Instead, see such challenges as the normal consequence of healthy racial dialogue and even as an invitation into deeper engagement.

By using my protocol, you can come to understand race in a personal and profound way. After this, you will discover how we can translate these personal insights about race into practices that effectively eliminate racial achievement disparities.

We are all learners, to some degree, in this examination of race. It matters not where you are on the continuum of racial understanding. What is important is your willingness to expand your racial consciousness, deeply explore your own racial identity, and better empathize with the corresponding perspectives and experiences of the racial other. Consequently, I invite you, the reader, to join with me in this journey toward becoming a racial equity leader.

1 PASSION

An Essential Characteristic of Racial Equity Leadership

Many reasons have been given why African American children are not excelling in schools in the United States. One that is seldom spoken aloud, but that is buried in the American psyche, is that black children are innately less capable—that they are somehow inferior. I want to start by dispelling that myth. . . . I write these words because what we need to know at a very deep level is that African American children do not come into this world at a deficit. There is no "achievement gap" at birth—at least not one that favors European American children. Indeed, the achievement gap should not be considered the gap between black children's performance and white children's performance—the latter of which can be considered mediocre on an international scale—but rather between black children's performance and these same children's exponentially greater potential. When we educators look out at a classroom of black faces, we must understand that we are looking at children at least as brilliant as those from any well-to-do white community. If we do not recognize the brilliance before us, we cannot help but carry on the societal views that these children are somehow damaged goods and that they cannot be expected to succeed.

—Lisa Delpit (2011, pp. 1, 5)

Teaching is a demanding profession. It requires remarkable skill, substantial knowledge, and significant effort. It would take little effort to describe the technical requirements of teaching, but teaching is not a technical job. The very best practitioner in education will fail without the proper mindset, that is, her personal and professional set of beliefs and attitudes about learning and teaching. Thus, in reality, one's racial beliefs and attitudes underlie everything necessary in teaching, particularly in the successful teaching of children of color and indigenous children. But what is involved in this proper racial mindset for engaging in the effort to eliminate racial achievement disparities?

Passion is the key. Having worked with thousands of educators, I have observed that those teachers and administrators who are most proficient at engaging *all* students of *every* race in rigorous studies also have a tremendous amount of passion for this particular work that they do. Passion, and specifically tightly holding on to a deep-seated, unyielding belief in the educability of the very children we fail, is what drives racial equity classroom leaders toward success.

For me, equity, rather than functioning as a program or initiative, is a value that we foster. Having a belief in the importance of achieving equity, and having the courage to apply passion to such a belief, is what fuels successful educators of underserved students. In a school that strives to eliminate racial achievement gaps, educators work toward promoting high achievement among all students and equitably providing the type of instruction that each student needs. When considering your own attitude, the following question should be posed: Is equity really your passion?

Just as people can become anti-racist once they begin to develop an authentic need to include people of many races in their personal lives, school leaders can become truly passionate for equity work as they discover a will to succeed with students of color in their school. This will or desire manifests itself as the driving and emotional force behind the work they do. Leaders with such a passion will begin to see equity as an essential characteristic of their school's success. They will clearly notice inequities where they exist and willingly focus on correcting them.

Educators need to locate this passion in order to transform schools. Observing schools with leaders who are truly passionate about equity is an incredible experience. These are amazing and dynamic schools that exude a great sense of community and enthusiasm. In these schools, continuous, rigorous learning by all and high expectations for everyone—including the teachers—are everyday experiences. Conversely, in schools lacking that sense of passion for equity, feelings of pessimism, failure, and hopelessness are omnipresent. These buildings are full of toxic adults who stave off meaningful reforms, and they are deadly places for the large numbers of children of color who typically attend them.

School leaders need to decide where they stand in relation to equity, and if they do not yet have passion for it, they must find some; passion is a prerequisite to succeeding in a school with a diverse racial population. Nowhere in our description of passion for equity do I suggest that the educator must be a person of color. Culturally proficient, racially conscious, courageous educators of all races can succeed with *all* students, but only after they locate and nurture their passion for equity.

The essence and hallmark of our passion is our heightened engagement and our willingness to change. There is little honor in holding back, limiting participation, accepting mediocrity, and finding comfort in the status quo. With passion, we engage our soul and our being in this work, along with our mind and our body. With passion, we reclaim our hope and belief in the possibility of a future devoid of racial injustice—a future governed by racial equity and a true quest for human equality. With passion, we will survive the conflict, the lack of support, and the passive resistance that comes with challenging institutionalized racism in our schools. And with passion, we will have the strength not only to *stand up for* what is right for our children, but to *do* what is right for them as well.

Passion is the cornerstone of racial equity leadership. Emboldened with *passion,* enabled with *practice,* and strengthened by *persistence,* we can create schools in which *all* students achieve at higher levels, achievement gaps are narrowed, and the racial predictability and disproportionality of high and low student achievement are eliminated.

TWO

What's So Courageous About This Conversation?

I Dream

I am from a clash of Color,
From an idea of love, modeled for others' perception.
I see me as I am, but am hidden from others' views.
I am who I am, but a living contradiction to my peers.
I see life as a blessing, a gift granted to me.
Why should my tint describe me?
Why should my culture degrade me?
Why should the ignorance of another conjure my presence?
Too many times I've been disappointed by the looks,
By the sneers and misconceptions of the people who don't get me,
Who don't understand why it hurts.
I dream of a place of glory and freedom,
Of losing the weight of oppression on my back.
I dream of the enlightenment of people,
Of the opening of their eyes.
I dream for acceptance,
And for the blessing of feeling special just once.
One moment of glory . . . for the true virtue in my life.
For the glimmer of freedom, and a rise in real pride.

—Used with permission of Pablo Vega, Junior
Chapel Hill High School, Chapel Hill, North Carolina

> What are your initial reactions to Pablo's poem? What parts of the poem resonate most for you? What parts of the poem present confusion for you? Judging from his work, what type of student do you believe Pablo to be? If Pablo were a student in your school, how might you respond to his voice? To what degree do you believe "Pablos" are attending your school?

Implicit in this poem are the moral reasons that schools need to address the gap in student achievement that exists among racial groups today. This poem was written by Pablo Vega, a student of Latino heritage, in roughly 15 minutes. His schoolwork indicated he was an average student. Yet, when given the opportunity during a Courageous Conversation workshop to share his personal feelings about his perceived place in society and the opportunities placed before him, he eloquently and effortlessly composed a poem that provides evidence of his extraordinary level of knowledge, skill, and intellect.

Pablo attended Chapel Hill High School in Chapel Hill, North Carolina. Chapel Hill–Carrboro City Schools (CHCCS) has been among the highest performing school systems in North Carolina for many years. According to one local news outlet, WRAL (2003), Chapel Hill schools were among the very best. The district's reputation was well known and publicized throughout the state and especially in the community. Using aggregated data, its average achievement scores consistently ranked in the top five in North Carolina in every subject.

Then, Chapel Hill took the courageous step of disaggregating the data and looking at the performance indicators by race. Students of color accounted for roughly 20% of the district's students, and new data showed they were scoring far below their White and Asian counterparts (Singleton, 2002).

Nettie Collins-Hart, then assistant superintendent in the district, described the newly revealed gap this way:

> The discrepancy is more glaring because we are so high performing. We are the number one school district in the state. However, if you compared African American students, not only was there an achievement gap here—as there certainly is in most school districts—but our African American children were not, in many cases, performing at par with other school districts that didn't have the resources and the reputation that we had. (Singleton, 2002)

In fact, whereas the district's White students were ranked at the top statewide, the district's Black students scored below the average for all Black students in North Carolina.

Faced with this reality, some educators in Chapel Hill admitted several years ago that they might not be quite as great as they had thought they were when it came to educating *all* students. They embraced the understanding that a truly first-rate school district is one where all students succeed, not just those of a certain race or background. At that time, they began to incorporate into their system the strategy of Courageous Conversation—a process that would help them foster success of *all* their students, no matter what the students looked like or where they lived.

Today, the vast majority of stakeholders in the district, including board members, administrators, teachers, families, and community members, have participated in Courageous Conversation to build racial understanding and discover what they can collectively do to close the achievement gap. Chapel Hill embarked on a rigorous equity program with great success and has persisted in those efforts. As a result, the racial achievement gaps among all groups are closing rapidly, as shown in more recent district reporting (CHCCS, 2004).

Increasingly, every student in CHCCS is guaranteed access to a successful education, including Pablo Vega and Black and Brown students like him. Pablo has experienced "the glimmer of freedom and a rise in real pride" described in his poem. He took valuable time in his senior year to participate in the professional development of educators in Chapel Hill; then, he graduated to attend a four-year college, and he intends to become a teacher.

> **REFLECTION**
>
> What achievement similarities and differences exist between your school system and the Chapel Hill–Carrboro City Schools? In what ways could your system benefit from similar equity efforts?

COURAGEOUS CONVERSATION

To exercise the passion, practice, and persistence necessary to address racial achievement disparities, all members of the school community need to be able to talk about race in a safer and honest way. Courageous Conversation offers a protocol and a strategy for school systems to eliminate racial achievement disparities. By engaging this strategy and learning the protocol, educators develop racial understanding, participate in interracial dialogue about race, and address racial issues in schools. According to Margaret Wheatley (2002), "Human conversation is the most ancient and easiest way to cultivate the conditions for change—personal change, community, and organizational change" (p. 3).

As schools engage in open and honest dialogue about racial achievement disparities, they can effectively address the obstacles to success that exist for all students. This dialogue is an educational necessity. Speaking about what needs to happen to begin closing the achievement gap, Julie Landsman (2004) writes,

> Teachers need to meet with parents, members of the community, students, and colleagues to discuss racism in our schools, our cities, and our states. Through dialogue with our students and their communities, we may find ourselves looking at learning, cooperation, and achievement in a more complex, interesting way. (p. 29)

Defining Courageous Conversation

Video

The Protocol
www.corwin.com/CCAR

I have defined Courageous Conversation, or the formal structure or protocol that exists for this type of dialogue, as

> utilizing the agreements, conditions, and compass to engage, sustain, and deepen interracial dialogue about race in order to examine schooling and improve student achievement.

Specifically, a Courageous Conversation

- *engages* those who won't talk.
- *sustains* the conversation when it gets uncomfortable or diverted.
- *deepens* the conversation to the point where authentic understanding and meaningful actions occur.

Having Courageous Conversations serves as a strategy for deinstitutionalizing racism and improving student achievement. I conceptualized and developed this protocol in 1995, while directing a statewide California project aimed at redesigning the admissions process in the state's public university systems to align with high school restructuring. Recognizing that school reform initiatives and traditional diversity training fail to consider the impact of race and racism on student achievement disparities, I created Courageous Conversation so that preK–12 and higher educators could examine why students of color were not gaining access to effective schooling and, subsequently, admission to college.

If we understand the need for dialogue about the racial achievement gap, the challenge becomes how do we open ourselves up to have a Courageous Conversation about the following questions:

- Why do racial gaps exist?
- What is the origin of the racial gaps?
- What factors have allowed these gaps to persist for so many years?

Some educators may say, with reason, that people are talking about race and student achievement more today than they ever have. The challenge, however, is to move beyond a basic awareness of the racial patterns found in student achieve-ment data to a more active, purposeful, and precise process that involves effec-tively inquiring about *why* the data show a gap.

An additional question also needs to be asked: If it had not been for federal legislation such as No Child Left Behind, and more recently Race to the Top and the Common Core State Standards, would educators be talking about racial gaps in achievement at all? If the answer is no, what does this suggest about willingness to investigate the intersections of race, teaching and learning, and achievement? Absent Courageous Conversation, I have found that the authentic, sustainable transformation of beliefs, expectations, and practices cannot occur.

Four Agreements of Courageous Conversation

The initial action for educators entering into Courageous Conversation is to commit to practicing the Four Agreements. Educators must agree to

1. stay engaged.

2. speak your truth.

3. experience discomfort.

4. expect and accept non-closure.

In my professional development work with school leaders, norms have often been established to guide difficult dialogue. I have discovered, however, that these traditional norms typically fall apart once race is put on the table. Specifically, when race surfaces as a topic for conversation, educators quickly become silent, defiant, angry, or judgmental. Courageous Conversation participants soon recog-nize that traditional rules and guidelines for dialogue are insufficient in interra-cial discourse about race. Thus, the Four Agreements serve as the bridge to engaging, sustaining, and deepening conversations about race.

Recognizing that these agreements exist as a foundation for the conversation enables those who would normally feel unsafe in such a conversation to feel safer, even while experiencing discomfort. Specifically, the agreements offer a safer space so that educators can engage their fears: For example, a White teacher may be afraid of offending or appearing racist, or a principal of color may fear becoming angry or being labeled as oversensitive or too emotional. Collectively, the agree-ments serve as a conduit for more meaningful interracial dialogue.

The Four Agreements of Courageous Conversation are explored in greater detail in Chapter 4.

Six Conditions of Courageous Conversation

To support the Four Agreements that define *how* we are to have the conversa-tion, the Six Conditions of Courageous Conversation guide participants through the subject matter they are supposed to talk about and remind them what topics they need to be mindful of during the interracial dialogue. Consequently, the agreements define the process, while the conditions outline the content and progression of Courageous Conversation.

The Six Conditions are as follows:

1. Establish a racial context that is personal, local, and immediate.

2. Isolate race while acknowledging the broader scope of diversity and the variety of factors and conditions that contribute to a racialized problem.

3. Develop understanding of race as a social/political construction of knowledge, and engage multiple racial perspectives to surface critical understanding.

4. Monitor the parameters of the conversation by being explicit and intentional about the number of participants, prompts for discussion, and time allotted for listening, speaking, and reflecting. Use the Courageous Conversation Compass (see Figure 2.1) to determine how each participant is displaying emotion—mind, body, and soul—to access a given racial topic.

5. Establish agreement around a contemporary working definition of race, one that is clearly differentiated from ethnicity and nationality.

6. Examine the presence and role of Whiteness and its impact on the conversation and the problem being addressed.

Unlike the Four Agreements, the Six Conditions are specifically ordered and necessarily sequential. The First and Second Conditions serve to *engage* us in a conversation about race, where such a conversation previously has not occurred. They provide a way to "test the waters," to determine how ready we are to dialogue with others, by having each of us consider our own *personal* racial experiences, beliefs, and perspectives. The Third and Fourth Conditions *sustain* the conversation and help to keep it moving once we have established a willingness to engage through mindful inquiry into those *multiple perspectives*, beliefs, and experiences that are different from our own. The Fifth and Sixth Conditions *deepen* the interracial dialogue about race by guiding us into the most difficult and least examined subject matters related to how we live and understand race. In this advanced aspect of conversation, we develop our understanding of *whiteness* and challenge our beliefs about our own association with and relationship to racial privilege and power. The conditions serve as an important scaffold for an increasingly more difficult, provocative, and authentic interracial conversation about race.

These Six Conditions of Courageous Conversation are explored individually and in greater detail in Chapters 5 to 10.

The Courageous Conversation Compass

Linda Darling-Hammond (1997) has said, "In order to create a cohesive community and a consensus on how to proceed, school people must have the occasion to engage in democratic discourse about the real stuff of teaching and learning" (p. 336). Part of this "democratic discourse" is providing enough time and space in the Courageous Conversation so that every educator's perspective and experience can be listened to and affirmed. The Fourth Condition of Courageous Conversation asks us to use the Courageous Conversation Compass to determine the place of engagement at which each participant in the dialogue is processing the content.

Video

The Compass
www.corwin.com/
CCAR

Figure 2.1 The Courageous Conversation Compass

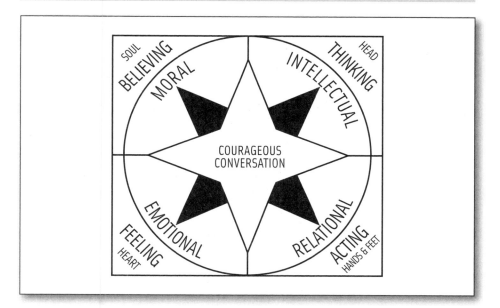

I developed the Compass as a personal navigational tool to guide participants through these conversations. It helps us to know where we are personally as well as to recognize the direction from which other participants come. Collectively, it leads us to a mutual understanding of our varied beliefs and opinions and helps us locate the sources of our emotions and actions or lack thereof.

On the Courageous Conversation Compass, I have identified four primary ways that people deal with racial information, events, and/or issues: emotional, intellectual, moral, and relational. These are the four points or cardinal directions of our compass.

- *Emotionally,* we respond to information through *feelings,* when a racial issue strikes us at a physical level and causes an internal sensation such as anger, sadness, joy, or embarrassment.

- *Intellectually,* our primary response to a racial issue or information may be characterized by personal disconnect with the subject or a steadfast search for more information or data. Our intellectual response is often verbal and based in our best *thinking.*
- *Morally,* we respond from a deep-seated *belief* that relates to the racial information or event. This belief has to do with the rightness or wrongness of a given racial issue. The justifications for one's moral views are often situated in the "gut" and may not be verbally articulated.
- *Relationally,* we connect and respond to racial information through our *acting* or what is most often characterized as specific behaviors and actions.

In a sense, emotional responses are seated in the heart, intellectual responses in the mind, moral responses in the soul, and relational responses in the hands and feet. This Compass together with the Six Conditions and Four Agreements fulfills the complete definition of Courageous Conversation.

REFLECTION

For the purposes of better understanding and personalizing the Courageous Conversation Compass, consider the following topics:*

- Affirmative Action
- Emergent Bilingualism
- The United States of America's First Black President
- Tribal Sovereignty of Indigenous Nations in the United States

As you say each of the aforementioned phrases and think about its significance, where do you initially locate yourself on the compass? If the phrase is not familiar to you, what does recognizing your lack of racial consciousness trigger? As you ponder the topic for a longer period of time and begin to connect it to your own personal experience, where do you travel on the compass? Do you experience significant or minimal movement?

*Readers outside of the United States should feel free to substitute here four context-specific, current racial topics before engaging in this reflective exercise.

A DIFFICULT CONVERSATION

Margaret Wheatley (2002) has asked, "What would it feel like to be listening to each other again about what disturbs and troubles us, about what gives us hope, about our yearnings, our fears, our prayers, and our children?" (p. 3). To gain full access to her question—*what would it feel like?*—we need to venture into a difficult conversation, one that clearly troubles educators and can make everyone downright uncomfortable. We believe that the ability to truly listen to and converse with each other will help educators improve education for *all* children—White included—and to better understand the racial experiences that impact their learning.

Educators typically have not examined and discussed race in their schools, because they fear they don't know how to go about this process correctly. Some justify inaction on racial achievement disparities by suggesting that no one knows how to impact them. Saying "we don't know how" allows educators to claim that they have done all they can do. Such suggestions do not produce improved results.

We suggest that the problem of educators not knowing what to do about racial achievement gaps or how to talk about race is not as devastating as the problem of educators failing to seek ways to close to the gaps.

IMPLEMENTATION EXERCISE

GOT PASSION?

Time required: 45 minutes

Materials required: For each participant, Courageous Conversation Journal and a copy of the worksheet that follows

1. Introduce the concept of Courageous Conversation with the following definition:

   Utilizing the agreements, conditions, and compass to engage, sustain, and deepen interracial dialogue about race in order to examine schooling and improve student achievement

2. Briefly describe the agreements, conditions, and compass, and inform the group that they will explore these in further depth later.

3. Based on the explanation in Part I of this book, describe *passion* as it relates to equity work.

4. Divide staff members into small groups of three or four people with whom they work closely, and give each member a copy of the activity worksheet.

5. Have each member of your group fill out Box 1 on the worksheet in response to the prompt,

   • What is a non–school-related activity about which I am truly passionate?

At this point, ask participants to share with the whole group what their passions are. Record responses on 8.5" by 11" pieces of paper, and post these around the room to establish a visual of the various passions in the community.

6. Have each member fill out Box 2 in response to the prompt.

   - What is it that I feel and that you would see as I engage in the activity about which I am passionate?

   Briefly share responses in the small groups.

7. Have each member fill out Box 3 with the following prompts:

   - What is my personal definition of equity/antiracism?
   - What is our collective definition of equity/antiracism?

   Briefly share responses in the small groups.

8. Determine as a large group collective definitions for both *equity* and *antiracism*. Make sure that the educators address both terms.

9. Have each member fill out Box 4 with responses to the following prompts:

   - When I am engaging in equity/antiracism work, what do I feel, and what do you see?
   - What qualities and characteristics are exhibited by school leaders who are engaging in equity/antiracism work?
   - In what ways do I personally exhibit these qualities and characteristics of equity/anti-racist leadership?

   Have participants discuss in their small groups what they have determined about their personal passion for equity/antiracism in their work in the school.

10. Have the larger group share reflections from small-group discussions.

11. Encourage participants to keep this exercise and future equity/antiracism work in their Courageous Conversation Journals.

GOT PASSION?

1. My Passion	2. Looks and Feels Like
3. Equity/Anti-Racism	**4. Leadership**

THREE

Why Race?

Most of us remain trapped in the narrow framework of the dominant liberal and conservative views of race in America, which with its worn-out vocabulary leaves us intellectually debilitated, morally disempowered, and personally depressed. . . .

Our truncated public discussions of race fail to confront the complexity of the issue in a candid and critical manner. The predictable pitting of liberals against conservatives, Great Society Democrats against self-help Republicans, reinforces intellectual parochialism and political paralysis. . . .

We confine discussions about race in America to the "problems" Black people pose for Whites rather than consider what this way of viewing Black people reveals about us as a nation.

This paralyzing framework encourages liberals to relieve their guilty consciences by supporting public funds directed at "the problems"; but at the same time, reluctant to exercise principled criticism of Black people, liberals deny them the freedom to err. Similarly, conservatives blame the "problems" on Black people themselves—and thereby render Black social misery invisible or unworthy of public attention.

Hence, for liberals, Black people are to be "included" and "integrated" into "our" society and culture, while for conservatives they are to be "well behaved" and "worthy of acceptance" by "our" way of life. Both fail to see that the presence and predicaments of Black people are neither additions to nor defections from American life, but rather constitutive elements of that life.

—Cornel West (2001, p. 2)

In what ways are the "presence and predicaments of Black people . . . constitutive elements of [American] life"? Does this also apply to other groups of color? How have the condition and experiences of Black people in America influenced your conservative and/or liberal views about race?

Arguably, great divisions exist between racial groups in the United States, because we lack understanding that each group possesses a unique racial perspective, and we struggle to empathize with the racial others' unique racial experience. To expand on what West (2001) wrote, White Americans expect that people of color should be "integrated into White society and culture" and become "worthy of acceptance by the White way of life" and establish Whiteness as the acceptable standard.

The collective message from the dominant racial group to people of color is that the problem of race stems from their inability to thrive in "mainstream" society. Although individual responsibility is an admirable American ideal, people of color face an enormous challenge as they attempt to find a foothold in a nation that has never fully respected them or granted them equality.

THE PROBLEM OF THE COLOR LINE

The existence of a racial achievement gap is not shocking when you consider the day-to-day schooling reality for students of color and indigenous students. During their formative years, they must negotiate the psychological turmoil prompted by oppression and different status, while at the same time they are viewed by the school system and the larger society as a problem. Until teachers discover a love, empathy, and authentic desire to reach their students of color, these children will not develop to their full social, emotional, and academic potential. Likewise, as educators engage in racial equity work throughout the school system, they discover that their souls are nourished by the heightened engagement of their students of color and indigenous students.

According to W. E. B. DuBois (1903/1996), "The problem of the twentieth century is the problem of the color line, the relations of the darker to the lighter races of men in Asia and Africa, in America and the islands of the sea" (pp. 15–16). This rings as true in the 21st century as it did when Dubois's text was first published in 1903. Without question, great strides have been made to establish equality through politics and law, but true racial equality in our habits of heart and mind remains elusive. To work toward equality requires tremendous effort on the part of all racial groups—the racially advantaged and the racially disadvantaged.

Racial inequality is not just a "Black problem" or a "Brown problem" or a "Native American problem." It is a problem that impacts all of us. Thus, for White educators to claim rightfully that they are not racist, they must take action in bringing about true racial equality and insist on racial justice always and everywhere. Similarly, if we as people of color want to claim ourselves to stand for racial justice, we must speak up and speak out even when we are a lone voice or feel threats to our social or professional position.

Education for All Students

The aim of this book is to help educators improve the achievement of *all* students while narrowing the gaps between the lowest and highest performing groups and eliminating the pattern by which racial groups predictably and disproportionately occupy the highest and lowest achievement categories. To achieve this aim, educators, families, and community leaders must embrace the motto that is included in the pledge we ask our students to repeat each morning: . . . *with liberty and justice for all.*

If we truly want liberty and justice for everyone, we *all* must work toward attaining equality. People of color must continue to draw individual and institutional attention to racial inequity and demand racial equality. As recipients of racial advantage, White people must embrace their responsibility to challenge the awarding and acceptance of privilege. Absent these essential and interconnected actions, racial inequality, and thus tension and racial divisiveness, will continue to erode our aspiring democracy.

To quote Cornel West (2001) once again,

> To establish a new framework, we need to begin with a frank acknowledgment of the basic humanness and Americanness of each of us. And we must acknowledge that as a people—*E pluribus unum*—we are on a slippery slope toward economic strife, social turmoil, and cultural chaos. If we go down, we go down together. (p. 4)

Racial Responsibility

White people are the primary guardians and recipients of racial privilege; therefore they also bear significant responsibility for the perpetuation of racial inequality. Given the clarity of both scientific thought and human logic when it comes to understanding race as socially constructed rather than biologically determined, racial inequality in our society evidences the presence of racism. Thus, White people must take greater responsibility for understanding and addressing racism. This is no insignificant prognosis for public education, given that the overwhelming majority of teachers, principals, superintendents, and school board members are White. Despite the extraordinary and groundbreaking efforts of civil rights leaders to bring about racial equality, sustainable reform will occur only when White people individually and collectively embrace and encourage change.

At the very least, White educators must allow change to happen. Without their active participation in this way, racial injustices will continue to be viewed by White people as a primary concern only for people of color.

Here is an excerpt from an Asian parent's letter to a Los Angeles elementary school principal in reaction to tense discussions among parents and staff as to whether or not they would hire another staff member of color:

> The most hurtful racially charged comment said to me in my entire life wasn't *Jap* or *Chink* or *gook* or any of about a dozen things in my life I've been called. The most hurtful thing came from someone I liked and respected a great deal; someone who I thought was smart and compassionate. We were arguing about a hiring decision in which race was a factor. My argument was that she was in a position to help the cause of people of color and that it was incumbent upon her to do so. She told me that, "Racism is a big problem; it's a global problem. I resent you for trying to make it my problem."
>
> The translation to my ears? "I'm White. Racism is your problem, not mine. I don't have to deal with it if I don't want to." What infuriated me was the contrast in our situation—people of color have to deal with racism whether they want to or not. The conversation turned sour after that and I've never been able to forget that when push came to shove, that was what she felt.
>
> That comment stuck with me for years. That argument contains the underlying resentment many people of color feel towards White people; the feeling that *racism is your problem, not mine.* And, I assume, it's an underlying feeling many White people feel towards people of color: *Stop trying to make racism my problem.* I feel that sentiment lies beneath some of the parents' unwillingness to go along with the changes [at the school].
>
> I submit that with racial inequities continuing to worsen and with de facto segregation continuing to worsen, we're slouching towards another race riot or worse—something as inevitable to me as the next earthquake. And at that point, it will become obvious that racism is all of our problem.

REFLECTION

What are your initial reactions to this Asian parent's voice? Do you believe that these sentiments may be shared by parents of color in your school system? What data might you use as evidence to support your belief? What personal action might you take in response to this parent's letter and the related concerns of other people of color and indigenous people?

The words that this Asian parent chose to engage the principal of her child's school are central to addressing racial achievement disparities in education. The most productive and progressive society is one in which every member has full and unencumbered access to academic success and emotional security. When one group feels marginalized, everybody is affected—including those who are in positions of power and privilege, who often perceive themselves to be unaffected by the experiences of the underserved. White Americans are born into a social position in which they must assure people of color and indigenous people that the dominant society has their best interests at heart. The cost of not offering this assurance is a continuation of the present racial division, de facto segregation, and disparate educational outcomes. In important discussions about how to improve our society and how to better our schools, race matters.

THE RACIAL GAP

> People don't want to talk about racism. They say it's all about class. Why is this so hard for people? There's a fear and people are more comfortable talking about poverty, or gender, but they avoid talking about race. Being a white person in the US is a "state of being." We are not conscious of it. Even if a school has one speaker come in to talk about cultural sensitivity, or does one workshop, that's not enough if the schools don't follow up with that training. There's a "white racial frame," and so often white privileges are invisible, throughout society but especially in the education system.
>
> —Julie Landsman (quoted in Regan, 2012)

The most troublesome achievement gap is the racial gap—the difference in student achievement between White and Asian students and their Black, Brown, Native American, Southeast Asian, and Pacific Islander counterparts. Without question, poverty and wealth impact student achievement as well. Statistically, however, even within the same economic strata, there is an achievement gap based on race. The University of California (UC), together with the College Board, prepared a study (Nakao, 1998) that vividly captured the racial gaps that appear when average SAT scores are broken down both by family income and by race/ethnicity (see Figure 3.1). While this study involves only applicants to the freshman class at one large public institution, the findings seem to hold more far-reaching implications about the intersection of race, income, and achievement across the nation.

Some readers might wonder whether these data from 1995 reflect the current situation. The answer is absolutely. And although, in this revised edition of *Courageous Conversations About Race,* we can now present more recent data, it is still important to note that the College Board and many other educational institutions rarely provide data for public consumption that compare achievement data by race, income, and achievement. At the time the UC/College Board study was made, investigations like it were quite rare. Even though more data have been gathered during the nearly two decades since, we recognize that the breakthrough study of

1995 offered relevant information about today's racial and income achievement patterns. For those who remain unconvinced about the saliency of race, I ask what significant racial reforms have occurred in the preK–12 system and in the American economic structure over the past 10 years that would create a dramatic shift in the data.

As is clearly shown in Figure 3.1, income does impact achievement: The scores of all races improve as their family income increases. However, wealth or poverty alone fails to fully explain the racial achievement gap, which persists irrespective of income level.

Figure 3.1 Average SAT Scores by Parental Income and Race/Ethnicity

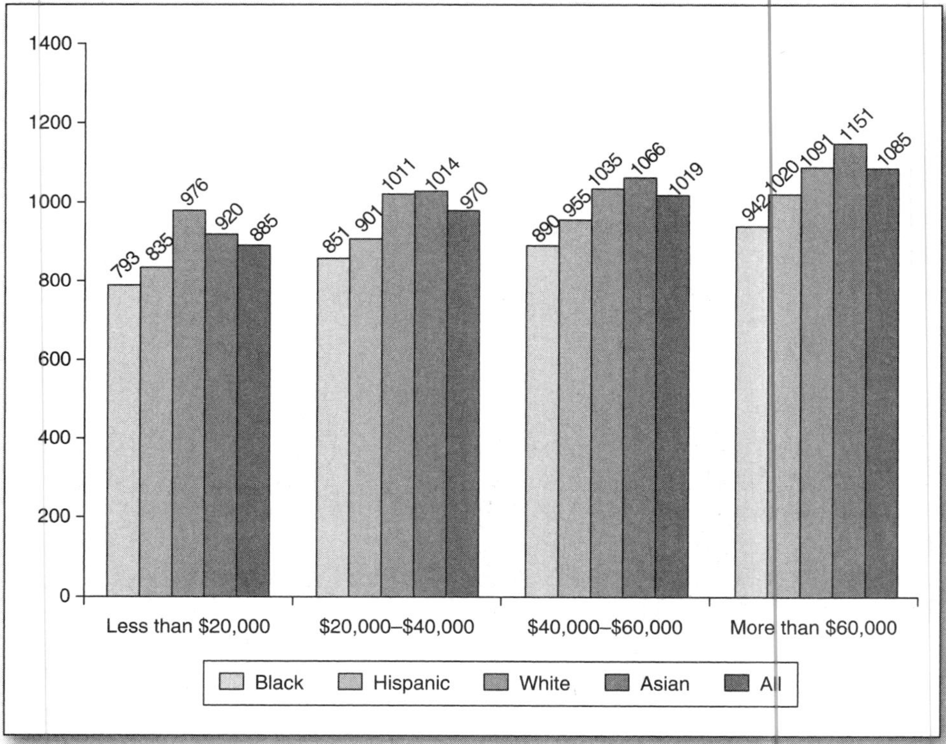

Source: National Center for Education Statistics, US Department of Education.

In most studies and reports, achievement gaps are addressed in terms of economic differences, and little or no connection is made to race. The UC data, which show the intersectionality of race and income, reveal important subtleties about racial achievement gaps. First, at every income level, Black and Brown students are outperformed by White students. Specifically, Black students are predictably the lowest performing group at every income level. Second, there is an astonishing achievement disparity between Black and White students who are equally poor. Third, we see that poorer White students actually outperform middle-income Black and Brown students. Consequently, even if we were to extrapolate the data to students in families with incomes of $200,000—clearly a greatly diminished pool of Black and Brown families—the racial gap would most likely persist. Back in 2005, when I made this prediction about what we would see if we extrapolated the data in this way, some readers disputed my hypothesis, believing instead that such high family incomes, regardless of the race of the family, would serve as an equalizing factor in terms of student achievement. In this second edition of *Courageous Conversations About Race*, I am able to display 2011 College Board SAT data (2010–2011, see Figure 3.2) that prove my point and validate my previous prediction about the power of race over income. In this more recent data set, the College Board also offers readers a more expanded view of racial factors by including American Indian students in the analysis. The fact that these underserved students were not represented in the 1995 study

Figure 3.2 2011 Average SAT Scores by Parental Income and Race/Ethnicity

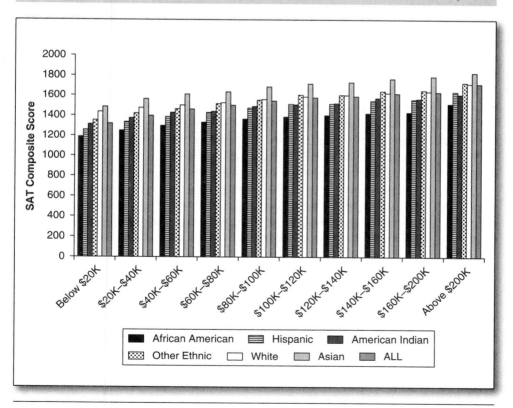

Source: Data derived from "College-Bound Seniors 2010 and 2011, Total Group Profile Report—ETHNICITY (Table 11)," Copyright © 2010–2011 The College Board, retrieved from www.collegeboard.org.

highlights the issue of "invisibility" facing American Indians, which research indicates to be our lowest achieving school-aged population (Editorial Projects in Education Research Center, 2011; Grigg, Moran, & Kuang, 2010; National Center for Education Statistics, 2013).

To suggest that the achievement gaps evidenced in the UC study, and more recently, the College Board analysis of SAT scores, have nothing to do with race or racism stands in the way of a complete explanation of the disparities within and between income levels. Of course, these studies also have the potential to provide evidence of the inherent racial biases in the SAT and suggest that institutional racism is deeply imbedded in American education. As Figure 3.1 shows, White students achieve scores that are quite similar across a broad income spectrum—varying over a range of only slightly more than 100 points. By comparison, the scores of all groups of color show substantial change from lowest to highest income groups: For Blacks, the range is approximately 150 points; for Latinos, almost 200 points; and for Asians, more than 230 points. In addition, White students predictably and measurably have higher achievement at the lowest income level. Figure 3.2 shows that these performance patterns, generally speaking, have continued to hold true over the past two decades despite dramatic changes in the test itself and in the scoring index, and despite the fact that the 2010–2011 analysis included a broader range of income levels than the 1995 study and an expanded racial classification. Why is this so? To address this question, we must consider ways in which the SAT and other standardized assessments of educational progress advantage White students and perhaps also those students who have learned to approach such assessments with a perspective or lived experience that is remarkably similar to that of White students.

For some readers, the high performance of Asian students evidenced in the 2011 College Board data serves as a distraction and challenges their ability to recognize and grapple with the continued lower achievement patterns of Black, Brown, and American Indian students. What must be understood here is that the impact of racism on schooling is different for Asian students than it is for other students of color and American Indian students. Often, Asian students face "positive" racial discrimination and stereotyping that defines their academic performance as superior to that of their White counterparts. Such institutional beliefs about Asian students' elevated acumen in say, math and science, for example, can serve to propel Asian students to excel in these and other subject areas. The same "positive" racial beliefs, however, can also serve to isolate Asian children in moments when they require support. As a former Ivy League admissions director, I submit from my professional experience that racist views about Asian students' one-dimensionality, suggesting that they are good at academics but not at athletics or leadership activities, creates quite a bit of stress in this community. Finally a fear sometimes held by White people—of being academically outperformed by Asian Americans—prompts a form of racial backlash that is neither "positive" nor productive. I will touch on this topic more in later parts of this book. For now, I invite readers to return to the Compass at the end of Chapter 2 and determine where they are located on it with respect to our discussion thus far of race, income, and achievement.

Socioeconomics and Race

When discussing socioeconomic background, it is important to consider the full weight of the descriptor. When educators consider reasons for achievement disparities among their students, the primary emphasis in considering socioeconomic background is placed on financial status—the *economic* half. More defining and perhaps sometimes confining, however, is the *socio* status, the aspect related to broader cultural nuances affecting an individual. Exploring students' socioeconomic status is an invitation for educators to dialogue about the students' cultural and economic backgrounds, where culture must include racial identity.

For people of color and indigenous people, the concepts of culture and race can be deeply overlapping, if not virtually synonymous. Furthermore, people of color and indigenous people are often identified by their racial/cultural identity first and then by their economic background. Although I am a middle-class Black man, I am seen in society's eyes as Black first and perhaps middle class second. The *socio* or racial/cultural status will always outweigh or trump the *economic* status in our race-conscious society; nevertheless, members of the dominant racial culture tend to search for and acknowledge primarily economic differences when explaining social stratification and academic achievement disparities. Why is it that White educators, especially, struggle to recognize that students' economic status is influenced, modified, and governed by their families' racial/cultural identity?

Furthermore, according to the data in the two studies I have cited, the students' *socio* or racial/cultural background appears to have a more powerful impact on participation and performance than their economic status. I believe this is because these racial/cultural factors significantly impact students' vision of the future and their expectations about what school will and will not offer them. I suggest that these racial/cultural elements are primary factors in the persistence of the racial achievement gap. Later in this book, I will explore the notion of racial/cultural status in greater detail.

Addressing the Racial Gap

The Courageous Conversation protocol provides a strategy to eventually eliminate these racial achievement gaps. Furthermore, such conversations foster and nurture the passion educators, students, and families need to address systemic racial inequities and the resulting achievement inequality. At Pacific Educational Group, based on our partnerships with numerous preK–12 and higher education systems, we have found the racial achievement gap to be the most difficult gap to address. However, we have witnessed that when educators make dramatic progress toward narrowing the gaps among students of different races, they also succeed at closing all related gaps, for example, gaps among students of different economic groups and with differing native languages.

Consider the evidence in the most recent report from the Chapel Hill–Carrboro City Schools (CHCCS, 2005) in North Carolina. This district had utilized the Courageous Conversation protocol for five years as a primary strategy for addressing racial achievement gaps. Not only did CHCCS show tremendous improvement in reducing racial achievement disparities, but it also made significant progress toward closing other gaps as well. In 2002, when schools were first required to meet federal average yearly progress (AYP) goals, only four schools in the Chapel Hill district were successful. Just two years later, 14 of the 15 schools in the district met the national goals and were recognized as "distinguished schools" on statewide rankings. According to the CHCCS (2004),

> The district as a whole showed a 94.2 percent proficiency rate, a statistic which included the district's students with exceptional education needs (Special Education) and students with limited English proficiency. In five schools, more than 95 percent of the students demonstrated proficiency on the tests.

RACE AS A FACTOR IN EDUCATION

As expectations, opportunities, resources, and access become equitable across all racial groups, the gaps close, because all students are supported in the differentiated ways necessary to achieve success. It is my belief that the most devastating factor contributing to the lowered achievement of students of color and indigenous students is systemic racism, which we recognize as the unexamined and unchallenged system of racial biases and residual White advantage that persist in our institutions of learning.

REFLECTION

To what degree do you and your colleagues believe race impacts student achievement? To what degree has race been a factor that is investigated in your school system's effort to address achievement disparity? Has this been an effort embraced by *all* educators—White included?

When schools address the issue of race head-on, dramatic results occur. Take, for example, Del Roble Elementary School in San José, California, a school of primarily Black, Latino, White, and Asian students. Del Roble, like many schools throughout the country, is characterized by a high rate of student transience and a large population of English language learners. Predictably, Del Roble has little if any categorical funding to support efforts in developing teachers to deliver a culturally responsive instructional program.

After disaggregating school data and discovering significant gaps among various subgroups of students, the staff at Del Roble joined with the community to begin using the Courageous Conversation Four Agreements, Six Conditions, and Compass. The protocol, which offered a new language, enabled teachers to examine instructional practices, a hallmark of creating an equitable school environment. In the case of Del Roble, educators, students, and families have successfully reduced their school's achievement gaps by focusing primarily on how students of different races experience teaching and learning. Evidence of their dramatic improvement is shared in the official school description written by the school's principal, Yvette Irving:

It is said that, in dreams, an oak tree symbolizes longevity, stability, strength, tolerance, wisdom, and prosperity. "Del Roble" is Spanish for "of the oak." It also names our school and represents all of the characteristics of the students, staff, and community in which it resides. Del Roble has its roots in local history having just celebrated its 30th year in existence. It is a stabilizing force for the community acting as a community center for adult education, neighborhood meetings, youth sporting events, and an evacuation site in times of need. The tree trunk is created by the staff who work inside the walls of the school, with support from the Oak Grove School District central office, and a community of parents, neighbors, and businesses that give it strength. Wisdom, emanating from the intentional and unwavering commitment to equity in access and outcomes for all students, is found in the Del Roble branches. The result—academic excellence—is achieved through acceleration in place of remediation, and differentiation rather than homogeneity. The core values of Quality Performance, Life-long Learning, Respect, Positive Interdependence, and Integrity are practiced by staff and student alike, and act as the leaves that blanket the children as they enter the school. These core values bring with them a tolerance for those who are different in ways both visible and unseen.

When you look at the accurate but impersonal statistics reflecting the Del Roble community you will find the following: 53% or 278 students participate in the NSLP (National School Lunch program), and we have a 23% mobility rate. 36% or 185 students are English Learners (EL). 48% of students have a primary language spoken at home that is not English, and 24 different languages are spoken on campus. Our racial diversity is reflected in 12% African American, 39% Latino, 20% Asian, 20% White, and 9% Other. Nationally, research implies that these statistics put the school at a disadvantage. The staff and community of Del Roble Elementary look at these statistics as our prosperity. With such diversity in the students who enter the doors of the school, the staff demonstrates innovation, collaboration, and determination as they educate and nurture the whole child.

The results of seizing this opportunity and implementing a comprehensive, standards aligned program in conjunction with an equity focus resulted in another set of "cold hard facts." Last year, 2002–2003, the school's Academic Performance Index (API) based on the state Standardized Testing and Reporting (STAR) results demonstrated a 43 point schoolwide growth from 712 to 754, compared with the prior year. Some subgroups exceeded overall school gains, with a 59 point growth for Latino students, 51 for Asian students and 23 for White students. The API also documented a 59-point growth for socioeconomically disadvantaged students. The school has the vision of *accelerating the rate of achievement of Latino and Black students, while sustaining the continued growth of their White and Asian counterparts.* This has been accomplished within the parameters of a limited school budget, since Del Roble receives no federal Title I funding, and with a staff wherein 65% of the teachers have 5 years or less experience. The school has also demonstrated success in increasing parent and community involvement, bringing back former Del Roble students as volunteers, developing partnerships with local businesses, and reducing disciplinary referrals. In addition we have created systemic change with racial representation in GATE (Gifted and Talented Education) now proportionate to the school enrollment, as it is in special education. The school's passionate belief is its responsibility to educate the whole child. Thus, the staff pursues professional development that not only supports them in effective teaching with standards aligned instructional materials, but that also helps them to foster a safe, happy, and healthy student. The school models what it hopes to teach its pupils. With the determination of staff, students, and parents, the vision becomes a reality.

The shared goal of staff and community is that each child who enters Del Roble leaves as a well-rounded, well-developed, life-long learner. This success is measured not only by the school's test results, but also in what each child becomes. By both measurements Del Roble has proven to be a success. "From little acorns, great oaks grow."

—Yvette Irving, Principal

In addition to standardized test data, Del Roble uses a second statistical analysis to measure whether student achievement growth is equitable across all racial groups. Using district and state data already disaggregated by race, Del Roble teachers calculate an *opportunity gap,* a statistic that compares rates of progress toward proficiency among racial subgroups. The opportunity gap measures the percentage of students in each grade who have already reached proficiency in comparison to the percentage of students who seem to be progressing too slowly to reach proficiency by the time they finish elementary school. As shown in Figure 3.3, Del Roble's opportunity gaps from the 2001–2002 school year ranged from 42.5% in second grade to 25.5% in fifth grade.

During those years, Black and Latino students were progressing at a slower rate toward proficiency than their White and Asian counterparts by a minimum of 25%. The school's improvement goal was to have all students reach proficiency by the end of sixth grade, and—as shown by these statistics—that did not seem likely to occur. At least that was the case until Del Roble educators began addressing the institutionalized racial challenges inherent in their school culture, climate, program, and structures.

Figure 3.3 2001–2002 Del Roble Math Proficiency Versus Opportunity Gap

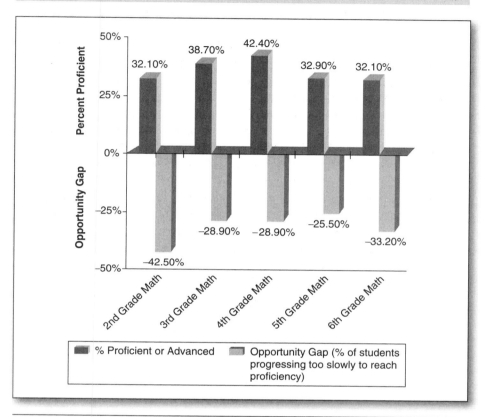

Source: Oak Grove School District.

The administrators and teachers at Del Roble created a dramatic turnaround in student achievement by acknowledging that racial biases existed in their own work and that these biases made it difficult for some students of some groups of color to succeed. The staff found these biases to be most pervasive in special education and GATE designation, hiring practices, and the teacher–classroom assignment process. In further addressing racial bias, teachers examined the curriculum used in their classrooms to see if the literature, for example, related to the culture of all students. The staff began to surface and share methods used by teachers who were succeeding with all students and to replicate those practices throughout the grade levels. Furthermore, Del Roble staff members actively fostered and nurtured relationships with families of color who had not traditionally been involved in school affairs. Most important, through effective utilization of the Courageous Conversation protocol, the entire staff became honest about their racial beliefs, expectations, judgments, and fears.

As a result of these efforts, the Del Roble community completely eliminated the opportunity gap in only one year's time. Concurrently, they also raised overall proficiency by an average of 15% per grade. This is not to say that all students suddenly were performing at the same level. What it does say, however, is that every student, regardless of racial background, was accelerating toward proficiency at an acceptable rate—the gaps closed, because students in groups of color that had traditionally performed poorly began progressing more rapidly than their White counterparts, toward mastery of the standards, as shown in Figure 3.4.

Figure 3.4 2002–2003 Del Roble Math Proficiency Versus Opportunity Gap

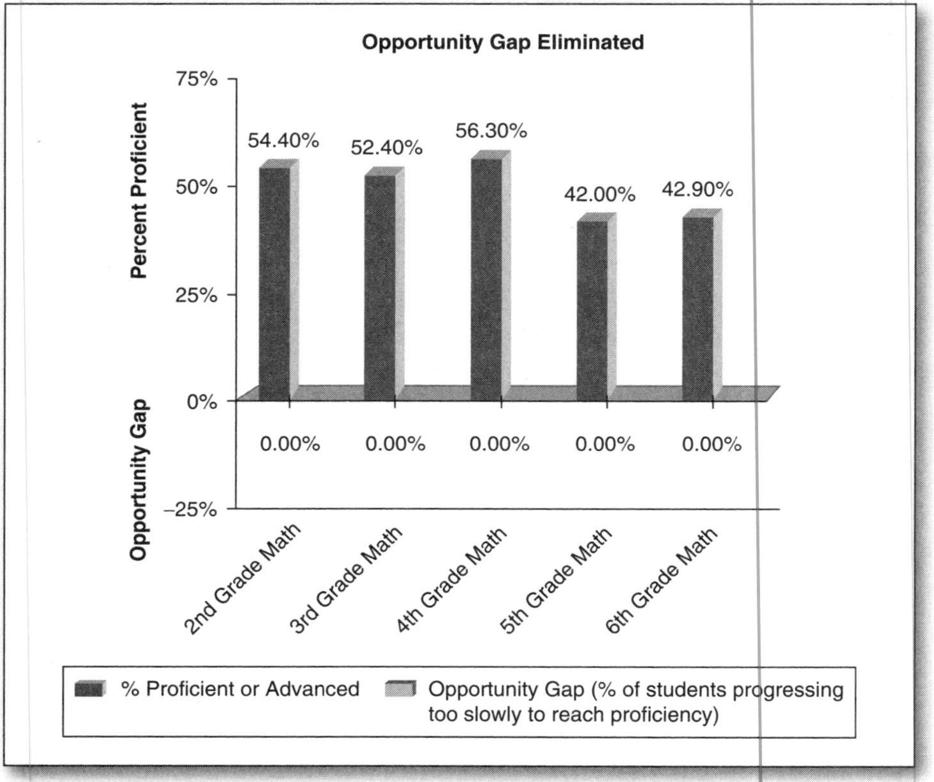

Source: Oak Grove School District.

By closing the opportunity gap, the school could now boast that by sixth grade, every student would have the knowledge and skills necessary to succeed in middle school. In other words, no children would be left behind. By promoting equitable, anti-racist education in their school, Del Roble closed the poverty gap, gender gap, and English language learning gap. By addressing race as an essential and foundational issue, Del Roble dealt effectively with *all* known factors impacting student performance.

Based on what you have read, what would you suspect to be the cultural (i.e., attitudes and behaviors) and structural (i.e., programs and policies) reforms that enabled Del Roble Elementary School to eliminate the racial gap? To what degree do you see similar reforms being instituted in your school system?

REFLECTION

DEALING WITH RACE

Recognizing that race is a significant factor impacting achievement requires that educators establish common understandings around racial issues. Too often, however, it seems that educators are reluctant to develop such understandings and instead blame the students themselves for the racial achievement gaps. Mano Singham (1998) explains this phenomenon in the following way:

> There is no real problem in the delivery system as such [especially in their own classroom] but only in the way that is received by different groups: that is, Black students don't respond to education in the proper manner. An alternative explanation is that the primary problem lies not in the way Black children view education but in the way we teach all children, Black, White, or other. (p. 12)

Many educators struggle to take personal and professional responsibility when it comes to meeting the needs of students of color and indigenous students who are not succeeding. They tend to focus on factors external to the school for explaining students' low achievement rather than examining their own instructional practices.

When dealing with issues of race, educators must become culturally proficient in relationships with students and families of varied racial backgrounds, experiences, beliefs, and understandings. As characterized by Lisa Delpit (1995a), teachers need to recognize "the haze of [our] own cultural lenses" (p. xv). Accordingly, as educators persist in Courageous Conversation and learn to address race more effectively, they will discover the limitations of their own views and recognize the validity of others'—even if some perspectives are radically different than their own. These different viewpoints, however, are not necessarily proof of racial division. More often, they merely serve as evidence that a person's racial/cultural lens encourages him or her to view the world accordingly and perhaps differently than someone of another racial background.

Addressing the impact of race in education is not a "feel good" experience. Nor is it an attempt to make White educators feel guilty, promote pity for people of color, or extract revenge on their behalf. Courageous Conversation provides the foundation for a systemic strategy to build responsibility through more thorough and authentic personal inquiry and engagement by educators, students, families, and the broader community. Educators participate in this difficult work of mastering the Courageous Conversation protocol for the sake of their students. Schools need to become places where effective education is guaranteed to every child. Effectively talking about race and addressing racism whenever and wherever it appears is an integral part of our responsibility to transform schools into inclusive, rigorous environments for ALL. Ruth Johnson (2002) puts it this way:

> It is about educators, students, and parents understanding the consequences of under preparation. It is about pointing out how and why some groups are under-prepared. Ultimately, it's about transforming the expectations and behaviors currently present in many schools and systems so that there are high-level options for all students. (p. 32)

ESTABLISHING COMMON LANGUAGE AROUND RACE

Developing and using common language in conversations about race helps establish critical understandings around how racial issues impact schooling. This is not to suggest that a single definition is available or even that one must be embraced. I do, however, believe that it is important that I provide a clear understanding of the meanings I intend when I use racial terminology.

Race, Racism, Racist

I refer to *race* as the socially constructed meaning attached to a variety of physical attributes, including but not limited to skin and eye color, hair texture, and bone structures of people in the United States and elsewhere. Thus, *racism*, generically speaking, can be defined as beliefs and an enactment of beliefs that one set of characteristics is superior to another set (e.g., white skin, blonde hair, and blue eyes are more beautiful than brown skin, brown eyes, and brown hair). Continuing with this decontextualized definition, a *racist* would be any person who subscribes to these beliefs and perpetuates them intentionally or unconsciously.

REFLECTION

Do you personally resonate with our definitions of *race, racism,* and *racist?* How are these definitions similar to or different from your own?

The aforementioned definitions work in any context, but when we view *race, racism,* and *racist* through the context of historical and contemporary American culture, and perhaps more broadly through a prism of Western culture, we can introduce a far more exact definition of *racism*. I believe that racism is the conscious or unconscious, intentional or unintentional enactment of racial power, grounded in racial prejudice, by an individual or group against another individual or group perceived to have lower racial status.

The scholars Gerald Pine and Asa Hilliard (1990) implicate far more people in perpetuating the debilitating realities of racism:

> Racism describes the combination of individual prejudice and individual discrimination, on the one hand, and institutional policies and practices, on the other, that result in the unjustified negative treatment and subordination of members of a racial or ethnic group. By convention, the term racism has been reserved to describe the mistreatment of members of racial and ethnic groups that have experienced a history of discrimination. *Prejudice, discrimination, and racism do not require intention.* (p. 595)

What I find most powerful in Pine and Hilliard's definition is the fact that racism does not require *intent.*

> How does Pine and Hilliard's definition of racism compare to your own? Based on this definition, do you perpetuate racism? If so, how? If not, why not?
>
> **REFLECTION**

In his article entitled *Racism,* Julian Weissglass (2001) broadly explores the nature of racism, its implications, and its distinction from the basic concept of prejudice:

> *Racism* is the systematic mistreatment of certain groups of people (often referred to as people of color) on the basis of skin color or other physical characteristics. This mistreatment is carried out by societal institutions, or by people who have been conditioned by the society to act, consciously or unconsciously, in harmful ways toward people of color. Racism is different from prejudice. A person of color can hurt a White person because of prejudice. The difference is that in this country, people of color face systematic and ongoing personal and institutionalized biases every day. (p. 49)

This description expands racism greatly by establishing it as the systemic perpetration of prejudice toward members of a particular race. It is important to note that for these acts to become systemic, they must emanate from the dominant race. Other groups do not have the racial power, presence, and position necessary to maintain the prejudicial acts over time and throughout society without abatement. Weissglass (2001) concludes by quoting Shirley Chisholm, America's first Black congresswoman, who said that "racism is so universal in this country, so widespread and deep-seated, that it is invisible because it is so normal" (p. 49).

REFLECTION

What reaction do you have to Weissglass's and Chisholm's assertions that racism is systemic, universal, invisible, and perpetrated by the dominant race? In what ways does this suggest that only White people can be racist? What is your belief?

Institutionalized Racism

Racism becomes institutionalized when organizations—such as a school, a district of schools, or a university—remain unconscious of issues related to race, or more actively perpetuate and enforce a dominant racial perspective or belief, for example, that racism is not a problem worthy of attention or redress. Despite efforts to reduce individual and collective racist acts, institutionalized racism persists in American culture and its educational systems due to educators' inaction as well as actions considered harmful to students of color. To serve students of color equitably, it is essential to challenge institutionalized racism and vigilantly reduce individual racial prejudices.

In explaining *institutionalized racism* in her landmark book, *White Awareness,* Judith H. Katz (2003) first quotes the *American Heritage Dictionary* definition of *racism:*

1. The belief that race accounts for differences in human character or ability and that a particular race is superior to others.

2. Discrimination or prejudice based on race.

She then adds the following qualification to illuminate institutionalized racism:

Prejudice plus power. (p. 53)

According to this definition, institutionalized racism equates to prejudice connected with the *power* to protect the interests of the discriminating racial group.

In further defining the nature of this power, Lindsey, Nuri Robins, and Terrell (2003), in their book *Cultural Proficiency,* define institutionalized racism as "the power to create an environment where that belief [racism] is manifested in the subtle or direct subjugation of the subordinate ethnic groups through a society's institutions" (p. 248).

It is important to consider this discussion of institutionalized racism as it pertains to schools. Rarely is intentional discrimination the central problem in the teacher–student relationship; rather, the discrimination includes unquestioned assumptions on the part of the institution within which these interactions take place. These assumptions—such as that Asian students are better at math, Brown parents don't support their kids in school, or advanced placement classes are too difficult for Black and Indigenous students—are at the heart of the racial achievement gap. Thus, institutionalized racism means to allow these negative assumptions to persist unchallenged by those having positional power. Unquestioned assumptions and unsubstantiated beliefs developed from limited experiences about the attitudes and abilities of student of color and their families are the basis for detrimental instructional practices that foster and preserve racial inequities in schools.

Henze, Katz, Norte, Sather, and Walker (2002) provide a shorthand formula to describe this type of institutionalized racism:

$$racism = racial\ prejudice + institutional\ power$$

They go on to establish a distinct difference between *individualized racial prejudice* and *institutionalized racism:*

> Certainly, any individual can perpetrate acts of racial prejudice towards another individual. Thus, Black people as individuals can be racially prejudiced against White people, Asians can be racially prejudiced against American Indians, and so on. But Black, Brown and American Indian people, individually or collectively, do not have the social, political, or economic power in the United States to alter the collective racial experience of White people. So in that sense, no matter how much racial prejudice individual Black Americans or other people of color might project towards White Americans, truly they cannot be said to be practicing institutional racism unless they are actively supporting the maintenance of racial power for White people. (p. 9)

REFLECTION

In what ways do you resonate with these scholars' definitions of *racism* and *institutionalized racism?* In what specific ways are their definitions similar to or different from your own?

The starting point in deinstitutionalizing racism is to believe first and fore-most that racism exists. Recall from an earlier discussion, the vast majority of school administrators and school board members, past and present, are White. Consequently, most educators—even those of color—are supervised and evalu-ated by a White person. When this is the case in a particular school, school system, or university setting, White educators experience a sense of racial superiority—whether consciously or unconsciously—manifested in their assumption that they uniquely possess certain skills and knowledge necessary for "appropriately" deal-ing with all students, parents, or even administrators and other teachers.

Because White educators feel somehow connected to the person who has always been in charge, their support of the White racial status quo equates to normal operational procedure. An educator, parent, or student of color who chal-lenges the White racial status quo is seen as a "troublemaker," "angry," or an "out-sider." Through Courageous Conversation, educators are able to discover a more effective response in which the predominantly White-led system authenticates the criticism rather than viewing it as an attack or dismissing the people of color rendering the critique.

Institutionalized racism also leads to conscious and unconscious feelings of racial inferiority for students of color and racial superiority among White students. For example, when White students enter an advanced placement classroom and see few if any students of color, they are unconsciously indoctrinated into White intellectual supremacy. These notions are typically unchallenged by educators, even as students of color learn about these classes, made up mostly of White students, and labeled as the "smart," "honors," "gifted," "advanced," "GATE," or "best" class. Not seeing others who look like them in these classes, many students of color and indigenous students will see themselves as being incapable of performing at equally high levels and feel unwanted in such classes or unworthy of taking them. Furthermore, because these classes are often taught by the more seasoned and respected teachers—the teachers who express passion for their work—the students of color are essentially taught by the system that they are *worth less* than White students.

According to Weissglass (2001), institutionalized racism fosters feelings of inferiority for students of color in the following ways:

1. The incorporation into institutionalized policies or practices of attitudes or values that work to the disadvantage of students of color (for example, differential allocation of resources, or tracking practices that consign many students of color to low tracks with less experienced teachers, from which they can seldom escape).

2. The unquestioned acceptance by the institution of White middle-class val-ues (for example, the scarcity of authors of color in many secondary schools' English curricula).

3. Schools' being passive in the face of prejudiced behavior that interferes with students' learning or well-being (for example, not addressing harassment or teasing, or meeting it with punishment instead of attempting to build communi-cation and understanding). (p. 49)

These unquestioned actions in schools are the most damaging aspects of institutionalized racism, because they stigmatize and marginalize students of color, thus creating gross inequities between them and their White counterparts. To eradicate these harmful practices, school communities must focus their efforts on intentionally and explicitly addressing systemic racial disparities, wherever they may exist.

Considering the aforementioned definitions of *racism* and *institutionalized racism*, where do you notice these phenomena most obviously and dangerously existing in your school system?

REFLECTION

Equity

Beyond establishing common language and understanding of what is meant by *race, racism,* and *racist,* another critical term for educators to develop meaning around when doing work in schools to eliminate racial disparities is *equity*. Equity is not a program or initiative and does not equate to "doing diversity work." Equity is a belief, a habit of mind that does not correspond to the beginning or end of the school day. Achieving true equity for all students must be a moral imperative, and it serves as a central and essential component of any attempt to eliminate racial achievement disparities. Lacking an individual and institutional purpose for racial equity, educators might experience a widening gap in achievement among students, because the root causes of such disparities remain unaddressed. In the long run, this will serve only to further disenfranchise students and parents of color. All students can benefit from a focus on equity, because an equitable school system is one that works to address the needs of each individual child.

I have developed the following definition for equity:

Educational equity is

- raising the achievement of all students, while
- narrowing the gaps between the highest and lowest performing students, and
- eliminating the racial predictability and disproportionality of which student groups occupy the highest and lowest achievement categories.

How does this definition of *equity* compare to the definition you have developed on your own or inferred from the previous chapters?

Equity is an operational belief that enables educators to provide whatever level of support is needed to whichever students require it. In the classroom, this means providing each and every student with what each individually needs to learn and succeed.

Furthermore, there is a distinct difference between *equality* and *equity*. According to DeCuir and Dixson (2004),

> In seeking *equality* rather than *equity*, the processes, structures, and ideologies that justify inequity are not addressed and dismantled. Remedies based on equality assume that citizens have the *same* opportunities and experiences. Race, and experiences based on race, are not equal. Thus, the experiences that people of color have with respect to race and racism create an unequal situation. *Equity*, however, recognizes that the playing field is *unequal* and attempts to address the inequality. (p. 29)

Equity is not a guarantee that all students *will* succeed. Rather, it assures that *all* students will have the opportunity and support necessary to succeed. In an equitable system, the barriers that inhibit student progress are removed. Students of color and their families can rest assured that the school will meet their needs to the same degree it meets White students' needs. Equity does not mean that every student receives an equal level of resources and support toward his or her educational goals. Rather, equity means that the students of greatest need receive the greatest level of support to guarantee academic success.

Anti-Racism and Leadership for Racial Equity

In coming to understand racism and institutionalized racism, it is not enough simply to become *non*-racist. Educators of all races should become *anti*-racists, which means to actively fight racism and its effects wherever they may exist.

Anti-racism can be defined as conscious and deliberate efforts to challenge the impact and perpetuation of institutional White racial power, presence, and privilege. It is critical that our examination of institutionalized White racism is not viewed as being against White people; rather, it is a way in which people of all races can gain the same level of access and privileges that White people tend to demand, to feel entitled to, and to take for granted. Anti-racism means working toward a realization of the ideals that the United States professes are true for all citizens. Specifically, anti-racism means that life, liberty, and the pursuit of happiness are guaranteed to people of color as well as White people.

To be anti-racist is to be active. Simply claiming to be non-racist and to "not see race in others" passively allows racism to continue. To eliminate racial achievement disparities, educators need to be aggressively anti-racist. Anti-racism is a deep, personal, and ongoing analysis of how each and every one of us perpetuates injustice and prejudice toward those who are not members of the dominant race.

Weissglass (2001) calls schools in which there are active anti-racist efforts under way "healing communities." In these environments,

> a wide range of anti-racism work will be going on. Educators will be identifying how their unaware bias affects their students, challenging any attitudes of low expectations, working with parents to help them support their children's learning, and identifying how racism becomes institutionalized in policies and practices. They will be questioning their curricula and pedagogy and working to make them more engaging to students of different cultures. (p. 50)

Anti-racist schools teach the history of how oppressed peoples have been treated in this country and support students of color and indigenous students and their families to challenge and heal from internalized racism. Anti-racist schools move beyond the celebration of diversity and create communities in which it is possible for students to talk about how they experience unfairness and discrimination and to heal. In these healing communities, adults' highest priority is caring about students and their learning.

As White educators are prompted to examine race and practice anti-racism, they need to be aware that White privilege counteracts their engagement by offering the opportunity to walk away from this conversation on race at times when it gets tough or personally uncomfortable. People of color and indigenous people face racial injustice daily and simply cannot avoid dealing with racism. Consequently, it is perhaps the greater injustice toward their colleagues and friends of color when White people choose not to deal with racial issues. To willingly partake of White privilege and be a bystander to racial inequity is actually to participate in the perpetuation of racism. Likewise, White educators who actively disengage from conversations about improving the achievement of students of color and indigenous students are racist, because anti-racism requires active challenges to institutionalized White racial power, presence, and privilege. There is no gray zone in anti-racist work.

Oprah Winfrey once said, "Racism is the day-to-day wearing down of the spirit. Anti-racism is the day-to-day goin' after the little things." Unfortunately for many White educators, "the little things" are not so apparent, and thus, addressing what are known as racial "microaggressions" rarely occurs in schools and universities. This fact makes me wonder whether the concept *anti-racist* is appropriate in the context of our current work, given one must be conscious of one's own daily racist beliefs and behavior in order to interrogate and correct them. For this reason, I tend to call on educators to be leaders who remain vigilant in their quest for racial equity. In my experience, establishing leadership for racial equity is not only achievable, but also recognizes the uneven application of our individual and collective consciousness, courage, and commitment when it comes to identifying, interrupting, and consistently working to eradicate racism in ourselves, our education systems, and our society.

DO WE HAVE THE WILL?

As educators, we need to ask ourselves, Do we have the *will* to educate all children? As Asa Hilliard (1995) suggests, providing quality education for all children is not a question of educators' experience or academic degrees; rather, it is a question of their personal willingness to fulfill their professional responsibilities:

> The knowledge and skills to educate all children already exist. Because we have lived in a historically oppressive society, educational issues tend to be framed as technical issues, which denies their political origin and meaning. . . . There are no pedagogical barriers to teaching and learning when willing people are prepared and made available to children. (p. 200)

REFLECTION

Do you believe that the knowledge and skills to educate *all* students already exist in education? To what degree do you feel that your school system has the will or passion to meet the needs of lower-achieving students of color?

Race matters in society and in our schools. The knowledge base to effectively teach all students—regardless of their race—already exists. Educators must decide whether to embrace this knowledge, examine their personal beliefs and practices, and engage in anti-racism for the benefit of their students. Hilliard (1995) continues, "If we embrace a will to excellence, we can deeply restructure education in ways that will enable teachers to release the full potential of all our children" (p. 200).

By understanding race and its impact on schooling, as well as by having a vision of equity and the courage to be anti-racists, educators will fortify their will. Only then can they truly recognize that to unleash the full potential of all children is within reach of any educator. As Ruth Johnson (2002) points out, "When asked what they would want for their own children, most educators inevitably say they expect the highest levels of education. Do other people's children deserve any less?" (p. 32).

To give all children the fair and equitable education they deserve, schools need to analyze how it is that they are serving or not serving their students of color. When addressing the racial achievement gap, race matters. It is critical that schools address issues around race to uncover whatever institutionalized biases exist that prevent students of color from reaching their fullest potential. Courageous Conversation serves as an essential strategy for educators in addressing racial matters and deinstitutionalizing racism in the educational arena.

IMPLEMENTATION EXERCISE

EQUITY TERMS

Time required: 45 minutes

Materials required: For each participant, Courageous Conversation Journal and the worksheet that follows

1. Make a copy of the following worksheet for each participant.

2. Before the discussion begins, have all educators answer 1a, 2a, 3a, and 4a by writing down what they believe each of the following terms means:

   Racism

   Institutionalized racism

   Anti-racism

   Equity

3. Ask for three to four volunteers to share with the entire group their personal definition for each term. Compare and contrast these definitions.

4. Present the definitions for each term based on what is presented in this chapter.

5. After the discussion, have each person answer 1b, 2b, 3b, and 4b by writing down a new definition for each term.

6. Divide all participants into small groups of three to four people. Have the groups discuss how their understanding of these terms has changed.

7. Bring the large group back together and allow people to share any conclusions.

8. Have the participants reflect on their personal learning and keep the worksheet in their journals for later reference.

EQUITY TERMS

1a. I have defined *racism* as

_____

_____

_____

1b. I now understand *racism* to be

_____

_____

_____

2a. I have defined *institutionalized racism* as

_____

_____

_____

2b. I now understand *institutionalized racism* to be

_____

_____

_____

3a. I have defined **equity** as

_____

_____

_____

3b. I now understand **equity** to be

_____

_____

_____

4a. I have defined **anti-racism** as

_____

_____

_____

4b. I now understand **leadership for racial equity** to be

_____

_____

_____

RACIAL AUTOBIOGRAPHY PART I

GLENN SINGLETON

Before kindergarten, I don't remember having a construct for race. I grew up in an entirely Black community in the inner city of Baltimore, where the only images of Whiteness I saw were on television. At Hilton Elementary School, all certificated and classified adults were Black; thus, interracial interaction was nonexistent. By fourth grade, I was attending YMCA camp for two weeks each summer, where I recall being fascinated by the hair texture and different body odors of White campers. In my young mind, differences existed between White and Black kids, but I never gave it too much thought. My family loved Hilton Elementary School, so much so that when we moved out of the attendance zone, they continued registering me as a student there by using my grandparents' address for fifth and sixth grades.

Today, I realize how integral it was to my educational success that I often saw my teachers in shopping centers, at social events, or at church on the weekends. This form of omnipresent accountability brought distress to me when I was caught misbehaving in school. Most of my teachers were not shy about "airing the class-room laundry" to our parents, and our families truly welcomed the information and responded accordingly. Never did I question whether my teachers understood me, my family, or our Black culture, as this was a shared experience. I believe that my K–4 teachers treated their students as if we were their own children, for better or for worse.

By the time I was in fifth grade, Baltimore, like many US urban centers, was again being forced to desegregate public schools. Like my mother's community in the late fifties, our neighborhood was abuzz about the possibility of its children being bused away from Hilton Elementary and leaving our highly qualified Black teachers behind. Fortunately for us, Hilton was an experimental site, where some teachers, rather than the students, were forced to relocate. My relationship with my fifth-grade teacher, Fran Finnegan, became the first of many interracial rela-tionships in which I would be involved. Mrs. Finnegan was said to be a wonderful suburban teacher, but in retrospect, it is clear she lacked the cultural proficiency necessary to advance our gifted class. She said it did not matter to her what color we were, but unfortunately, our inquisitive minds could not share her perspective. She was really White in our eyes and subject not only to our curiosity but also to our childish malice. I guess the many years of family and community members returning from their workplaces having had unfavorable experiences with "the (White) man"—who I later discovered could also be a White woman—permeated our consciousness, creating a sense of distrust of and dislike for our struggling White teacher.

As a class, we were quite aware of Mrs. Finnegan's racial foibles, and we also knew from experiences with Black teachers what it felt like to have teachers who truly knew and liked us! To her credit, when most of the White teachers departed

Hilton after little more than a semester, Mrs. Finnegan felt an unexplained need to hang around. With the White teacher exodus, Mrs. Finnegan was also forced to get to know the Black teachers, which I believe enabled her to begin figuring us out and improving the quality of her instruction. The days when we made Mrs. Finnegan break down in tears quickly dissipated into a new era of culturally responsive instruction. What a shock it was to hear my mother refer to my White teacher as "Sista Finnegan" after attending a parent/teacher conference. Now that she has retired from Hilton Elementary School, Mrs. Finnegan lives on as one of our family's most influential and memorable teachers.

Given my success at Hilton Elementary School, I wonder why I was "strongly encouraged" by my mother to attend a private school for middle and high school. I recall feeling torn between the excitement of Park School's well-resourced, extravagant campus and facility and the desire to walk to school with my neighborhood friends. The message I received explicitly from home and implicitly from the Park School community was "If it ain't White, it isn't Right." My best friend, Jimmy, and I were sent to Park School together, so I wasn't alone, except for the fact that Park School administrators never allowed us to be in the same classes. It seemed to me that Jimmy was responsible for diversifying one half of our class and I the other. We would huddle for lunch each day and for class photos once a year. Jimmy's athletic prowess eventually earned him distinction, as he could adapt his football and baseball skills to soccer and lacrosse, the only sports options available to Park students. I also played both sports but found little of my soul on the manicured athletic fields.

The state-of-the-art theater called out to me when I was forced into summer school before seventh grade. What a shock and a blow to my confidence to move from the ranks of gifted in the Black community to remedial among my White soon-to-be peers. While Park faculty "refreshed" the "slower learners" in summer school, the administrators opened the elitist doors of its professional theater each summer to inner-city teenage artists who staged Black musicals such as *The Wiz* and *Purlie.* But come fall, the Black teenagers had all returned to their inner-city schools and taken the Black musicals, energy, and spirit with them. I was left with the theater and a long list of Gilbert and Sullivan or Rodgers and Hammerstein productions in which I would need to fit my Black body into White roles. Today, I am still known as the "Black Pirate King" from our eighth-grade production of *The Pirates of Penzance* by a school that adamantly insisted that they did not see color. Performing arts transformed me into a singing, dancing cowboy in *Oklahoma* and a racist White gang-leader in *West Side Story.* My new roles brought with them a host of lasting racial identity struggles.

Mastering the advanced curriculum in the classroom mirrored the theatrical requirement that I think and act White. Park was increasingly impressed by my ability to imitate their culture so precisely. I received the highest award for my contribution to life on campus. The corresponding reward to my family and

(Continued)

(Continued)

neighborhood were feelings of alienation and internalized White supremacy as I embodied long-lasting self-hatred.

While it was clear by junior year that I might be first in the family to graduate from college, beginning a Black college tradition at Morehouse, Morgan, or Howard was out of the question, given my counselor felt an Ivy League university such as Penn, Brown, or Cornell would bring greater prominence to any Park School alumnus. I left Park deeply connected to the institution, my education, and my faculty and friends partly because I was extraordinarily proficient in Whiteness and poised to further assimilate at the next higher level.

At Penn, I chose, based on my experience at Park, to embrace the White community and neglect all things Black. In the mainly White dormitory, I befriended White students and eventually pledged a "very White" fraternity, Sigma Chi. How deep was my investment in Whiteness by this stage? So much so that I found nothing wrong with shouting "All Honor to His Name" as my overtly racist White pledge master read the names of the known White supremacist founders. My initiation was just short of a Ku Klux Klan rally complete with white hooded robes, fire-lit torches, and a cross burning—defined as the blazing symbol of the fraternity. Given that we never truly studied this heinous American past at Park School, I was dangerously naïve. There are many painful memories related to Sigma Chi that I have buried; I am now convinced it was not the best choice for my spirit.

I believe I eventually went to work as an admissions director at Penn partly because I knew how to be White at the university, and I was well respected for my well-honed assimilation efforts. Traveling to New England to recruit students served as a racial wake-up call. Not only did many White high school educators and Penn alumni disrespect me racially, but I was often not considered to be the "real" Ivy League admissions director. Many had trouble with a Black man having such power. As a university administrator, I got to see my alma mater in a completely different way. I watched talented students of color come to Penn and not fit in culturally. I could truly see the forced process of assimilation that had been my own daily diet as a student there and then as an administrator.

Five years later when Penn moved me to California to direct the West Coast admissions office, I initially believed the hype surrounding the wonderful diversity and interracial solidarity in California. I guess I was amazed to see how close together the different races lived, worked, and played. I also learned quickly that it was not "politically correct" to talk about race in the Golden State. Although the East was incredibly segregated by comparison, I felt safer being Black in Philly, Baltimore, and New York City. In California, I could never quite figure out how people felt about me racially, whereas the racial writing was, both literally and figuratively, on the wall back East. *More to come . . .*

FOUR

Agreeing to Talk About Race

Discussions and debates about racism create anxiety and conflict, which are handled differently by different cultural groups. For example, Whites tend to fear open discussion of racial problems because they believe that such discussion will stir up hard feelings and old hatreds. Whites tend to believe that heated arguments about racism lead to divisiveness, loss of control, bitter conflict, and even violence. Blacks, on the other hand, believe that discussion and debate about racism help to push racial problems to the surface—and, perhaps, force society to deal with them.

—Gerald Pine and Asa Hilliard (1990, p. 596)

Courageous Conversation is an ambitious attempt to break down the racial tensions and ignorance that hobble our progress as a nation. By utilizing the protocol to engage, sustain, and deepen this dialogue, those who already possess the knowledge gain the opportunity to share it, which is not only healing but also insightful. For those who do not have the knowledge yet, they learn how to access it, develop insights about their own and others' racial identity, and grow tremendously from that experience. In building mutual understanding, educators discover what they need to collectively foster equity and diminish both overt and, for some, more subtle racial conflict.

To ensure personal engagement, honesty, endurance, and persistence in the dialogue about race in schools, the first formal step in this process is for educators to commit to honoring the Four Agreements of Courageous Conversation: to stay engaged, experience discomfort, speak your truth, and expect and accept non-closure. As preparation for making this commitment, however, educators need to consider their own racial consciousness. White educators might ask themselves: Am I aware that racial inequity exists, and am I capable of addressing it? Educators of color might ask: Do I unwittingly support institutionalized racism in our system, and am I willing to speak up and confront the inequities I experience personally and see negatively affecting our students of color and indigenous students?

RACIAL CONSCIOUSNESS

One of the most difficult aspects of Courageous Conversations about race, whether those engaging in it are White, of color, or indigenous, is admitting that they may not know all that they have claimed to know or honestly believed they knew. With limited racial consciousness, many educators—Whites especially— feel inhibited when conversing about race and racial issues, and/or find themselves lacking in knowledge and understanding about their own racial experience as well as about those who have different racial backgrounds and perspectives.

Pamela Noli is a White educator in the San Francisco Bay Area. In the early part of her career, Pam felt that she was doing an immense amount of good for the teachers, students, and families of color with whom she worked, because she deeply cared about their welfare. It was this sense of empathy and caring that guided much of her decision-making process.

She began her teaching career in California's San Joaquin Valley and chose to work in schools that primarily served Latinos. She was there by choice, and she knew that she loved the children. However, she assumed that the love she felt could overcome her lack of actual knowledge about her students' lives. She thought that if she cared enough, she could make the right decisions for her students.

At the time, she was married to a Latino, had a Latino last name, and lived in a Latino farming community. Even though she learned more and more about some of the people of color in her town and what created their sense of community, she came to realize how much more she had to learn. As she says,

> I still really didn't know what I didn't know. I thought that because I loved so much that I did know, till someone said, "You know Pam, you're the most dangerous person in this conversation, you White liberals." That was exactly what she said to me! She continued, "White liberals are the most dangerous people in the conversation about race because you think you know because you care, but *you don't know what you don't know.*" You don't know what you don't know!
>
> It was so true for me.
>
> When I was going to college at Fresno State I was on the march with Cesar Chavez in Sacramento, but I was completely there as a missionary. I didn't know at the time, but as I reflect back, I was there helping those *poor Brown people.* I didn't know what I didn't know, but I thought I did. (Singleton, 2002)

For Pam, acknowledging that *she did not know what she did not know* was the hardest realization in coming to terms with her racial consciousness and how it affected her work with students of color. A huge shift for Pam in her own consciousness was separating the fact that she cared from what she actually knew.

While educators of color often know about their own racial experience, they may lack an understanding of how to advance interracial dialogue in a productive way. Jamie Almanzán is a biracial former middle school teacher of Mexican American and White American descent who worked hard to develop a profound sense of who he is racially. The more that Jamie developed his consciousness around how race was impacting him and the students he served, the more he felt the need to share his insights with his colleagues, who were predominately White. The staff's resistance to engage in dialogue about Jamie's important discoveries caused internal conflict and great tension between him and his colleagues. Like many teachers of color in similar situations, Jamie eventually chose to retreat to the privacy and solitude of his own classroom, as he felt that it was no use trying to get his colleagues to understand his point of view or the viewpoints of many of his Mexican American students and their families. Clearly, his inability to facilitate interracial dialogue with school-based adults did not serve his students' best interest either.

To overcome these challenges, both of these educators participated in Courageous Conversation professional development. For Pam, this protocol and strategy provided her with a way of attaining the knowledge she needed to understand what the lives of her students of color were really like. For Jamie, Courageous Conversation helped him to facilitate effective interracial dialogue in the school setting. Armed with these skills and knowledge, these two educators increased not only their capacity to care but also their effectiveness in the classroom and with colleagues. Courageous Conversation fortifies the passion, practice, and persistence educators need to build racial consciousness and impact more profoundly their schools' learning environments.

I Don't Know What I Don't Know

The first step in developing racial consciousness is acknowledging that "I don't know what I don't know"—a simple phrase with profound implications. Consciously, we use what we think we know when we share with others our beliefs and opinions. Equally powerful, however, is what we don't know or what we incorrectly assume we know. These two domains of knowledge—*I don't know I don't know* and *I don't know but I think I do*—are ultimately the most limiting in the way we lead our own lives. When we function based on a set of assumptions without accurate funds of knowledge about what is real, we develop a myopic and distorted view of self and of others.

In terms of our own racial experience, we may have a limited understanding not only of the lives of people of different races but even of how our personal racial identities impact our own lives. Many White people struggle to recognize that they have a racialized existence and that their color, indeed, affords them privilege and opportunity in our society. Likewise, people of color and indigenous people may distrust the motives of White people collectively without actually discussing this distrust with the individual White people in their lives. To develop racial consciousness is to challenge our assumptions, and thus build our funds of knowledge through actual lived experiences. This will allow us to live more authentically within our own racial experience and deal more honestly with the racialized existence of others.

To develop our racial awareness, as diagrammed in Figure 4.1, the Racial Consciousness Flow Chart, we must deliberately move out of "I don't know I don't know" through the different stages of consciousness until we reach "I know I know."

Figure 4.1　Racial Consciousness Flow Chart

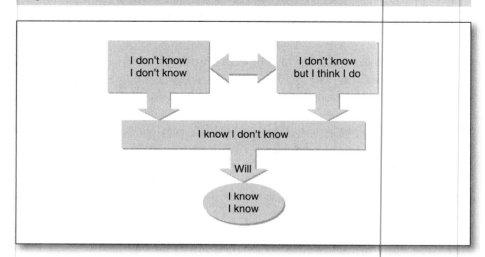

Moving Through the Stages

To advance through the stages as we confront racial issues on a daily basis is a consciousness-raising experience. When we act based on ignorance, we are functioning in the stage "I don't know I don't know." Likewise, if our assumptions guide us but have not been verified, we are in the stage of "I don't know but I think I do." From either of these stages, we can experience an awakening of our consciousness by acquiring information that challenges our assumptions or equips us with new knowledge. At this point, we move into "I know I don't know." From here, we can exercise our *will* by actively engaging in the expansion of our knowledge and understanding. As we do this, we move into the final stage, "I know I know." Only at this point do we begin to exist in full consciousness and become secure in our belief that our fund of knowledge is sufficient.

The following story illustrates how we move through these different stages of racial consciousness awareness:

A White female teacher is asked whether or not Black students in the school are underrepresented in honors and Advanced Placement (AP) courses in comparison to White students. Having never considered this and being unaware of the racial enrollment in these courses, she instinctively responds no. Ignorant of the realities of White overenrollment in the honors and AP classes, her consciousness at this moment is in the stage of "I don't know I don't know."

Next, the teacher expresses the belief that there is no racial achievement gap in the honors and AP program. This belief is in the stage of "I don't know but I think I do," because she is operating from an assumption that students of all races who qualify for these courses excel to the same degree.

Following this, the teacher is presented with statistical data highlighting the achievement gap between Black and White students in honors and AP courses. This is now a consciousness-raising experience informing the teacher that her fund of knowledge related to the intersection of race and student course placement has been limited. At this point, she advances into the stage of "I know I don't know."

Based on this experience, the teacher must exercise her *will and engage her passion* to discover the reality of the achievement gap, which might include discussing with honors and AP students of color why they succeed and don't succeed. This should lead her to explore other racial inequities that exist in her school. By doing this, she has elevated her consciousness into the stage of "I know I know." Secure in this newfound knowledge, the teacher becomes much more effective in her own classroom with all students.

> **REFLECTION**
>
> Think of an experience when your racial consciousness was developed. Name and reflect on the discovery, then trace it through the stages outlined previously.

It is important to reach this deepest level of racial consciousness to connect effectively with students, parents, and colleagues of different races. White educators must understand that although racial consciousness for many people of color is acute, giving voice to it remains a challenge. Educators of color can likewise recognize how difficult engaging in this conversation is for a White person, often because of the limited amount of thought given to understanding one's White racial experience. Consequently, the productivity of interracial relationships, professional as well as personal, depends on how authentic we all become in our own racial consciousness.

This need to raise our individual and collective racial consciousness and advance from "I don't know I don't know" toward "I know I know" is more about where the adults are rather than the students. Educators eventually will need to determine the distance that exists between their own racial consciousness and that of their students. Large gaps in racial consciousness between teachers and students can create dissonance, especially when students feel that a teacher does not understand them. Although many educators of color and indigenous educators may possess a sufficient level of racial consciousness, failure to voice their understanding has a similar devastating effect on our underserved Black, Brown, and Indigenous children. Consequently, what typically occurs in both of these situations of disconnect is that the student will disengage from learning before the adult attempts to raise his or her own racial consciousness or raise his or her voice and foster meaningful engagement.

As educators experience consciousness-raising opportunities in their schools with the overarching goal of rising to the stage of "I know I know" in their own racial consciousness, they prepare themselves to fully engage in Courageous Conversations about race.

FOUR AGREEMENTS OF COURAGEOUS CONVERSATION

To participate effectively in interracial dialogue about race, the first step is to commit to honoring and practicing the Four Agreements of Courageous Conversation. By committing to these, participants agree to

- Stay engaged
- Experience discomfort
- Speak your truth
- Expect and accept non-closure

Embracing these agreements will allow educators to engage, sustain, and deepen interracial dialogue about racial identity, racism, and the racial achievement disparities that exist between White students and students of color or indigenous students.

The racial climate and culture in our country and our schools equip us with well-developed skills for disengaging from racial issues. Consequently, we have created lasting and hidden racial conflicts that impact all of us. These agreements, however, secure in participants the commitment and persistence needed to address these conflicts as they surface during Courageous Conversation. As described by Frederique Wynberg, a White staff developer and proponent of equity work in Vallejo, California,

It takes Courageous Conversation to get to the point where you can actually think about race—as a White person—without feeling defensive. Or, for people of color, without feeling both defensive because you're now part of a White institution and also very angry because of what is going on in society and what's institutionalized. (Singleton, 2002)

For White educators, educators of color, and indigenous educators, committing to the Four Agreements is the first step required to counter the problematic norms that traditionally occur during interracial dialogue about race. At the end of this chapter, you will have the opportunity to commit personally to these agreements and to try leading others in making the same commitment. With this accomplished, you will be ready to begin Courageous Conversation, assured by an understanding that all involved in the dialogue are fully committed to the process.

Stay Engaged

Participants in Courageous Conversation must stay engaged. This is a personal commitment each of us makes, regardless of the engagement of others. Staying engaged means remaining morally, emotionally, intellectually, and relationally involved in the dialogue. To stay engaged is to not let your heart and mind "check out" of the conversation while leaving your body seated at the table.

This may be more difficult than it sounds, because educators traditionally do not talk about race unless the racial challenge is unavoidable. Many White Americans have been culturally conditioned to not talk about race. While Whites maintain this silence, many people of color and indigenous people—in the United States and beyond—converse about racial matters daily, if only among themselves. Consequently, little "before the crisis" interracial dialogue about race ever takes place. Collectively in the United States, racial topics tend to be "hot button" issues that either cause people of color to become vocally angry or make White people silently defiant or disconnected. Given this accepted pattern of interracial disengagement among the vast majority of Americans, it is no wonder so many racial challenges continue to exist within our larger society.

Collective disengagement also exists in schools. When a dramatic racial achievement gap persists, the children of the school pay the ultimate price for the adults' unwillingness to engage in difficult interracial dialogue. Whenever the topic turns to race, many educators seem to disengage by (a) redefining the conversation to focus on poverty, family structure, or any of a number of diversity issues other than race or (b) becoming silent, perhaps staring off into space, and letting out a deep and drawn-out breath to signal lack of interest or discomfort with the conversation.

REFLECTION

Can you think of a time in a personal and/or professional circumstance when race became a topic of conversation and you either actively changed the subject or avoided the conversation altogether? What did you believe caused you to react in this manner?

The challenge is to resist the natural inclination to move away from the conversation. In our experience, most educators will not want to talk about racial issues. School leaders need to be aware of this as an initial step in creating the necessary safer space for staff to stay engaged. If this relative safety is not created, those at the table will stand up and walk away, whether literally or figuratively.

By individually committing to stay engaged in Courageous Conversations about race, educators can guard against the learned tendency to disengage. By collectively making this commitment, we can fully embrace the conversation and ensure that it deepens our focus on eliminating racial achievement disparity and propels our efforts to do so.

Speak Your Truth

It was Martin Luther King Jr. (1968) who said, "I do not see how we will ever solve the turbulent problem of race confronting our nation until there is an honest confrontation with it and a willing search for the truth and a willingness to admit the truth when we discover it." Speaking your truth in Courageous Conversations about race requires a willingness to take risks. Speaking your truth means being absolutely honest about your thoughts, feelings, and opinions and not just saying what you perceive others want to hear. Too often, we don't speak our truth out of fear of offending, appearing angry, or sounding ignorant. In a sense, we opt for preserving an external peace over sharing our internal truths. But until we can become completely and audibly honest, the dialogue will remain limited and ultimately ineffective.

When it comes to racial matters in our society, we have learned to not say what's on our minds—to not speak our truth. This, however, often leads to deeper confusion, mistrust, and misunderstanding. Many beliefs concerning race are based on misconceptions and half-truths. This can occur when a member of one race believes that a member of another race agrees with or supports her simply because the other person said nothing. Without speaking his truth, the educator who has remained silent has allowed his own beliefs or opinions to be misinterpreted or misrepresented.

Lisa Delpit (1988/1995b) has labeled this phenomenon the *silenced dialogue;* in it, teachers and parents of color tend to get quiet in the presence of more verbal White educators. In her essay, "The Silenced Dialogue: Power and Pedagogy of Educating Other People's Children," Delpit suggests that this silence occurs because educators and parents of color often feel their racial experiences are deprecated or invalidated by White educators. She goes on to write,

> [White educators] do not perceive themselves to have power over the non-White speakers. However, either by virtue of their position, their numbers, or their access to that particular code of power of calling upon research to validate one's position, the White educators had the authority to establish what was to be considered "truth" regardless of the opinions of the people of color, and the [educators and parents of color] were well aware of that fact. (p. 26)

This silence is likely to occur in faculty meetings, in the principal's office, and even during informal conversations when people of color describing a racist experience or situation are told, "Aren't you exaggerating it a little?" "That (White) person really didn't mean it that way," or "You probably just misunderstood them." As this happens time and time again, people of color and indigenous people grow silent, refrain from sharing their stories and opinions, and no longer speak their truth. This silence, however, is now seen as implicit agreement; others believe that the educators and parents of color actually agree with what is happening in the primarily White institution. Delpit (1988/1995b) writes that when educators of color are silent, then "the White educators believe that their colleagues of color did, in the end, agree with their logic. After all, they stopped disagreeing, didn't they?" (p. 23).

For example, if only one Brown educator sits on a bilingual committee at a school, but—caught in the silenced dialogue—that educator says nothing as a policy is pushed forward, the school claims it has total support. Then, should the Brown community protest, the school points out that the Latino serving on the committee never said anything against the policy, which must be an indication that he or she supported it. What White educators in this and similar situations fail to take into account, however, is that the silence does not necessarily mean that the Brown educator agreed with the policy or felt safe to express his or her true feelings about it. It only means that he or she was silent.

The silenced dialogue can also occur among White people. Henze et al. (2002) explain why educators may be afraid to address conflicts or tensions that have racial dimensions in an honest, forthright, and truthful manner:

> They may be afraid that doing so will lead to an increase in conflict or that they will then be targeted by the original perpetrators. They may simply not want to raise the issue because it is too painful to talk about or they know that other people will be uncomfortable. Many schools have a code of silence about race and ethnicity, a value system that says it's best to be colorblind. In a colorblind school, there is no safe place for someone [of color]. (p. 46)

In this "colorblind school" where silenced dialogue is practiced among White educators, there may be a perceived lack of racial problems, but this is typically only because racial issues are redefined, ignored, avoided, and/or dismissed.

As Lena Williams (2000) writes in *It's the Little Things*, Whites often don't speak their truth in regard to racial issues, because they are afraid of making a misstep and having to defend what they say, their actions, or their race. Consequently, White people may rarely share their own authentic racial stories and beliefs, but rather they may talk about what happened to a White friend or tell a colleague of color what they believe he wants to hear. White people need to speak their own personal truth, as this is the only way for them to fully engage and develop their racial consciousness. Even though they may fear appearing racist at first as they expose inner thoughts and beliefs, speaking honestly is the way that

White people can first become more fully cognizant of their own racial experience and subsequently develop deeper understanding of the racial perspectives and experiences of others.

REFLECTION

Can you recall a time when race was the topic of conversation and you became silent and/or shared something that was less than your truest feeling in fear of what other's response might be?

All educators—Whites, people of color, and indigenous people—must share the responsibility to engage and speak their truth in Courageous Conversations about race. In fact, people of color will be more likely to open up when White people simply validate their experiences without shutting them down, interrogating them, or redefining their experience into more familiar diversity terms. A White person can never "own" the experience of a person of color, just as a person of color cannot "own" the White experience. We can only become experts in defining our own racial experiences and personal realities. Part of our struggle is rooted in our relative inability to search for meaning in the racial perspective of others, no matter how different another's experience may be from our own.

When it comes to dealing with race, one of the greatest challenges in American culture and especially in our schools is that White people, people of color, and indigenous people don't share their honest feelings about race. For a Courageous Conversation to occur, we need to engage, which means we break our silence and speak our truth.

Experience Discomfort

Because of the problematic racial conditions in our society, Courageous Conversations necessarily create discomfort for participants. Rather than experience the discomfort in interracial dialogue, many people often put an emphasis on how we are all alike instead of addressing our obvious differences. Typical diversity trainings are focused around not getting participants upset or too uncomfortable. Traditional diversity training, however, has been unsuccessful in helping schools eliminate racial achievement disparities. The Courageous Conversation protocol and strategy for achieving racial equity, on the other hand, asks participants to agree to experience discomfort so that they can deal with the reality of race and racism in an honest and forthright way.

In my work with school systems and universities both across the nation and around the world, I have challenged educators to deal openly and honestly with their racial challenges. On occasion, I have been accused of "dividing the staff." The reality is that I have simply brought into the open the troubles that already exist but have been deemed "non-discussable." If educators experience division as they deal with issues of race and equity, I suspect that they were already silently divided. Although discomfiting, giving voice and meaning to this racial divide can begin the process of healing and transformation.

Likewise, it is disingenuous for school systems to address the racial achievement gap in a cursory or "feel good" way. Educators need to engage in this dialogue authentically. To do so, participants need to be personally responsible for pushing themselves into a real dialogue—the kind that will make them uncomfortable but also will lead to real growth. Such conversations require that people open up and examine their core racial beliefs, values, perceptions, and behaviors. But as people speak their truth, tremendous emotion and fear may surface, thus creating personal and collective discomfort. For many White educators, discomfort unmasks their fear linked to offending people of color or indigenous people when expressing perceived biased or unsympathetic racial views and perspectives. On the other hand, educators of color and indigenous educators most often avoid uncomfortable dialogue out of fear of expressing intense anger and being misunderstood, ignored, or even punished by their White colleagues.

To develop authentic interracial relationships, we must break our collective silence. Staying within the parameters of the Courageous Conversation protocol, however, affords participants greater safety while managing this dialogue. As they increase their tolerance for the discomfort, they will also increase their ability to address the most challenging institutional circumstances associated with racial achievement disparity.

Expect and Accept Non-Closure

The remaining Agreement of Courageous Conversation encourages participants to recognize that they will not necessarily reach closure in their racial understandings or in their interracial interactions. The normal way of dealing with challenges faced by schools is to search for the "solutions." In Courageous Conversation, however, solutions are revealed in the process of dialogue itself. Simply put, we cannot discover a solution to a challenge if we have not been able to talk, specifically and intentionally, about that challenge. Furthermore, the magnitude, complexity, and longevity of our racial struggle and strife, particularly in the United States, rule out any possibility of discovering a "quick fix." In this conversation, the solutions discovered are ever forming and ever changing. Therefore, participants must commit to an ongoing dialogue as an essential component of their action plan. This is how to manifest the agreement to expect and accept non-closure.

Typical professional learning opportunities offer educators a binder in which specific steps and goals are listed. These seem concrete and may even appear sequential. The suggestion is that by the time each exercise or activity in the binder is completed, a solution will be found to the challenge being addressed. If such a binder existed for addressing racial achievement disparities, I would happily present it.

This, however, is not the case. Rarely has the issue of race been addressed in the traditional professional learning opportunities for educators, and it has never been presented as essential learning. I believe that much of this neglect is due to the fact that no neat and tidy tasks, processes, or timelines with guaranteed solutions currently exist. Courageous Conversation, however, triggers a moral, intellectual, relational, and emotional shift that allows participants to revisit their many professional development binders of previous trainings with a newly developed racial lens and language. If we expect and accept non-closure in racial discourse, then the more we talk, the more we learn; and the more we learn, the more appropriate and promising will be our individual and collective actions and interventions.

REFLECTION

As you reflect on the Four Agreements of Courageous Conversation, which do you believe will be the most difficult for you to embrace and practice? Why is this so? Which will be the easiest?

The Courageous Conversation can at times be difficult but is also rewarding. Given that everyone enters this dialogue at a unique place, some will take longer to arrive at a basic understanding of what race is and how it impacts their lives, and for some it will take longer to be ready to talk about how race impacts student achievement. Others may be ready almost immediately to begin examining how race impacts the classroom, program, department, or systemwide policies. Everyone, however, must stay collectively engaged throughout this continuous, challenging, and always evolving dialogue.

The Four Agreements of Courageous Conversation require commitment by each individual involved in the school improvement effort. These Agreements prepare educators to authentically engage in Courageous Conversation. Furthermore, they allow stakeholders to manage the conversation as real change begins to occur. Some school systems engaged in racial equity work have added additional agreements to supplement these four. As long as you exercise extreme caution to not dilute the Four Agreements, I encourage you to consider the culture of your system and determine what other agreements might help your colleagues remain committed to Courageous Conversations about race.

IMPLEMENTATION EXERCISE

FOUR AGREEMENTS OF COURAGEOUS CONVERSATION

Time required: 45 minutes

Materials required: For each participant, Courageous Conversation Journal and the two worksheets that follow

Present the Racial Consciousness Flow Chart to your group, and discuss the following:

- What does it mean to admit "I don't know I don't know"?
- What are the inherent weaknesses of "I don't know but I think I do"?
- How can admitting "I know I don't know" impact a teacher's efforts?
- What kind of *will* needs to be enacted to advance from "I know I don't know" to "I know I know"?

1. Have each participant identify three areas where their knowledge exists for each stage of the Racial Consciousness Flow Chart and reflect briefly with a partner.

2. Share with the group the meaning and rationale for each of the Four Agreements of Courageous Conversation:

   Stay engaged

   Experience discomfort

   Speak your truth

   Expect and accept non-closure

3. Divide the participants into small groups, and have them discuss the Four Agreements using the following prompts:

   - During a conversation about race, has anyone ever experienced *disengagement* from the conversation? How did it impact the dialogue?
   - Has anyone ever felt *discomfort* during a conversation on race? If so, did you work through the discomfort successfully, or was it left unresolved?
   - Which emotions prevent you from *speaking your truth* during interracial conversations about race? Which conditions can make it safer for you to deal with your racial fears and speak your truth?
   - Why is it necessary to *expect and accept non-closure* when dealing with race?

4. Have each participant complete and sign the following Four Agreements of Courageous Conversation document. After they complete this, have them keep the document in their Courageous Conversation Journal.

Discuss with the group how having committed to these agreements will impact the staff's dialogue about student achievement in your school or school system.

RACIAL CONSCIOUSNESS FLOW CHART FOR EXERCISE

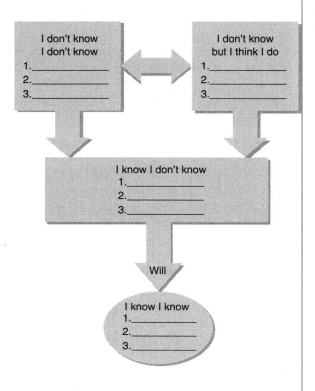

FOUR AGREEMENTS OF COURAGEOUS CONVERSATION

I agree to . . .

- Stay engaged.
- Experience discomfort.
- Speak my truth.
- Expect and accept non-closure.

My signature below indicates my commitment to engage, sustain, and deepen interracial dialogue about race.

_____
Educator's Signature

CURTIS LINTON

RACIAL AUTOBIOGRAPHY

I grew up White, male, middle class, Mormon, educated and heterosexual in the suburbs of Salt Lake City, Utah. Where I lived, I defined the norm. I was the third of my siblings to attend Jordan High School—all model kids, all student body officers, and all honors students. My teachers were just like me, and my parents were both teachers. The only surprise I could have offered was to not succeed. Thus, my privileged lens on the world while growing up was one of excellence and high expectations.

Growing up, race and difference were novelties to be explored, but never personally lived. Race in my sphere was defined by color, never by White. I believed success depended on high expectations, creativity, knowledge, and hard work—as exhibited by the half-dozen successful Brown and Black boys on my football team and the handful of high-achieving Asian students in my honors and AP classes. Whether confidently road-tripping across North America, adventurously backpacking through Europe, or faithfully living in France as a Mormon missionary, I unknowingly represented a privileged White racial norm everywhere I went.

But the challenge with privilege is that it is a blind experience, unlike entitlement, which is conscious. Privilege is the door already opened and the right to determine what is right—for everyone—without doubt. Privilege is not devoid of conflict, doubt, and suffering, but it provides freedom to work through these challenges without lasting impact. Being White in a world that privileges White has been my racial experience. Every day, I must consciously acknowledge this reality— I might disagree with racial privilege, but it is freely granted every day.

In 2002, I produced a professional development program for the *Video Journal of Education* on Courageous Conversations About Race and its impact in schools. Working on this awakened me to a consciousness of race that has permanently altered me.

The first time I met Glenn Singleton was during Day 1 of this program, while filming his presentation. Having grown up Mormon, I learned, when I stepped outside the community I grew up in, what it felt like to be outside the norm and a misunderstood curiosity. I connected quickly and intensely with Glenn's descriptions of his own life story, of being different and feeling outside the norm, even when accepted by others. Despite knowing little about the realities of race and racism, I clearly heard Glenn describe my own unique experience.

For several months, we filmed Courageous Conversations with Glenn across the United States. Reflecting deeply on the realities of race, my questions started to come and my doubts arose. I was clearly in the zone of productive disequilibrium—knowledge had been presented to me that both connected to

(Continued)

(Continued)

and disagreed with my own experiences. Eating dinner with Glenn one night, the reality of race hit me: Feeling marginalized because of my Mormonism was a chosen experience, whereas Glenn's being Black was a born experience. Therein was the difference—I invited prejudice if I chose to announce my heritage, whereas Glenn invited racism just by being present. This newfound White consciousness coalesced into an understanding that I had been granted societal normalcy and opportunity without ever asking for it.

Two years later, Glenn and I coauthored the first edition of *Courageous Conversations About Race*. Growing beyond racial naiveté, I had become intellectually adept at defining race, racism, and institutionalized racism, even conducting workshops on educational equity. But I had much more to learn about the realities of race.

In 2005, my wife Melody and I adopted our son, Dominic, and four years later, our daughter, Maya, both of whom came from African American heritage. Finding myself to now be the father of Black children, my construct of race shifted again. I wasn't a Black father of Black children but a White father of Black children, with no specific training to be such. As I held their beautiful dark bodies within my pale arms, my racial consciousness skyrocketed. This was no longer an intellectual project, nor a cultural experience. These were my kids. They were Black. And they lived outside the norm in a racially unjust society.

Within our home, they are children to be raised. They grow, they fight, they fall, and they wake up in the night and want to be loved. But outside the home, they are Black kids subject to the same prejudices and inequities as any child of color. They are truly living a third cultural experience—they are not White, and their parents are not Black. They are racially Black growing up culturally White. The presence of these beautiful Black children changed everything in my White existence.

Raising Black children in a dominant White world is a rich yet challenging responsibility. Like teachers, parents tend to revert back to their own experiences when facing difficulties. But I cannot do this. If I raise my kids the way I was raised, I am raising them as though they are White and can assume privilege on the path to success. But they are Black, not White. This racial reality presents itself always and everywhere—in family, religion, education, and society. Daily I ask myself, "How can I norm my children's experience so that they can have the respect, opportunity, and excellence I had?"

My family has fully loved Dominic and Maya—never once have I doubted that my children are treated as though they are any less worthy than their cousins. But my family grew up racially ignorant like myself. As she had done with her other grandsons, my mother once gave Dominic a monkey doll and called him "my little monkey." Even though I knew she did this with no ill intent, I had to challenge her label and explain that it was different with a Black grandson because of racial stereotypes. Norming race requires challenging even loved ones when they display ignorance, prejudice, and stereotyping.

Likewise, it has been difficult navigating the religious heritage in which we grew up. The Mormon Church has a long history of racial discrimination and has struggled to honestly address this—as did I when I could not explain why my church had once used doctrine to institutionalize racial oppression. In trying to make Mormonism work for my family, I became frustrated and disillusioned. Honoring the identity of my children became much more important than protecting the past of my church.

Similarly, public education powerfully perpetuates institutionalized racial inequity. Despite overwhelming research showing how, no diverse US education system has ever led all students to succeed academically. Rarely are there schools that implement culturally relevant and equitable educational practices. Luckily, we found Wasatch Elementary, where diversity is celebrated, difference is normed, success is constant, and equity is guaranteed.

Norming difference has become our family mantra. Our kids would not naturally fit in an all-White neighborhood, nor in an all-color one. We had to find a neighborhood where difference was much more the norm. Deliberately, we moved into the Avenues neighborhood of Salt Lake City, since it is statistically diverse in terms of race, religion, politics, sexual orientation, education, and socioeconomics. No one statistical grouping defines this particular neighborhood, hence difference is normed for us.

Furthermore, my wife and I started the Domino Foundation to support transracial adoption families like our own through multicultural classes, Courageous Conversations, social events, and opportunities for these kids of color to just play with other kids of color—a rare experience for most of these children. We run the Domino Foundation so that these kids can be the norm every once in a while. Some have accused us of overthinking our family's racial identity, but as White parents of Black children we have to change and alter our own realities in order to more fully support our kids within theirs.

Despite all these personal efforts, my racial privilege persists unchecked. This is the most insidious inequity of all. No matter how hard I try to give up my own racial privilege and build a more equitable world, I am always a White man walking with the unconscious privilege my racial identity affords.

Often after a workshop or Domino event, someone will thank and congratulate me for being a "champion" of this work. Thus, within the very act of working toward racial equity, I receive additional praise and credibility and become even more privileged for challenging privilege! How can I norm difference in society for me, my children, and others when society continuously insists on reinforcing the realities of White racial privilege?

PART 2 PRACTICE
The Foundation of Racial Equity Leadership

The key here is not the kind of instruction but the attitude underlying it. When teachers do not understand the potential of the students they teach, they will underteach them no matter what the methodology.

—Lisa Delpit (1995a, p. 175)

When a school system's educators have developed sufficient *passion* for addressing its racial achievement disparities, leadership needs to develop the skills necessary to tackle institutionalized racism. For this reason, *practice* is the second quality of systemic racial equity transformation. By developing and implementing effective practices, educators find meaningful opportunities to use and enhance the knowledge, skills, and capacity they have gained through Courageous Conversation.

Educators who strive to achieve the vision of an equitable school or higher education system refrain from blaming underserved students for the system's failures. They see it as their moral imperative and professional responsibility to acknowledge where schooling is ineffective and specifically where instructional practices are unsupportive of student success.

We must aim to create a nation of high achievers regardless of background. Some Americans seem to believe that disparity and disproportionality in achievement among racial groups is inevitable—the result of obvious differences in the economic and educational resources that different groups can access. But this doesn't explain why some schools—indeed, some whole districts—serving poor children and large numbers of children of color achieve much better results than districts with comparable demographics do. Indeed, if the causes of underachievement rest primarily in families or the students themselves, these better results should not be possible. Perhaps it isn't poverty or racial/ethnic background in and of itself, but rather educators' response to these and other characteristics that suppresses educational achievement (Johnson, 2002, p. 6).

It must become unacceptable for educators to not guarantee equitable access and opportunity to all students groups. Student success cannot be left to chance. As described by Kati Haycock (Education Trust, 2009), the "old way" of schooling leaves a great deal to chance, because

- curriculum is left up to individual schools or teachers.
- teachers "broadcast" the content—a kind of one-size-fits-all approach.
- some students "get it" and some don't.
- teachers don't exactly know which students are really getting it . . . and they couldn't do much about those who aren't anyway.

The old way of schooling places sole responsibility for learning on the students and guarantees the same results we have always had. In the "new way" of schooling, however, educators accept full responsibility for teaching, and *little is left to chance:*

- All teachers teach a common, coherent curriculum that clearly lays out what kids are supposed to have learned at each step of the way.
- Teachers use a variety of strategies to help students master a common set of knowledge and skills—individualized instruction.
- Teachers know which students aren't getting it the first time and which students are falling seriously behind.
- Teachers can tap into a variety of strategies for providing additional instruction to students who don't get it the first time or who are falling seriously behind.

The new way to educational success involves teachers acquiring the skills or *practices* they need to ensure that every one of their students succeeds. Once again, *little is left to chance.* Teaching is centered and focused around getting each and every student to perform at or above the standards. When instruction is matched to the needs of the individual student, then education begins to transcend the perceived limitations of race, culture, and background.

I believe that language and communication provide the foundation of culture. Specifically, those ideas, thoughts, and perspectives that people are able to effectively exchange with members of their community become the basis for establishing shared values, attitudes, and behaviors. In essence, only when educators have established both a language and process for communication about racial matters will they be poised to restructure their schools, classrooms, curricula, and relationships with students and families in ways that improve student engagement and performance.

In my work with preK–12 and higher education systems both in the United States and abroad, Courageous Conversation has served as that essential protocol that not only offers language but also a comprehensive communication strategy for transforming debilitating beliefs about learning and teaching. Adding to the Four Agreements and the Compass, the Six Conditions of Courageous Conversation guide us through the requisite content and processes of racial dialogue in a way that allows educators to feel relative safety as they examine the points at which race intersects schooling.

The conditions are sequential and progressive, and they intentionally build on each other. Also, I offer the conditions in three tiers—engaging, sustaining, and deepening—each of which encapsulates two conditions and is framed by a guiding statement.

Tier 1—The ***engaging*** conditions

> *Engage* through your own *personal* racial experiences, beliefs, and perspectives while demonstrating respectful understanding of specific historical as well as contemporary, local, and immediate racial contexts.

Tier 2—The ***sustaining*** conditions

> *Sustain* yourself and others in the conversation through mindful inquiry into those *multiple perspectives,* beliefs, and experiences that are different than your own.

Tier 3—The ***deepening*** conditions

> *Deepen* your understanding of *Whiteness,* and interrogate your beliefs about your own association with and relationship to white racial privilege and power.

As educators consider the specific meaning defining the tiers and guiding statements, they will find that each condition adds depth and complexity to the conversation. As you develop greater understanding of the conditions in the following chapters and engage in the suggested reflections, exercises, and implementation activities, you will master the *practices* needed to internalize Courageous Conversation and subsequently enhance your focus and effectiveness in addressing racial achievement disparity in your school or higher education system.

FIVE

The First Condition

Getting Personal Right Here and Right Now

It is pretty clear the achievement gap has roots in school and non-school factors, but if you tell teachers the gap has two sources, they want to fix the out-of-school stuff first. They never get around to doing the things they can do.

—Kati Haycock, Director of The Education
Trust (quoted in Barnes, 2004, p. 70)

Rather than blaming factors external to schools for causing the racial achievement gap, educators should address the critical factors within their control that influence student achievement, such as the qualifications, expectations, and cultural proficiency of educators, the rigor of the curriculum, and the effectiveness of instruction.

Eliminating racial achievement disparities begins with an examination of self rather than of others. For this reason, the First Condition of Courageous Conversation invites us to

establish a racial context that is personal, local, and immediate.

Specifically, educators need to address their own racial attitudes, beliefs, and expectations as they relate to their students of color and indigenous students as well as their White students. When the conversation focuses initially on the educators' own racial consciousness, identity, and experiences, they can better understand the way in which they may be interpreting their students' academic interests and engagement.

PERSONAL, LOCAL, AND IMMEDIATE

To develop a fuller understanding of race, we must first look deeply and intro-spectively at our own racial existence as a doorway to understanding the com-plexities of race in America. This is why the First Condition of Courageous Conversation prompts participants to examine their own personal, local, and immediate circumstances related to race. In doing this, we engage in the dialogue by carefully examining our personal racial identity development and experiences linked to racism.

Examining the impact of race in our own lives serves as a precursor to examin-ing the impact of race in the larger context of a school. As we become personally aware of our own racialized existence, we can more deeply understand the racial experiences of others. Without doing this, we will continue to assess the racial experiences of others through our own distorted lens. The foundational level of racial awareness must be personal, local, and immediate. Thus, heightening racial consciousness begins with self-examination and is bolstered by continuous racial inquiry and reflection.

REFLECTION

Before you opened this book, how consciously aware of race were you?

You have already noticed in our racial autobiographies, which appeared at the ends of chapters 3 and 4 of this book, that as coauthors of the first edition, Curtis Linton and I could not have come from more different racial backgrounds. Precisely because I am Black and grew up in Baltimore, Maryland, and Curtis is White and grew up near Salt Lake City, Utah, we have experienced radically dif-ferent racial realities. Both of us have led intensely racialized lives that we needed to analyze critically prior to understanding each other. One important difference, however, in our journeys toward personal racial consciousness—and a difference that we believe is reflective of the experience of our respective racial groups—is that I have long been aware of the impact of race in my life, whereas Curtis had only recently come to recognize himself racially. Given that our first step was to examine race in our own individual lives, Curtis needed to accelerate his racial examination, while I had to be patient during Curtis's process of inquiry and dis-covery. For me, it was also important that I pay close attention to Curtis's process of discovery, as his racial reality and circumstances, I believed, were quite similar to those of many White educators who inhabit schools and universities. Having this kind of mutual introduction to race not only led us to a far greater understanding of and empathy for how race impacts our respective lives, but also provided insight about how to work with interracial teams of educators in a variety of school and university settings.

Between the chapters in which I explore the Six Conditions of Courageous Conversation are several more powerful racial autobiographies. These narratives were written by racial equity leaders, of different races, who join me as practitioners and professional facilitators of Courageous Conversation. These are personal reflections on how race impacts individual lives. Racial autobiographies are a tool for developing and deepening personal understanding of and insights about race. They not only provide a process for racial discovery but also serve as illustrations of what it means to establish a racial context that is personal, local, and immediate. Highlighting the First Condition, the racial autobiographies also show the progression that each individual has followed to build his or her own racial consciousness. As you read each of these narratives, pay close attention to the questions the writer raises with respect to his or her own leading edge of racial learning. As racial equity leaders, our ability to formulate thoughtful inquiry around our own personal, local, and immediate racial identity development is a powerful illustration of our own authentic practice of the agreement to expect and accept non-closure. I am hopeful these carefully chosen and well-crafted racial autobiographies will serve as models for your own work in racial self-definition and in your pursuit of racial equity.

> **REFLECTION**
>
> What can you recall about the events and conversations related to race, race relations, and/or racism that may have impacted your current perspectives and/or experiences?

THE IMPACT OF RACE ON MY LIFE

The First Condition of Courageous Conversation focuses on the way in which race impacts each of us, right here and right now. Imagine that a billboard sits above the road on your commute to work beckoning you to address the following question:

> *To what degree*
> *does race*
> *impact my life?*

The emphasis here is on "my life," because to engage in Courageous Conversations requires making race personal. As racialized conversations become tougher for us, our tendency is to speak more impersonally. The pain of facing racism, coupled with the propensity of the dominant White culture to minimize or deny racist acts, might encourage people of color to generalize what is actually a personal impact of racism. In addition, many White people have a tendency to talk about racism only from the perspective of how people of color and indigenous people are oppressed rather than considering what role they might play in that oppression. We cannot talk about race collectively as a nation, family, or education system until we have individually talked about race in our own lives—personally, locally, and immediately.

REFLECTION

To what degree and in what ways does race impact your own personal life?

Consider the billboard once again:

Race in my life?
0–100%

The billboard now asks for you to determine what percentage of your life is impacted by race.

REFLECTION

Determine the percentage of your life, from 0 to 100%, that is impacted by race.

As you examine this prompt further and begin to deeply investigate race personally, you will come to recognize that race impacts every aspect of your life

100% of the time. This total impact of race occurs whether you are conscious or unconscious of the impact and whether you spend time with people of the same race or of a race different than your own. Because people are defined by their racial identity in this society, race is constantly present and having an impact on your experience and perspective. This is to say that the impact of race disappears only when you no longer have your skin, and thus, the omnipresent skin that you are in defines your omnipresent racial impact.

What if you arrived at a percentage lower than 100? Most likely, you determined your level of racial *consciousness* rather than racial *impact*. People who answer the question with the lowest percentages typically do not view interactions with White people or White cultural experiences as racial. Low percentages are also derived by people who do not wish to characterize themselves racially, choosing instead to connect us all to one human "race." Although this idea may be noble, and humans do belong to the same species, in the United States, as well as in other parts of the world, race is defined today by physical traits. Many White educators find it difficult and perhaps disturbing to consider themselves part of a racial group; ironically, the word *race* conjures up only images of and experiences with people of color. Educators of color, on the other hand, tend to quickly acknowledge the universality and omnipresence of race in their lives.

If you are White, it helps to think not only of outwardly racist comments or actions but of the ways in which race may play out in your personal relationships, opportunities, and sense of security throughout your community and beyond. Although Curtis Linton grew up in a predominantly White community where race was rarely discussed, the impact of race on his life was still 100%: He felt racially secure in this society and benefited greatly from a schooling system that was geared to serve primarily White children.

Sometimes, people of color and indigenous people will list an impact percentage lower than 100 because they exclude time spent interacting with people of their own race. But race still dominates these interactions, as people of color and indigenous people often feel safest, racially speaking, when spending time among those of their own race, just as White people do. If you are a person of color or indigenous person, consider how race plays into your life every day, how it affects the way others treat you, and whether it has had an impact on your schooling, career, and your place in society. As it was for Curtis, the racial impact is also 100% for me, as I grew up in an all-Black neighborhood in Baltimore, Maryland. Similarly, it was still 100% when I graduated from my all-Black elementary school and went on to attend a predominately White middle and high school.

The question, "Race In My Life?" is intended not so much to generate an assessment of race's impact but to initiate an ongoing conversation about racial consciousness and the degree to which educators are aware of how and when race permeates their personal and professional interactions. Once everyone realizes that race is always impacting our experience, the far more provocative question emerges: To what degree am I conscious of this 100% racial impact in my life?

DEGREE OF RACIAL CONSCIOUSNESS

Discussing the role of race in our lives invites us to refer back to the Racial Consciousness Flow Chart introduced in the previous chapter and repeated in Figure 5.1.

In identifying how conscious you are about how race impacts your life, you are labeling the degree to which "I know I don't know" or "I know I know." This means that the difference between that percentage and 100% is how much "I don't know I don't know" or "I don't know but I think I do."

The percentage at which we believe that race impacts our lives can be viewed as our racial consciousness. The ability to effectively converse about race is determined by the degree to which we can consciously place the lens of race in front of us as we examine our own personal interactions with family and friends. Ultimately, educators need to view the experiences of students, work of colleagues, patterns in achievement data, school policies, and effective ways of engaging parents and the communities of color and indigenous stakeholders through the lens of race. The success of Courageous Conversation, however, hinges on the willingness and ability of participants to examine *themselves* racially and not prematurely divert the dialogue to an examination of their students. Educators cannot effectively consider their students' racial beliefs, attitudes, and behaviors before they have carefully investigated their own.

RACIAL CONSCIOUSNESS
VERSUS RACIAL UNCONSCIOUSNESS

As shown here, if you consider your racial consciousness as a fraction, the denominator of 100 signifies the total impact of race and the acknowledgment that race permeates everything in modern American society as well as in many other societies around the world. The numerator represents the degree to which you are racially conscious personally, locally, and immediately. The difference between the numerator and the denominator is racial unconsciousness. Just as in any proper fraction, mathematically speaking, the numerator can never be larger than the denominator. Thus when educators believe that racial impact in their lives is

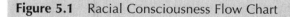

Figure 5.1 Racial Consciousness Flow Chart

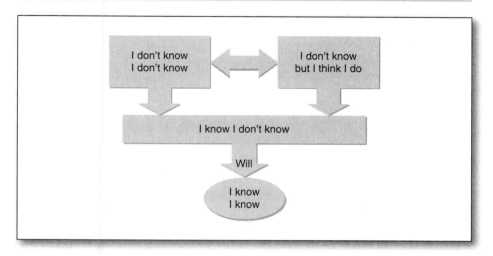

low, say 40, so too must 40 be their absolute highest level of racial consciousness. Ironically none of us achieve 100% consciousness about anything, and especially not about race.

$$\frac{\text{Race in my life} = ?\% \ (\textit{Racial Consciousness})}{100 \ (\text{Racial Unconsciousness} + \text{Consciousness})}$$

We need to challenge our racial unconsciousness in the conversation to reach a greater understanding of race in our own lives. This unconsciousness causes the greatest discomfort in interracial interaction, as often experienced by White educators working with colleagues, students, and families of color or these same cohorts of indigenous people. This is because people of color, like me, tend not only to be more conscious of our own racial experience but also understand a great deal about White racial culture as well, because we live in a White-dominated society. Simply put, racial discomfort is heightened when racially dominant people of lesser consciousness are required to interact with racially targeted or oppressed people of greater consciousness in circumstances in which the racially dominant, or White people, possess greater power and authority or have a high level of confidence in their own ill-formed racial beliefs.

Over time, educators engaged in Courageous Conversation will better understand the inherent rises and dips in their own racial consciousness. It is precisely this movement that creates the sense of discomfort on which authentic dialogue is predicated. As educators practice these skills through Courageous Conversation, they will continually build their own racial consciousness and their ability to understand the racial reality of those with whom they interact. By arriving at their own personal, local, and immediate understanding of race in their own lives, they can begin to effectively address the omnipresent impact of race on the schooling of their students.

REFLECTION

Describe *race in my life* in terms of your perceived racial consciousness and racial unconsciousness. In which situations and circumstances do you believe yourself to be most racially aware? In which circumstances do you feel you would benefit from having greater racial consciousness?

IMPLEMENTATION EXERCISE

RACE IN MY LIFE

Time required: 45 minutes

Materials required: For each participant, Courageous Conversation Journal and the worksheet that follows

Introduce the First Condition of Courageous Conversation:

Establish a racial context that is personal, local, and immediate.

Ask participants why it is important first to address race personally and individually before trying to understand it at a group or societal level.

1. Provide each individual with a copy of the worksheet and have them answer the prompt:

   • How much is my life impacted by race?

   Have them consider the degree, from 0–100%, to which race impacts their life, and write that figure in the box.

2. Divide the participants into small groups of four to five people, mixing races if possible. Have the small groups share their percentages with each other and consider the following prompts:

   • What are our highest and lowest percentages?
   • What are the reasons for discrepancies or similarities in our percentages?

3. Explain to the entire group that this percentage is our racial consciousness. Refer to the Racial Consciousness Flow Chart (Figure 5.1) and discuss how this percentage identifies what "I know I know." The difference between our racial consciousness percentage and 100% is our racial unconsciousness, or what it is that "I don't know I don't know" in terms of how race impacts us.

4. Reiterate to the group that this first of the Six Conditions of Courageous Conversation deals with race personally, locally, and immediately, and have each participant complete the rest of the handout by addressing how

   - My race impacts my life emotionally.
   - My race impacts my life relationally.
   - My race impacts my life intellectually.
   - My race impacts my life morally.

   Remind participants that they need to address how *their own race* impacts their own lives—*not the race of others*. Have each person in the small groups choose one of these prompts to share with the others in their group.

5. Bring everyone back together and pose the following question for an open discussion:

   - How does my own race impact me personally, locally, and immediately?

6. Have everyone keep the worksheet in their Courageous Conversation Journal.

FIRST CONDITION OF COURAGEOUS CONVERSATION

Establish a racial context that is personal, local, and immediate.

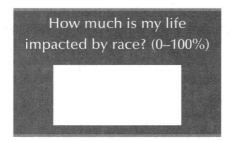

How much is my life impacted by race? (0–100%)

My race impacts my life

- Emotionally:
- Relationally:
- Intellectually:
- Morally:

RACIAL AUTOBIOGRAPHY

MELISSA KRULL

As a white child growing up on the lower west side of St. Paul, Minnesota, I have vivid memories of life within a family of seven. For some of these early years, we lived in one half of the duplex my parents owned along with my grandmother. When I was really young, mom stayed at home with the kids and dad worked long hours in real estate. Money was never abundant, but somehow we all got what we needed. Our community would best be described as middle to low income. Our neighbors and school friends were largely white and Latino. We lived in an integrated neighborhood, and no one really had much in terms of money. Large families were common, and living among our friends of color seemed normal to me.

From first grade through eighth grade, I attended St. Matthew's Catholic School. We were a practicing Catholic family. We attended church on Sundays and once during the week at school. I remember having to wear a doily on my head when attending church and having to bring my prayer book. We wore uniforms, went to confession, said the rosary, and walked through the Stations of the Cross. Our teachers were nuns, and our school leader was the monsignor, who was a holy, staunch, and robust man of Catholic faith. All of these school leaders were White in spite of the fact that we were a diverse neighborhood and school.

I have memories of socioeconomic differences among us and of our racial differences, but they were not enough to cause me to think much about race. The racial slurs that were bantered about by White kids and by our classmates of color were commonplace. We affectionately and playfully accepted the use of racially derogative nicknames for our friends of color. Kids of color seemed fully immersed in the school culture with us—well liked and included, so we thought.

Many of us moved on to the Catholic high school together. I don't remember thinking about another option, and yet there was a public school near our home. My siblings had gone to the Catholic high school, and I knew that I would follow that path. Going to a public school was not really a consideration. I had no teachers of color, only Christian brothers and sisters and lay teachers. All White. As a high school student, I lived, learned, and socialized with more White students and fewer students of color. My racial identity, then, was something that I was less than conscious of through my 12 years of schooling. While my Catholic upbringing became the lens through which my life decisions and actions were framed, the fact that there was an absence of racial understanding through those formative years is now disappointing and disturbing. Today I understand the lasting and injurious effects of a moral compass devoid of racial justice.

It was not until well into adulthood that I realized race was and had been a significant part of my life. As I pursued a career in education and moved into teaching, administrative work, and eventually superintendent work, the construct of race became clear to me after two sequential events occurred: first, the passage of the No Child Left Behind Act (NCLB), requiring the disaggregation of data by race, and second, a few years later meeting Glenn Singleton. Both were, for very different reasons, profound for me as an individual and as a school leader.

Pursuant to NCLB, as superintendent I recall reviewing the disaggregated racial data in the Eden Prairie, Minnesota, school system for the first time and recognizing that we, as a largely White, affluent school district, did in fact have significant racial achievement disparities. I wrestled with revealing this truth to the community. I anticipated there would be tension as we made known to our stakeholders our decision to look at how *all* of our children, without exception, were performing. I understood it was on my watch that these data were, for the first time, being made evident. I felt responsible for leading the necessary work to stop the trajectory that was leaving many of our children of color behind. For me, that's when it became impossible to ignore the racial predictability of our effectiveness as an educational system. Eden Prairie Schools began a long journey of attending to the obvious racial disparities that had been hidden within an educational system that reveled in significantly high scores for many students and celebrated numerous AP scholars, National Merit Scholars, and premier athletic teams.

A few years later, at the urging of two of my administrators, I attended a meeting of superintendents and met Glenn Singleton. This one-hour meeting transformed my view of my life's work permanently. Glenn brought to my attention the urgency of intentionally embracing racial equity work on behalf of *all* students. While I don't recall the specifics, I do recall making a phone call from my car to my colleague at work and saying to him, "This is it; *this* is *our* work moving forward." Thus began my *real* racially conscious journey as a superintendent.

Glenn became a regular consultant in Eden Prairie Schools. It was during his trainings that I learned and developed most as a racially conscious leader. I realized then that only when I as superintendent acted, engaged, and modeled using the protocol for Courageous Conversations would the rest of the system begin to change. I learned that as superintendent I needed to be fully present in the learning, not sequestered in my office or attending to things less important than eliminating our racial disparities. I learned that nothing else would matter more. If I was serious about closing these gaps in teaching and learning, I had to engage personally and recognize, as a white female superintendent with privilege, that I lacked deep understandings about race that I had easily overlooked my entire life, even while I was surrounded by people of different races.

I grew to recognize that any pain or struggle I might have experienced professionally was nothing compared to the discomfort the children and families felt who had been systemically underserved their entire school career due to the color of their skin. Recognizing *I* had always been provided opportunities, access, and choice—enabling me to gain the education I wanted—was central to my learning.

(Continued)

(Continued)

I realized that as superintendent, I could make a significant and positive difference in the experience of many students and staff. The more I *decided* to care about race, the more I could learn and authentically lead this important work. All of these focused, lived experiences as an educational leader brought me and many others in my district to a place of deep engagement and understanding about race, equity, and education. Our results became reflective of our learning, as our racially predictable achievement gaps narrowed with "all deliberate speed."

During these transformative years, my beautiful daughter Helen arrived in my life. My journey as a White parent of a Brown, Guatemalan child framed a new racial experience for me and my daughter. Today, as I negotiate her schooling and watch her navigate her own childhood experiences, I am certain of the impact racial equity has on the socialization of all children. Seeing this through my mother eyes provides yet another dimension for truly understanding the dynamics of race, equity, and education.

As I write this autobiography, my racial consciousness continues to unfold and emerge. For example, I recently listened to a story on Minnesota Public Radio about a 43-year-old Black man named Eric Garner. The story began by describing an incident between Mr. Garner and police officers in the New York City Police Department (NYPD). Garner was described as a large man with "presence" who resisted the claims the NYPD made about him As the story unfolded, it became clear to me that there was a misunderstanding between this man and the officers. As it was related in the story, Garner was forced by the officers into a chokehold—a banned NYPD practice—and brought to his knees and then onto his back while gasping for air and repeating, "I can't breathe." Eric Garner died in this confrontation. The racial violence described in this story resonates today with my own sense of the racial injustices prevalent in our specialized education services, where predictable racial educational achievement disparities persist at the highest levels. Today, not only am I aware of the extent of continued racial inequities, but I understand the need to think, believe, and act with an internal compass dedicated to the moral imperative of eradicating racial inequities in every moment of every day.

SIX

The Second Condition

Keeping the Spotlight on Race

In My Heart

Why do you stare at me in the stores?
Is it because my skin is darker than yours?
Must you contaminate the American society
With your petty stereotypes?
Is it your hatred that blinds you,
Or is it your ignorance that feeds you?
I am from a culture of proud warriors and loving mothers.
But where I live now
They want to destroy our culture.
They can never stop what is kept in my heart.
But is it still here?
Am I looked down upon?
Well, don't look down on me unless you are picking me up.
Your hatred was made to tear me up.
It will never succeed.
In a time of freedom,
Racism is still here.

—Used with permission of Jamyan Brooks
High School Senior, Chapel Hill, North Carolina

What thoughts and/or questions arose for you as you read this student's poem? How do the student's perspectives about race connect to your own *personal, local, and immediate* racial experience?

This poem illustrates the student's hyperawareness that others view him primarily as a racial being. As he comes "from a culture of proud warriors and loving mothers," he sees himself as more than Black. But he is exhausted by his reality: Non-Black members of American society see him in stereotypical ways that force him to fit within a preconceived mold. In this poem, this highly conscious student asks all of us to look more clearly at our racial prejudices and to grant him the equality, respect, and high expectations that he has thus far been denied.

ISOLATING RACE

The Second Condition of Courageous Conversation encourages us to

isolate race while acknowledging the broader scope of diversity and the variety of factors that contribute to a racialized problem.

This condition focuses on the critical need to address race explicitly and intentionally. In doing so, educators not only deepen their understanding of race but also develop skills to acknowledge and address those other diversity-related factors, such as economic status, gender, and religion, which often contribute to a racialized problem. Through our careful and isolated examination of race, educators not only discover new meaning in race but also more authentically recognize the intersection of race and other aspects of human diversity and culture.

My experience suggests that when educators attempt to address too many phenomena coupled with race initially, they tend to converse about those other topics—say, poverty or family values—instead of race, because those topics are often easier to negotiate. It is extremely difficult to keep the conversation focused on race and not drift off into topics that are less emotionally charged and about which people feel more knowledgeable. How common it is for the topic of race to surface during an examination of achievement data of students of color or indigenous students, and someone says, "Well, what about poverty?" Then someone else might say, "And what about language?" Suddenly, the conversation loses focus around the challenge of race and is predictably redefined to any number of other diversity issues.

Furthermore, we have found that many prominent educational researchers and practitioners express solid understandings of other diversity topics but fail to explore or even recognize race as a viable factor affecting school culture and student achievement. Given our suggestion from the previous chapter—that race impacts 100% of our life experiences—how odd it is that popular educational research, theory, and practice virtually ignore and sometimes explicitly reject any notion that race matters in schooling processes and outcomes. Never do we suggest that race is the only factor for educators to consider as they struggle to improve schools. But, how can race at the very least not play a role in our cycle of inquiry regarding eliminating persistent racial achievement disparities? In short, I recognize race is never the only factor that we must consider when addressing the way things are in preK–12 and higher education. Unfortunately, though, often it is the missing or avoided factor for educators seated at the so-called school reform table. The Second Condition of Courageous Conversation assists educators in avoiding the tendency to divert attention from race.

Redefining Race

Putting race on the table and keeping it there is a struggle because of the tendency to redefine institutional racial issues as internal factors that are more accessible and familiar to us, or perhaps as challenges that are external to school and district operations. Specifically, educators often develop an understanding of the fact that Black, Brown, and Indigenous students are not meeting standards by naming family, community, and the behavior of the students themselves as reasons for the problem rather than by examining how race influences school culture, the quality and delivery of instruction, and curricular choices. In essence, a race-blind approach and strategy encourages educators to blame students for what they bring to school, something over which educators ultimately have little personal control and, therefore, for which they can feel little responsibility. The following justifications for low student performance are drawn from interactions with educators grappling with the issue of racial achievement disparity, prior to their developing racial consciousness:

- Family

  No value for education

  A natural dislike for reading

  Parents don't read to their kids

  Parents are uneducated

- Poverty

  Parents are always working

  There is no money for books

  They can't visit museums or travel

  Kids have to work to support the family

- Community

  No value for education

  No respect for authority

  No good role models

  Kids feel too unsafe to focus on school

  Bad influences like drugs and gangs

- Language

  The students don't understand English well enough

  Since the parents can't speak English, they can't help their kids

  A lack of proper English proves a lack of intelligence

  I (the teacher) can't speak their language, so I can't help them

- Mobility

  We (the school) are not responsible for their lack of learning, since they just arrived here

  How can we help a student who is just going to move again?

  The student isn't stable enough to learn

Each of these excuses for the racial achievement gap carries the same message: It's not a school problem; it's the student's/the family's/the community's problem, and so on. Current and critical research, however, indicates that each one of these factors can be addressed effectively in a school environment (Education Trust, 2009). Without question, these commonly mentioned factors can affect a student's learning, but data show that none of these excuses can prevent any group of students from achieving at high levels. What is also important to understand, as it relates to the Second Condition, or isolating race, is that an educator's own personal racial beliefs, attitudes, and behaviors will greatly impact how and what a student effectively learns and is able to do.

Race Is Pervasive

When we isolate race, we gain tremendous insight into just how pervasive a role race plays in our society and our world. Whether blatant or subtle, raw or sophisticated, issues of race are foundational in much of public discourse, in media presentations, political campaigns, and public debate over economic development, urban renewal, new school construction boundaries, and textbook adoptions. And yet, race as a topic remains difficult to surface and even more challenging to examine in isolation from other social factors.

Consider your initial reaction to the following advertisement, which was published in a number of nationally circulated periodicals:

Naughty?

Nice?

This is by no means a complex illustration, and there is no right or wrong reaction; but what is quickly evident is that the ad at some level willingly plays on commonly held racial stereotypes, values, and beliefs. This is simply one tiny example of how pervasively race is embedded in society.

Where do you locate yourself on the Courageous Conversation Compass when you first glance at this advertisement? Upon further examination and pondering of the advertisement, what, if any, movement on the Compass occurs for you? If you were to personalize this advertisement, what meaning does it hold for you in terms of your own personal, local, and immediate racial experience?

REFLECTION

This advertisement clearly communicates multiple messages. When asked to isolate race, however, we focus our examination on an understanding of the racial tone that underlies the messages. For many people, the Volkswagen advertisement immediately conjures up deep thoughts and sound connections to race. Consider as evidence the following popular responses educators have given to the advertisement over the past five years in Courageous Conversation seminars:

- Black is naughty while White is nice
- Black is bad and White is good
- White is "Right"
- White is boring
- Black is evil
- Black opposing White
- Black is rebellious while White is conservative
- Black and White don't go the same direction; they are oppositional
- Face-off

These age-old references to the Western civilization Black and White racial binary seem to persist not only in media but also in literature, the arts, and our everyday euphemisms in the United States and beyond. Unfortunately for some, such images leave lasting personal scars and stimulate anger; others, who see racial messages as innocent or unintentional, may adopt a more defensive posture or altogether disregard them as insightful or impacting. Herein lies the apparent conflict that prompts the need for Courageous Conversations about race.

Defining Color

Even academically or intellectually speaking, race has a pervasive influence on our thinking schemas, as shown by the following edited dictionary definitions of *white* and *black:*

> White: 1 a: free from color; 2 a: being a member of a group or race characterized by reduced pigmentation and usu. specif. distinguished from persons belonging to groups marked by black, brown, yellow, or red skin coloration; b: of, relating to, characteristic of, or consisting of white people; c: marked by upright fairness; 3: free from spot or blemish: as a (1): free from moral impurity: innocent; c: not intended to cause harm; d: favorable, fortunate; 6 a: conservative or reactionary in political outlook and action

> Black: 1 a: of the color black; b (1): very dark in color <his face was ~ with rage>; (3): heavy, serious; 2 a: having dark skin, hair, and eyes: swarthy <the ~ Irish>; b (1) often cap: of or relating to any of various population groups having dark pigmentation of the skin; (2): of or relating to the Afro-American people or their culture; 4: dirty, soiled; 5 a: characterized by the absence of light; 6 a: thoroughly sinister or evil: wicked; b: indicative of condemnation or discredit; 7: connected with or invoking the supernatural and esp. the devil; 8 a: very sad, gloomy, or calamitous; b: marked by the occurrence of disaster; 9: characterized by hostility or angry discontent: sullen; 12: characterized by grim, distorted, or grotesque satire

> **REFLECTION**
>
> When examining these definitions through the isolated lens of race, what do you see? In what ways do these definitions reflect familiar societal views of and behaviors around race? What potential stereotypes do you see in the making or being fortified by these definitions?

Isolating race as we consider these definitions, we see that *white* is endowed with "upright fairness," "free from moral impurity," "favorable," and "fortunate," whereas *black* is considered to be "serious," "swarthy," "dirty," "wicked," "calamitous," and "angry discontent." Are these not some of the characteristics that many members of society attribute to White and Black people, respectively?

Racial Impact

The advertisement and the definitions clearly offer understandings about issues other than race, but race plays a significant role in interpreting their full meaning and, therefore, is worth careful consideration and examination. Rather than picturing cars, substitute the image of student achievement data disaggregated by race, and consider your personal response to the patterns you see. The data can lead educators into conversations about the multiple factors impacting achievement disparity, including teaching, learning, school culture, and family involvement. But the data also invite Courageous Conversations about the role race plays in student performance, discipline, and engagement.

When we isolate race, we expand our consciousness about the role race, racial identity development, and institutional racism play in our society. Clearly, the color of the paint on a car cannot cause different performance, nor can cars be "naughty" or "nice." But it is not such a big leap to see how purposeful personification of the cars extends our thinking to determining who is appropriate for selling, buying, and driving them. Although we cannot determine the motives of the advertisers or the focus groups that helped select any given advertisement, we can get clear on what impact the image has on various racial groups' beliefs, experiences, and behaviors.

Based on your own personal racial confirmation, clarification, or discoveries thus far, answer the following questions using a lens or filter of race:

- How does it feel to be characterized as naughty or nice or to be unidentified altogether?
- Do these characterizations or omissions affect your level of engagement and achievement?
- Who benefits/suffers from these existing racial representations?

REFLECTION

UNPACKING RACE

Our Second Condition of Courageous Conversation—isolate race—prompts participants to bring race front and center in the conversation so that they may better examine and understand its impact. More specifically, at this point, educators "unpack race," hoping to understand the deeper meaning without distraction of other, albeit related issues.

When I was in seventh grade, my family elected to place me in an independent, predominantly White, Jewish, suburban day school. As one of a handful of students of color in the middle school, I was never allowed to "unpack" my racial identity, nor did my White teachers ever choose to acknowledge, much less "unpack," their racial reality or publicly examine their racial beliefs. Consequently, I was left struggling and searching throughout my time at Park School to explain what I was experiencing. I lacked any meaningful or constructive opportunities to talk about the primary cause for my unease: race.

The educators at Park School prided themselves on being race neutral and colorblind, which I view as the antithesis of the Second Condition, because we all have racial perspectives that impact our daily racial interactions and experiences, whether we are conscious of them or not. Nevertheless, I stood out as one of only four Black students in my class. I was hypervisible and thus a magnet for individual and institutional scrutiny. In my first year at Park School, a graduating Black senior I didn't know very well discreetly wrote in my yearbook:

> To Glenn, I wish you the best of luck in this crazy place. As we both know, because you are Black, you can only achieve as much as a White by being educated. Continue to strive hard and you will reach the goals that you have set. Just believe in yourself and what you can do and life will be that much easier to bear. Love, Wanda.

While Wanda's advice may have constituted some of the most important words written in my yearbook, these were not the words of wisdom for which I hoped. By the end of my first year at Park School, I was already trying to gain the approval of my White classmates and teachers, who seemed more interested in having me change how I spoke, what I ate, the music I appreciated, and the clothes I wore. Ironically, the Park School community professed itself to be colorblind, but they immediately noticed that I was racially different. Some classmates labeled where I came from as a ghetto and thus found it difficult to relate to my "culture." In order to "fit in," my only choice was to "pretend" that I, too, was White.

As many students would, I responded to growing marginalization by assimilating to Park School's "normalized" White ways of being. Again, as early as the end of my first year at Park, I had begun the process of racial assimilation; many of my White friends and teachers eventually claimed to "not see you as Black." My "refined" choices in music, food, and clothing had transformed my racial identity but had not changed the fact that race had become a buried consciousness in my life.

To survive in this primarily White school, I had to separate myself from my own community, which my classmates implicitly considered inferior. Such identity changes may have helped me fit in better, although I never fit in *totally* at Park, because I was always pretending rather than being my authentic self. The forced process of racial assimilation also prevented me from being fully a part of my family and my larger Black Baltimorean and American community, which I previously had relied on for emotional, cultural, and spiritual sustenance.

Desegregated schools face the challenge of providing quality education for racially marginalized students, while their staff members, for the most part, have not acquainted themselves with the experiences, perspectives, or understandings associated with being a person of color. Without "unpacking" race, White educators often attempt—whether intentionally or unintentionally—to make their colleagues of color as well as their students of color conform to the normalized conditions of White culture. By professing themselves to be colorblind, educators essentially indicate that no cultural differences exist between White people and people of color. Clearly, no one at Park School really believed that I was White and Jewish. In fact, the administration prided itself on selecting a highly diverse student body. So why, then, were they quick to comment that "we don't see color" or "we don't think of you as Black," once I began to comment on my personal, local, and immediate racial experience and inquire about what I perceived to be institutional racial biases? For educators, students, and families of color, challenging White educators' mythical colorblindness can lead to their further marginalization and often even stand in the way of their receiving critical resources, support, and advancement.

> **REFLECTION**
>
> Consider your own affiliations, such as your workplace, religious institution, social clubs, and recreational places that you frequent. What is the racial composition? If racial diversity exists, are tensions present due to race or racial differences? In what ways has this been addressed—or not addressed? If little racial diversity exists, why is this the case?

We believe that many educators fail to meet the needs of the growing number of students of color and indigenous students because this challenge is often labeled "diversity work" rather than effective pedagogy. Certainly, race is one of many categories of diversity, but making instruction accessible to students of color and indigenous students is not a matter of diversity: It is our responsibility to ensure quality education for all. Only when educators isolate race as a topic in their school improvement discussions are they certain to focus on issues that directly impact students of color, indigenous students, and White students alike. Isolating race helps educators to understand race and simultaneously to develop real solutions to racial achievement disparities.

IMPLEMENTATION EXERCISE

ISOLATING RACE

Time required: 45 minutes

Materials required: For each participant, Courageous Conversation Journal and a copy of the handout that follows

1. Introduce the Second Condition of Courageous Conversation:

   Isolate race while acknowledging the broader scope of diversity and the variety of factors that contribute to a racialized problem.

   Ask the group why it is important to isolate race in the conversation rather than avoiding it altogether or addressing it in conjunction with other diversity issues such as poverty and gender.

2. Based on whether you are facilitating a group of district administrators, secondary teachers, or elementary teachers, pass out the appropriate handout.

3. Inform the participants that you are going to examine the racial makeup of the school or school system. By creating this racial demography map, you can begin isolating race and statistically examining how it impacts achievement.

4. Divide the participants into small groups of four to five people, mixing racial groups if at all possible. Assign each team one of the sections, such as Student Body or Community Participation, on the handout. At your next meeting, each team should submit a written report of findings to the facilitator and prepare to share with the entire group the following data:

   - Prior to collecting and examining any data, what did we believe to be the racial composition of the section that we were about to investigate? Why did we believe this composition existed/persisted?
   - According to the data, what is the racial composition—White, Black, Brown, Asian, Indigenous, or multiracial—of each of the racial subgroups in the section you worked on?
   - What are the patterns you identified in your section in terms of the racial composition?
   - What preliminary explanations have you identified that explain these patterns? Include the following:

     Participation and nonparticipation

     Accessibility, opportunity, and inclusiveness

     Prejudice and discrimination
   - What are some initial ways that these discrepancies can be addressed?

5. At your next meeting, have each group report its findings.

6. After reporting, pose the following questions for an open discussion:

   • What racial beliefs are operational in our school or school system? How do the data we collected confirm or refute our racial beliefs?
   • In our school or school system, do we have a problem with racial inequity in terms of representation, participation, and/or achievement?
   • Do we need to address these racial issues? If so, why and how?

Additional Exercises

1. Select several educators from a variety of departments or upper grade levels and have each identify a student of color or indigenous student. Have the teachers document how they see race impacting the students' schooling experience by selectively shadowing and conversing with these students during a full day. Have the educators report to the entire staff what they noticed and learned.

2. Guide grade-level or departmental teams in doing a racial audit of their curriculum, similar to the Volkswagen analysis. What racial messages and images are present in texts, bulletin boards, websites, teacher representation, school announcements, and so on? How do the images and messages correspond with the racial composition of the student body?

SECOND CONDITION OF COURAGEOUS CONVERSATION

Isolate race while acknowledging the broader scope of diversity and the variety of factors and conditions that contribute to a racialized problem.

RACIAL MAKEUP OF OUR SCHOOL SYSTEM

Identify the racial composition of every subgroup under each section of your school system. This can be done through quantitative analysis of data or qualitative observation.

➢ District Administration

　　i. Superintendents and assistant superintendents
　　ii. School board
　　iii. Staff development department
　　iv. Curriculum department

➢ District Student Body

　　i. All district students
　　ii. Graduation rates
　　iii. Dropout rates
　　iv. Disaggregated student achievement

➢ District Personnel

　　i. Classified staff
　　ii. Unclassified staff

➢ Community Participation

　　i. District PTA
　　　　1. PTA leadership
　　　　2. PTA membership
　　ii. School board attendance
　　iii. Other district–community partnerships
　　　　1. Police
　　　　2. Colleges/universities
　　　　3. Local businesses
　　　　4. Others

Include the following racial/ethnic identities as they pertain to your school system:

- Black
- White
- Brown/Latino
- Asian

- Southeast Asian
- South Asian
- Pacific Islander
- Middle Eastern

- American Indian (Indigenous)
- Biracial
- Other racial identities or subgroups as needed

RACIAL MAKEUP OF OUR SCHOOL

Identify the racial composition of every subgroup under each section of your secondary school. This can be done through quantitative analysis of data or qualitative observation.

➤ School Student Body

    i. All students
    ii. Attendance rates
    iii. Graduation/dropout rates
    iv. Retention rates
    v. Referrals and suspensions
    vi. Free and reduced-price lunch participants
    vii. Gifted and talented / advanced placement / honors
    viii. Special education/remedial
    ix. Disaggregated student achievement

➤ Community Participation

    i. School PTA
       1. PTA leadership
       2. PTA membership
    ii. School meeting attendance
    iii. Parent-teacher conferences
    iv. Volunteers
    v. Other school–community partnerships
       1. Police
       2. Colleges/universities
       3. Local businesses
       4. Others

➤ School Staff

    i. Principals and assistant principals
    ii. School governing board
    iii. Counseling department
    iv. Teacher leadership teams
    v. School staff
       1. Classified
       2. Unclassified

➤ Extracurricular Participation

    i. Student government
    ii. Extracurricular activities (athletics, dances, drama, debate, academics, clubs, etc.)
       1. Advisers and coaches
       2. Student participants
    iii. Extracurricular spectator attendance (all events)
       1. Student attendees
       2. Staff attendees
       3. Community attendees
    iv. Before- and afterschool advisers and student participants
       1. Athletic programs
       2. Academic programs

Include the following racial identities as they pertain to your school, or other races or subgroups as needed:

- Black
- White
- Brown/Latino
- American Indian (Indigenous)

- Asian
- Southeast Asian
- South Asian
- Pacific Islander

- Middle Eastern
- Biracial
- Other racial identities or subgroups as needed

PATRICK SÁNCHEZ

I am Pat Sánchez, the youngest of seven children who grew up in an entirely Latino community in San Luis—a southern Colorado town about an hour north of Taos, New Mexico. I am a very proud Mexican whose family has roots in Colorado that go back more than 300 years. Though our home was modest, it was exceptionally rich in tradition, culture, language, legends, and beliefs. The people who made up my community all had similar backgrounds—a mix of Spaniards who spoke seventeenth-century Spanish, and indigenous people, mostly Navajo and Apache and some Ute. My family lineage is both Navajo and Spanish. My lived experience prompts me to pass down oral history and traditions and talk to my own children about how important it is to be a Mexi-CAN.

I recall my earliest encounters with race were the questions I posed to my parents as a young child—is "wetback" a bad word? Why do we sometimes call ourselves Mexican, and other times we call ourselves Spanish? Even as a young child, I was unknowingly cognizant of the conflicting ideologies my parents and grandparents had most likely grappled with their entire lives.

My parents' response evidenced a lack of clarity regarding why these conflicting ideologies existed; they mentioned that "they just don't speak our Spanish or understand our culture." Our discussion left me with a myriad of follow-up questions.

An additional formative event involved our monthly family trip to Alamosa, Colorado, where we would purchase groceries and supplies for the ranch. On one particular outing, my Navajo grandmother, and güero, hazel-eyed Spanish grandfather joined us on the trip. Being the baby of the family, I recall engaging in persuasive nagging, which led to a full-on tantrum at the store demanding change for the mechanical horse at the end of the checkout line. Moments later, a White farmer in line behind us remarked, "Why don't you Mexicans go back to Mexico?!"

I remember watching my mother do her best to help my father regain his composure, as he expressed both anger and confusion with this man's words. As we loaded our groceries into the car and began our trip home, I recall listening to the adults in my life discuss the situation at length. Toward the end of their conversation, I remember my grandmother calmingly reminding us that we need to feel sorry for the White man and pray for him, because it will take a long time to teach him. Her words resonated with me then, and I have continued to carry them with me throughout my life.

I fondly remember the opportunities I had to sneak off with my grandmother, hear her talk endearingly about the Navajo ways, and learn from her experiences regarding how it felt for her as a child when the güeros started moving into the San Luis Valley. She told me stories from her grandmother who remembered when "the border had crossed us," meaning the US border had been extended into Mexico so that she now lived in the United States, and how the güeros exhausted all of the wood and wildlife, and then later in her life did not honor their treaties about use of our land. My mother, who was notably perceptive, was keen in identifying people who "had two faces," which, along with being lazy, were two of the biggest insults to character in our community.

My experience in school was overshadowed by the bad reputation my older brothers had left from their time there. Their fighting, drug dealing, and violence had clearly prevented my teachers from giving me any sort of clean slate. I recall my first day of sixth grade when Mr. G took attendance—he saw my name, pointed to me and said, *"Listen, I had both of your brothers, and I am not going to tolerate any BS from you. But, I will make you a deal, if you sit in the back, and do not disrupt the class, I will pass you."* At that time, this sounded like a great deal. I agreed to it and later made the same deal with several other teachers as well.

October of freshmen year brought much darkness to my world. My brother Stan, closer to me in age, was shot in a drug deal gone bad. This made me angry and led me to seriously consider taking the wrong path with the wrong friends. I was alarmingly accustomed to the rampant low expectations of adults throughout my school, and I had become a master of flying below the radar in my educational journey.

Then—a pivotal moment in my narrative took me out of the darkness. Senior year, when I received my class schedule, I noticed a crucial mistake: It listed AP Biology with Mr. Bernal. So, I knocked on his classroom door to let him know about the mistake—he was teaching, but waved me in to sit at his desk while he finished his class. When the bell rang, and before I could even say a word, Mr. Bernal remarked, *"You got your schedule, and before you say anything I want you to know that I spoke with your parents and we agreed that these are your choices. You either take my class and do your best so you can graduate, or you can go work on the ranch. I know you are smarter then you act, and so do your parents. So, what is it going to be?"* Upon reflection, I now realize this was the tipping point for my educational trajectory.

Later in my senior year, Mr. Bernal once again went to bat for me. After arguing with a counselor who disagreed with my taking any sort of college or career preparatory classes, he invited me to take the Armed Services Vocational Aptitude Battery (ASVAB) test. Before I began, Mr. Bernal pulled me aside, reminding me of our agreement to always do my best. So, I proceeded, and I recall the look of pride on Mr. Bernal's face when I completed the test—I had scored above the 98th percentile nationally.

I am now the superintendent of a struggling inner-city district with nearly 8,000 students. When I walked into this role two years ago, I began my reform work in a school district that was second from the bottom in the state for academic achievement. I also was informed of a findings report from the Office for Civil Rights, relative to accusations prior to my arrival that Latino students were not treated fairly in our district. Armed with this information, I began the process

(Continued)

(Continued)

of rebuilding trust and rapport with all of the district's employees, families, and community members. Our district is approaching a student population that is 90% Latino, and I have spent a great deal of time reestablishing communication and trust with this growing Latino community.

But a small contingent of privileged, vocal, and influential community members was displeased with our success in reestablishing trust in the Latino community. As a result of these improved relationships and my choosing to focus on equity, our district halted a nine-year decline in performance on state tests. Still, although I attributed our success to the eradication of deficit thinking about our kids and the community we serve, that same privileged, vocal, and influential community contingent suggested we must be cheating to get those kinds of results.

Recently one morning, I was driving to work after dropping off my son at school and heard something rolling around in the back of my truck. When I arrived at work, I looked in the back and discovered a rock that had been wrapped with a note surrounded by a rubber band and thrown through my window.

> "mr SANCHEZ" you Mexican loving piece of s***, You are destroying our district, Go back to your country, this is AMERICA , F*** you and those other Mexican lovers, we are watching you, watch your back, F*****!!!!

This pivotal moment was my most recent racial event. How disappointing to once again—like when I was a child in the grocery store—experience how little progress we have made in our ability to authentically discuss race. For a brief, dark moment, I reflected on how I would have responded to a situation like this 20 years ago as a cholo. Back then, I had that deep anger boiling under the surface and was the one quick to resolve issues with anger-fueled violence. I recalled spending much of my high school experience with the Chicano version of the television show "Sons of Anarchy."

But further reflection reinforced my steadfast belief regarding the critical importance of improving our nation's skill set to discuss race—because *race* does matter. It is important for leaders of color to learn how to harness our own induced anger and transform it into productive action, so we deeply engage in this critical equity work, because it is the right battle and we are clearly at war.

How can we create school systems in our society that support us in developing this skill set while simultaneously eliminating the frequency of negative, sometimes violent interracial interactions?

SEVEN

The Third Condition

Engaging Multiple Racial Perspectives

We are trapped in our history and our history is trapped in us!

—James Baldwin

A s Baldwin so eloquently writes, it seems impossible for any of us to fully separate our current reality from our history of experiences. Even if we *could* do so, why would we, given that there is so much to learn from what has happened in our individual and collective pasts, especially with regard to race, race relations, and racism? We can uncover critical perspectives and develop deeper interracial relationships as we examine our interrelated histories, which continue to nourish the foundation of our daily racial interactions.

The Third Condition of Courageous Conversation prompts participants to

normalize social construction of knowledge, thus engaging multiple racial points of view in order to surface critical perspective.

To *normalize social construction of knowledge* is to acknowledge the process through which racial meaning is inherited, interpreted, and passed on from one generation to the next. Each of us creates meaning around our current racial reality based on how we have experienced and understood our near and distant pasts. The Third Condition enables educators to develop will, skill, and capacity for listening to and engaging with others' contrasting and conflicting racial perspectives and experiences. In our discussions around race, educators must formally recognize and respect that people offer a broad continuum of willingness and ability to examine and understand racial matters.

Where and how people have grown up creates the lens through which they see the world racially. This is known as the *social construction of knowledge* about race. If everyone involved in a Courageous Conversation brings somewhat of a unique social construction of racial knowledge, then there will necessarily be *multiple racial points of view* to consider. Because we view this as a normal phenomenon of our interracial existence—especially in education—the Third Condition of Courageous Conversation invites participants to normalize social construction and multiple racial points of view to surface contrasting, conflicting, or critical perspectives.

SOCIAL CONSTRUCTION OF KNOWLEDGE

We see things not as they are, but rather as we are!

—Pastor Douglas Fitch, Glide Memorial Church

Tremendous complexities exist around race as a socially and politically constructed phenomenon, because race both *exists* and *does not exist* in the United States specifically and more generally throughout the Western world. In spite of the specific racial meanings that we have learned to associate with skin and eye color or hair texture, all human beings are scientifically of one species. Only socially and politically do we exist in the variety of racial groups we have learned to define and recognize. With respect to race, how, where, and with whom we live, work, and play forms our personal and collective racial contexts and is at the heart of how we interpret race in our lives and define race in the lives of others.

Racial issues are not about physical skin color but rather stem from the meaning and value people assign to skin color. Remarkable variance exists in how different racial groups determine, define, and describe their own collective racial experience as well as the experiences of "the racial other." Clearly, then, it is important to recognize that definitions of race and shared racial experiences in the United States of America are derived from national, state, and local community contexts. My work in various African countries and throughout Canada, Australia, and New Zealand, as well as my leisurely travel to six of the seven continents, supports a similar notion of how racial meaning is constructed. Through developing a greater understanding of these contexts, we can better understand the thoughts, beliefs, and feelings that people of each "racial group" bring with them into Courageous Conversation.

In Chapter 9, a description of the Fifth Condition of Courageous Conversation provides an opportunity to explore briefly how history has shaped current racial realities. What we hope to indicate in the Third Condition is just how much historical perspective about race is passed down from one generation to the next, thus shaping the way people view contemporary racial images and their interracial interactions. For example, if you think back to the Volkswagen advertisement presented in the previous chapter, both the racial information that you recognized and that which you failed to see are parts of your personal process of socially constructing knowledge about race.

REFLECTION

Can you think of a time when someone you knew did something that you viewed to be racially unjust or even racist, but the person engaged in the action saw it differently? Describe the differing historic and contemporary racial contexts that you believe influenced your point of view and the other person's contrasting one.

Internalization and Transfer of Racism

As people of color and indigenous people are continuously subjected to racist acts, an eventual internalization and transfer of racism often occurs. This is a process in which people of color begin to believe all that they hear about their own racial image, potential, and power. When people of color internalize negative racial messages, they may lose hope, thus buying into notions of second-class or subservient citizenship. Eventually, this conditioning or racism undermines their confidence and ability to function successfully in the White-dominant culture. According to Weissglass (2001),

> The patterns of internalizing and transferring racism (insults, criticism, slurs, and violence) are rooted in genocide, slavery, subjugation, conquest, and exploitation. When people are hurt and not allowed to heal through emotional release, they are pulled to re-enact the hurt on someone else. Since People of Color have rarely been able to act out their hurt on Whites, they tend to act it out on family members and other people of Color. These behavior patterns tend to get passed on from generation to generation. (p. 50)

Similarly, White people can develop skills to not see and acknowledge the impact of race, and specifically racial advantage, in their lives or the pervasiveness of institutionalized racism. This is called *structured colorblindness* and is found within a White belief that people of color and indigenous people are less successful because they try less, or worse, because they are inferior to White people. Internalizing such beliefs of White supremacy is quite harmful to White educators and the White children they teach.

SURFACING CRITICAL PERSPECTIVES

Multiple points of view about race, racial identity development, and racism serve to sustain interracial dialogue, because critical perspective surfaces. But the various racial points of view can also bring the dialogue to an abrupt conclusion. The

Third Condition of Courageous Conversation suggests that it is normal for different racial groups to offer different racial points of view as determined and defined by their shared racial experiences. Even more confusing, however, is the fact that people of the same racial group may also diverge in their point of view in spite of having a shared racial context.

Recall for a moment my racial autobiography, which I shared at the end of the Chapter 3. Clearly, my view of White racial culture changed dramatically after graduating from an all-Black elementary school, in which the presence of Whiteness was limited to books and media, and then enrolling in a predominantly White middle school, where not only were books and media still White, but also 100% of the educators and 95% of the students were White. My changing viewpoint affected not only my beliefs and attitude but also my behavior, both in White contexts and in my own Black community. In this relatively short period of time, race—as a social and political construct—did not change in Baltimore, but what race meant to me, and perhaps to those who knew me, certainly changed dramatically.

By making normal or "normalizing" the presence of multiple racial points of view, we avoid a situation in which one way of understanding race—typically a dominant one—invalidates other points of view and thus invalidates other racial expressions and experiences as well. Although it may not be done maliciously or even intentionally, it is nonetheless not uncommon for White educators to discount, disparage, or deny the racial views of educators of color. Perhaps only because the dominant culture does not witness or experience a situation or circumstance in the same way as people of color and indigenous people, there may be a gentle insistence that all people see it the "White way." To sustain a Courageous Conversation, educators must avoid forcing onto others their own individual and collective racial point of view, which often means enforcing a dominant White racial understanding of schooling as normal and correct.

REFLECTION

Think of an interracial situation or conversation that was dominated by a White racial point of view. What was the prevailing tone? Was the process inclusive or not? What was the outcome, and was it satisfactory to all participants?

Counternarratives

When multiple points of view are embraced, educators are better able to locate and understand racial conflict as well as become aware of racial bias. Essentially, they uncover the *counternarrative,* a critical perspective that reveals and explains the impact of racism. Only through surfacing an understanding of how racism is experienced by those most keenly aware and conscious of it can educators arrive at a critical racial perspective about student engagement and the actual impact on and effectiveness of their teaching for underserved students of color and indigenous students.

In my experience, as White educators normalize multiple points of view, they come to a much deeper understanding of the cumulative effect of racism for people of color. Rather than feeling personally challenged, guilty, put off, or offended by this process, they often come to feel greater personal and professional empathy and responsibility. As educators of color and indigenous educators witness this transformation of their White colleagues and discover their true lack of racist intent or malice, they are less likely to be guarded and suspicious in their commentary and interactions.

This mutual redefinition and resulting belief in the possibility of effective interracial relations invites the necessary exploration toward a critical perspective of how students and families of color and indigenous students and families experience school.

Validating Multiple Points of View

By normalizing social construction of knowledge and thus engaging multiple racial points of view, participants in Courageous Conversation surface critical perspectives that open the door to new ways of looking at the challenge of effectively educating all students. Many participants find it difficult—and this is the essence of this Third Condition—to listen to the racial views of people of color and indigenous people as intently as they listen to White ideas about race, and they are also challenged to allow people of color and indigenous people the same variation in their views that they allow among White people.

As a North American culture, we often recognize, embrace, and promote people of color and indigenous people whose racial ideology is aligned with more conservative White ideologies. Often, these people of color or indigenous people express a point of view that exists outside the majority viewpoint among people of color. The appointment of Clarence Thomas to the US Supreme Court is illustrative of this phenomenon. His appointment provided a way to racially diversify the Supreme Court without diversifying its racial ideology. This same phenomenon can exist in schools, where largely White staffs are more sympathetic to the voices of educators, students, and parents of color when they impart an understanding about the impact of race on schooling that is closely aligned to the dominant White point of view.

Some readers misunderstand my intention in the Third Condition where I call for us to "validate" multiple racial perspectives. I am not requesting that you agree with or find truth in another's contrasting or conflicting interpretation of his or her racialized experience. My intention is not that we validate another's story but rather we validate that each of us has a story, and more than likely, our stories will be somewhat different. The Third Condition is designed to support each of us in giving voice to our own racial experience, however we may interpret that experience to have occurred. Subsequently, through the Fifth and Sixth Conditions, Courageous Conversations participants will be able to deepen their discovery, insights, and understanding about where racial truth exists in the stories about race that we tell. Finally, keep in mind that the Third Condition of Courageous Conversation does not request or require that participants agree, which is precisely the reason for which we agree to expect and accept non-closure. The Third Condition merely encourages educators to embrace and entertain diverging points of view as a way of engaging with race in a deeply critical way.

REFLECTION

Consider the following racially "loaded" topics:*

- Affirmative Action in college admissions
- The killing of Trayvon Martin
- The DREAM Act
- Indian gaming

First, isolate race (the Second Condition) and try to give voice to at least two conflicting points of view for each topic. Next, determine the factors that have shaped your own social construction of knowledge on these issues. What seems to be the dominant viewpoint among your family members, friends, colleagues, and social circles? How closely do their racial ideologies align with your own opinion?

*Readers outside of the United States should feel free to substitute here four context-specific, current racial topics before engaging in this reflective exercise.

As participants engage in Courageous Conversation, the First Condition (focusing on the personal, local, and immediate) and the Second Condition (isolating race) serve as the foundation on which the multiple points of view and the critical perspective (the Third Condition) can rest. Once these are engaged— and, in a sense, discovering or reaffirming that race impacts each of us all the time—the Third Condition of Courageous Conversation invites educators to speak their truth about their varied racial experiences and perspectives. Rather than bringing conversation to a silent halt, these conflicting viewpoints serve as the doorway to sustained dialogue and as an opportunity to surface critical perspective about race, racial identity, and institutional racism.

IMPLEMENTATION EXERCISE

ENGAGING MULTIPLE RACIAL POINTS OF VIEW

Time required: 45 minutes

Materials required: For each participant, Courageous Conversation Journal and a copy of the poem below

1. Explain and explore the Third Condition of Courageous Conversation:

    Normalize social construction of knowledge, thus engaging multiple racial points of view in order to surface critical perspective.

    Based on your reading, describe for the group the following terms:

    - *Normalize*
    - *Social construction of knowledge*
    - *Multiple racial points of view*
    - *Critical perspective*

2. Ask the group how the application of this condition can create a safe environment for people to share their honest opinions and feelings about race and racism.

3. Conduct a listening exercise. Divide participants into groups according to their race (racial affinity groups), and have them read the poem "I Dream" by Pablo Vega, which is on the worksheet.

4. Invite each educator to provide an individual response to the following question:

    - What is Pablo saying about the impact of race on his life both inside and outside of school?

    Have members of each racial affinity group share their responses with others in their same group, and create a unified interpretation of the poem that highlights the shared meaning and understanding arrived at by all or most of the group members.

5. Bring all of the participants back together, and have each affinity group present its interpretation of the poem.

6. Invite the participants to examine each racial affinity group's interpretation of the poem, summarizing the multiple racial viewpoints and surfacing the critical racial perspective, or the *counternarrative,* and revealing ideas of which most people in the room were not aware.

    - What were the similarities and differences among racial viewpoints?
    - What social constructions were apparent in each group's interpretation?

- What value to the group's understanding came from hearing multiple racial points of view regarding Pablo's experience as described in "I Dream"?
- How can these multiple viewpoints be more fully honored in all conversations?

7. Have each participant reflect on this conversation in his or her Courageous Conversation Journal.

I Dream

I am from a clash of Color,
From an idea of love, modeled for others' perception.
I see me as I am, but am hidden from others' views.
I am who I am, but a living contradiction to my peers.
I see life as a blessing, a gift granted to me.
Why should my tint describe me? Why should my culture degrade me?
Why should the ignorance of another conjure my presence?
Too many times I've been disappointed by the looks,
By the sneers and misconceptions of the people who don't get me,
Who don't understand why it hurts.
I dream of a place of glory and freedom,
Of losing the weight of oppression on my back.
I dream of the enlightenment of people,
Of the opening of their eyes.
I dream for acceptance,
And for the blessing of feeling special just once.
One moment of glory . . . for the true virtue in my life.
For the glimmer of freedom, and a rise in real pride.

—Used with permission of Pablo Vega
Chapel Hill High School, North Carolina

REFLECTION

What is Pablo saying about the impact of race on his life both inside and outside of school?

LEIDENE KING

RACIAL AUTOBIOGRAPHY

Walking to my gate, I pass an African-American male. We nod in acknowledgment of one another and continue on our ways. Arriving at my gate I find a seat and begin to situate my carry-on and work bag. I look up and catch the gaze of a White female staring at me. As our eyes meet, she hurriedly looks away. After sitting for several minutes, I approach the gate with a question about my boarding pass. Two gate agents, both African American females, are sitting behind the counter and are in the midst of conversation. I stand and wait, remaining unacknowledged. After a moment, a White male comes and stands in line behind me. The two women promptly stop their conversation and come to help me, and then the White male behind me. As I return to my seat with my boarding pass question answered and new questions running through my mind, an Asian male, age about 60, looks at me with a wondering glance and then returns to his reading.

From my earliest recollection, my race has been salient. I was recently asked, "Leidene, who are you in your humanity, beyond race?" As I contemplated the question, I realized that I have no idea. For me, there is no "me" without race. My race is inextricably linked to who I am. And some ask, isn't it because you look for it, you expect it to be that way? It's clear to me that those who ask such questions haven't lived race as I have and don't live race as I do. As a result, they attempt to construct their understanding of my racial experiences without my racial experiences, but rather with their own. This seldom works.

So, back to my earliest recollection of race. I'm in kindergarten, and a friend asks me, "What are you?" I am fascinated by and excited about the question. "I don't know," I answer. I seek the answer to this question from the person who in my five-year old world knows all, my mom. Soon after my mom gets home from work, I ask her, "What am I?" My Chinese mom who married my African American dad and was initially disowned for marrying a Black man shared, "You're Black and Chinese, Leidene." I wasn't quite sure what that meant exactly, but I was delighted to have an answer to share with my friend. When I see my friend at school the next day, I excitedly share with her, "I'm Black and Chinese." She says, "Cool," and we finish singing, dancing, and doing what kindergarteners do. No biggie. Initially, I felt really special being asked, "What are you?" But that specialness diminished with the increasing frequency of the questions, the staring, the comments all suggesting to me that I was not quite where I belonged, though I felt I was exactly where I belonged.

By the time I reached the upper grade levels of elementary school, some girls would say things like "you think you're cute" or "you are conceited" with a good bit of hostility. And my thinking I was cute or being conceited seemed related to my skin being light and my having "good hair." From such regularly occurring

(Continued)

(Continued)

experiences, I learned that what I look like means something—sometimes it's good, and sometimes it could land me on the receiving end of hostility. Taking all this in, I share with my mom one day that I think some of the girls at school don't like me because I'm light-skinned. My mom readily let me know that wasn't true, which I internalized as me possibly though improbably misunderstanding my classmates and/or my mom being unable to help me with what I was experiencing. I learned to get along with my classmates. I became very likeable. I played down what I looked like and worked to fit in. So when the girls at school had cornrows with beads at the ends, I got them too. When gold hoop earrings with your name on them and nameplate leather belts were in, I got those too. They couldn't tell me I didn't belong here. Clearly, I did.

Onto college. One of my closest college friends and I were talking about growing up, what it was like, et cetera, and after I shared with her some of what I did to fit in, she said, "Oh, that's why you talk like that?" I thought "talk like what?" She meant, "Talk 'Black.'" Until that moment I hadn't consciously thought about how or why I talk the way I do. Because she looked African American, a need to talk a certain way didn't compute, because she was Black and that was an accepted, undisputed, and unquestioned truth. Her dark skin granted her automatic acceptance within her racial community. Who I am, however, was questioned regularly until I learned to preemptively quell such examination with the way I spoke, dressed, or did my hair.

In doing race work professionally, I've learned that people who look like me are sometimes referred to as "racially ambiguous." You look at me and don't necessarily know what my race is. Moreover, "what I am" according to others, changes with geography. In Phoenix, for example, I am Mexican or a *Chicana por la causa.* In Harlem, I'm Puerto Rican or Dominican. In my mother's homeland, Hawaii, I'm local or *Kama'aina.* Then there are those who refer to me as mixed or biracial. I once embraced this latter description until I recognized that the biracial category was established as increasing numbers of White people had children with people of color and wanted their children to be classified as "both." When I was growing up, if you had one drop of color in you, you were colored, not White, and this attitude was even stronger for folks who were born before I was. Biracial was not an option for me—nor is it for President Obama.

My racial identity—what I am—continues to be brought to my attention either directly or indirectly just about daily. Such a focus from others prompts an involuntary, personal recognition of my race accompanied by a sense of racial "otherness." This circumstance has led me to seek and secure communities of acceptance like my sorority and other organizations for Black women, where what are you, racially speaking, is a given rather than a question.

When the African American Brotha and I exchange nods, this reminds me that I do belong. When the White woman stares at me in the airport, she reminds me that I am often a source of curiosity to be pondered and figured out. When my Black Sisters have me wait in a manner they don't require of the White male, I wonder if they've learned their own lack of importance and reflect that in how they have treated me. Finally, when the Asian male possibly recognizes a part of himself in me but not quite—each of these recurring moments remind me of "What am I" and all that goes into my knowing how to answer that question. I wonder how many of us desire a racial place to belong—a place to simply be without having to answer the questions, what are you and why are you here?

EIGHT

The Fourth Condition

Keeping Us All at the Table

We Need to Really Talk

I am overwhelmed.
Don't make me wash the colors, the heritage, the languages—
I don't want to.
We need to really talk . . .
as though no one is judging
but everyone is listening.
It's easy to forget that life is complex enough that love and hate,
acceptance and fear grow in one.
Don't just like me, ask me, make me question,
make me uncertain and in this time of doubt,
let's do something.
Forget stereotypes,
lose our words to internal thoughts.
I am not saying we're going to move the world,
but we can provoke a shift in our minds,
moving away from ignorance, discrimination,
and the belief that
we understand without experiencing.

—Used with permission of Janaka Lagoo
Sophomore, Chapel Hill, North Carolina

As so eloquently stated by this African American sophomore in Chapel Hill, North Carolina, a significant challenge to addressing race interracially in the United States is our ability to actually just talk about it. Mainstream American culture reinforces a message that race is something we simply don't talk about, especially if our discussion group includes members of different races. But absent open and honest dialogue between people of different races, there is little hope that racial aggressions, misunderstandings, and tensions will lessen. This is especially true in our schools, where the culture of silence surrounding race serves only to perpetuate racism and to exacerbate racial achievement disparities that exist among students.

My numerous experiences participating in both successful and unsuccessful interracial dialogue have enabled me to consider exactly what sends a well-intentioned conversation into dangerous territory. Typically, Courageous Conversation begins with participants examining race in their own individual lives. Making race personal, local, and immediate is what I refer to as the First Condition. Often, my struggle is to help participants stay focused on the impact of race in their own lives, given the "hot-button" nature of the subject and the reality of how race intersects so many other issues.

The Second Condition of Courageous Conversation fortifies our focus by instructing us to isolate race. While we might want to examine how race affects someone's economic or gender status, we first need to discover what race is and how it impacts our lives. The Second Condition guides us toward recognizing that although race is always a factor in life experiences, people have different levels of consciousness of this omnipresent racial impact, based on their upbringing, the current racial context in which they live, and how they identify racially.

The Third Condition of Courageous Conversation sets the stage for ushering in multiple racial points of view and critical racial perspective. It is here that participants search for their own personal meaning regarding any racialized situation and recognize that others will do the same. Because diversity of racial opinion can breed contention among participants, we often notice the potential for conflict for the first time at this point of the conversation. Acknowledging that different points of view are both normal and necessary to surface critical perspective, or the *counternarrative* about race, enables participants to survive the storm of conflicting racial viewpoints. Critical perspective will indeed sustain the conversation and advance it toward a deeper level of racial inquiry; but conflicting racial opinions also heighten discomfort and challenge educators' commitment to stay engaged.

For this reason, the Fourth Condition of Courageous Conversation specifically focuses participants on the dialogue process as a way of ensuring greater safety and sustained, deeper introspection. The Fourth Condition provides an opportunity to examine intentionally and consciously who is engaging, how they are engaging, and from where on the Courageous Conversation Compass they are entering and moving about in the dialogue. The Fourth Condition of Courageous Conversation asks participants to

> *monitor the parameters of the conversation by being explicit and intentional about the number of participants, prompts for discussion, and time allotted for listening, speaking, and reflecting. Use the Courageous Conversation Compass to gauge where you and other participants are in*

terms of your emotional, intellectual, moral, and relational proximity and connection to a given racial topic.

Paying attention to the formal elements of conversation fosters greater safety for all involved. With maximum safety comes an increased willingness on the part of all educators to step courageously out of their comfort zones and take the risk of speaking their truths.

REFLECTION

What do you believe to be some of the necessary parameters for effective interracial conversations about race to occur?

INTERRACIAL DIALOGUE

Why is interracial dialogue so difficult? To begin with, we are socialized to understand and comment on race differently based on our own racial affiliation. Of course, it's not true that *all* White people will respond one way while *all* people of color or indigenous people respond another way, but some racial patterns in the interracial dialogue have emerged in my research and practice. For example, many White Americans have been raised to believe that it is racist to notice race—that it is virtuous to be colorblind, so to speak. Thus, many White educators view talking about race as inappropriate, particularly while in mixed racial company. Conversely, people of color and indigenous people must notice race in this country as a variety of racial situations are still damaging to our mind, body, and soul—and indeed may be fatal if ignored.

Just over 40 years ago, segregation of White people and people of color was indeed legal in the United States. Although racial desegregation is the law of the land and achieving racial equality is an avowed goal, not a day goes by when people of color and indigenous people are not publicly labeled as some form of burden to this country's progress. Descriptions such as *alien, violent, lazy, immoral, illegitimate, at-risk, low-performing,* and *disadvantaged* must be overcome by hard-working, patriotic people of color and indigenous people every day. Thus, it is virtually impossible for people of color to not notice color or to ignore White people who seem to have difficulty with the existence of people who are not White. Consequently, people of color and indigenous people tend to bring more experience and a resulting greater racial consciousness to the conversation. As people of color, many of us talk about race all the time to ourselves as well as to anyone else who will listen!

Racialized Communication

Another reason why the interracial conversation is so difficult is that people enter it having very different communication styles and desired outcomes. For many people of color and indigenous people, a productive conversation about race is, in and of itself, healing, whereas for many White people, the conversation is often viewed as threatening, especially when it appears to have no concrete resolution, focused action, or determined result. Understanding these and other predictable and patterned racial experiences helps educators engaged in Courageous Conversation to anticipate and identify their own behavior as well as the behavior of their conversation partners.

Distrust typically exists on all sides of the interracial conversation. For example, many educators of color believe that White educators, generally, don't want to talk about race and have a hard time listening to and accepting as valid the racial perspectives of people of color. Many White educators, on the other hand, fear people of color and indigenous people will label them racist should they misspeak or fail to express their racial viewpoint with absolute precision and confidence. Keeping this in mind allows participants in Courageous Conversation to monitor for these problematic circumstances. Lisa Delpit has done a significant amount of research identifying these difficulties in interracial dialogue. In her article, "The Silenced Dialogue," Delpit (1988/1995b) shares the thoughts of a Black educator teaching in a multiracial urban elementary school regarding her interactions with many of the White teachers with whom she works:

> When you're talking to White people they still want it to be their way. You can try to talk to them and give them examples, but they're so headstrong, they think they know what's best for *everybody,* for *everybody's* children. They won't listen; White folks are going to do what they want to do *anyway.*

What Delpit captures here is the frustration of a teacher of color who wants to have a conversation about race but feels she can't do so effectively, as shown in her concluding statement, "It's really hard. [Whites] just don't listen well. No, they listen, but they don't *hear.*"

This teacher's challenge could have been addressed by focusing on the Fourth Condition of Courageous Conversation, which alerts White teachers, in this case, to talk less, listen carefully, and reflect more on what is being said. The Fourth Condition might have helped reduce the Black teacher's frustration by providing upfront insights surrounding how and why White people tend to struggle with conversations about race. According to Linda Chambers, a Black principal retired from Johnston H. Cooper Elementary in Vallejo, California, "Race is a very taboo subject. It's like it's there and it's in your face, especially if you're an educator of color; but White educators don't typically think about race, they don't talk about race" (Singleton, 2002). As I implement Courageous Conversation in various settings, I have found that difficulties in discussing race stubbornly persist among educators despite the public and political efforts to address racial achievement disparities.

White Talk Versus Color Commentary

Historically and still to some degree today, racial discourse in the United States is governed by the cultural parameters of the dominant White population. Consequently, when discussing race and racial issues, White people tend to engage from a place of certain authority, even though they have quite often been remiss in conducting their own racial introspection. In contrast, people of color and indigenous people initially tend to communicate in the interracial forum in a more cautious and tempered manner. Having observed and participated in countless interracial dyads and larger teams of educators attempting to conduct meaningful discourse about racial matters, I have documented predictable patterns in conversation. As a result, I have identified eight characteristics that describe the nature of the communication that occurs in typical interracial conversations about race. I have grouped and labeled these patterns *White Talk* and *Color Commentary,* each of which is described below:

White Talk

- Verbal: Focused on talking and offering racial meaning through word choice, voice tone, and intonation

- Impersonal: Focused on the sharing of racial perspectives or experiences of someone not immediately present or involved in the conversation
- Intellectual: Focused on what one thinks (or has read) with respect to race

- Task oriented: Focused on engaging in dialogue for the purposes of solving a problem or getting something accomplished

Color Commentary

- Nonverbal: Focused on offering racial meaning through facial expressions, body movements, and physical gestures
- Personal: Focused on sharing one's own personal racial narrative, perspectives, or experiences

- Emotional: Focused on what one feels (or has experienced) with respect to race

- Process oriented: Focused on engaging in dialogue for the purposes of feeling present, connected, or heard

Although the eight characteristics emerge in predictable and patterned ways in interracial dialogue in which race is the topic, I am not suggesting that *all* White people or *all* people of color and indigenous people will follow the pattern of White Talk or Color Commentary based solely on their racial affiliation. Rather, these patterns are characteristic of how people of racial groupings *typically* rather than stereotypically respond when faced with racial subject matter in interracial discourse.

Initially, some people feel that these characteristics represent stereotypes—that only a few White people or people of color succumb to the characteristics of White Talk and Color Commentary. I argue that they go well beyond stereotype to represent *patterns* of racial discourse based on monitoring thousands of interracial conversations about race over nearly two decades, happening among both male and female educators of various ages, economic backgrounds, and geographic locations throughout the United States and various countries abroad.

Finally, for many White readers especially, who have previously failed to even recognize themselves as having membership in a group, much less a culture, based on their race, my determinations about communication patterns are jolting and perhaps seem offensive. Pursuant to the agreements in Chapter 4, I ask that you stay engaged while leaning into the discomfort that you may be feeling now. Additionally, recall the Third Condition, introduced in Chapter 7, which requests that you "normalize multiple racial perspectives," given that we each socially construct meaning about race.

As we probe deeper into the conflict inherent in the very ways we talk about race, the Fourth Condition of Courageous Conversation enables us to create a balance between White Talk and Color Commentary. My experience tells me that without careful monitoring and intervention, all four characteristics of White Talk will be dominant in the dialogue, simply because more White educators are present in our schools and thus involved in the Courageous Conversation. When the discussion is predictably and significantly unbalanced, fewer people for whom Color Commentary is natural and normal will feel they have had the opportunity or the encouragement to participate. By examining and better understanding these eight characteristics, educators have the opportunity to bring balance and sustenance to Courageous Conversations about race.

REFLECTION

Think of an interracial conversation about race in which you recently have been involved. Can the overall conversation be characterized more by the features of White Talk or Color Commentary? Which of the characteristics best defines your own personal contributions to the dialogue?

Identifying and remaining conscious about how we differentially communicate and exercise control in conversations based on our racial identity is critical to interracial understanding and progress. Table 8.1 provides further examples of White Talk and Color Commentary.

REFLECTION

Describe your own typical communication style using the terms of White Talk or Color Commentary. How and to what degree does your typical communication style change when race is the presenting topic and you are in an interracial professional setting such as a staff meeting, parent conference, or classroom situation?

Of course, not all White people engage in White Talk, and not all people of color and indigenous people engage in Color Commentary. In fact, to survive and advance in educational contexts usually governed by White people, people of color typically learn and practice White Talk, because it is the language of power and influence. Likewise, some White people have developed Color Commentary characteristics as a way of being more effective and accepted in their conversations with people of color and indigenous people.

Table 8.1 Understanding White Talk and Color Commentary

White Talk	*Color Commentary*
Verbal: Characterized by loud, authoritative, and interrupted speech. Value is placed on expressing oneself and controlling the conversation.	**Nonverbal:** Characterized by silent respect for as well as disconnect from the one talking and/or positional/cultural authority. Communication takes place through body motions and other nonverbal expression.
Example: Who speaks first, longest, and most often	Example: Folded arms, silence, sighs, rolling of the eyes, refusal to offer direct eye contact
Impersonal: Typically spoken in third person. Prone to explaining opinion through use of other people's stories or experiences.	**Personal:** Typically spoken in first person. Great value placed upon sharing one's own story and experiences.
Example: "My best friend who is Black. . . . " "I am married to a person of color who thinks that. . . . " "I grew up around Asians and they said. . . . "	Example: "The police pulled me over because I am Black. . . . " "As an indigenous person, I don't trust White people. . . . " "We believe that [such-and-such a place] has a problem with indigenous people."
Intellectual: Dialogue is abstract and disconnected from immediate and local reality. More interested in quantitative analysis of one's thinking.	**Emotional:** Dialogue is centered on an immediate and local racial reality. More interested in qualitative analysis and feelings.
Example: "Statistics say. . . . " "Do the data really suggest that it is because of race?" "I once read that. . . . " "[So-and-so] said. . . . " "Can you give me a citation that supports that?" "What university did he attend?" "He studied with. . . . "	Example: "I don't feel as though you like or respect me as a Black teacher. . . . " "I feel alone here as the only teacher of color. . . . " "I get so angry when they speak for me, misinterpret and misrepresent me. . . . " "I don't trust. . . . " "I don't feel safe."

(Continued)

Table 8.1 (Continued)

White Talk	*Color Commentary*
Task oriented: Organized around the need "to do" something and to find solutions. An impatient focus on locating tools and strategies to address racial issues. Views the racial challenge as a technical problem in which the solutions exist and simply need to be unearthed. Sees introspective conversation as a waste of time.	**Process oriented:** Organized around the need "to be" respected, validated, and affirmed. Developing trust in others occurs through the examination of racial attitudes and beliefs in public. Racial challenges are viewed as adaptive problems that require us to deal with our inner thought processes and to explore our biases to create undiscovered solutions.
Example: "When are we going to get to the actions? I'm tired of talking. . . . " "What does talking about race have to do with the achievement gap? Give me a strategy."	Example: "How do you feel about this Brown student?" "How do you believe your students of color feel about you as a teacher?" "How do Latino faculty feel about working in a predominantly White school?"

Balancing Power in Communication

Consider this common illustration of how White Talk and Color Commentary can collide, resulting in a nonproductive exchange:

A White teacher prepares to be in conference with an indigenous family. As the parents sit down, the time-conscious teacher dives right into a list of what the student has and has not accomplished according to the grade-level standards. With achievement data in hand to support her assessment, the teacher continues by explaining what types of support she is trained to provide and what assistance might not be possible, given her time with respect to the large number of children in the classroom. The teacher then politely suggests to the parents what they need to do for their child at home to ensure success.

Now finished, the teacher has talked only about the "to do's" and the data. Breathless, angry, and flustered, the parents unsuccessfully fight back intense emotion as they challenge the teacher with one question: "Do you like my child, and is her spirit safe while in your care?" After saying this, they begin to express to the teacher how special they believe their child is and how important it is that their child feel appreciated by the teacher. Not prepared to converse at this level, the teacher grows flustered and launches into a defense of her practice. In the end, both the parents and teacher fail to engage in meaningful dialogue about the student's experience.

This interracial conversation lacked an effective balance in communication styles between the participants. The White teacher's conversation manner was extremely verbal, impersonal, intellectual, and task oriented. Predictably, the parents were nonverbal as they fearfully absorbed and processed the assessment of their child. Without question, the teacher must inform parents of what their child needs "to do" to achieve academic success. But educators should do this in a way that balances White Talk and Color Commentary when attempting to communicate cross-racially. Effective interracial conversations require time for trust building through first-person sharing and examination. Only when we have established ourselves personally, locally, and immediately can we engage in safer interracial dialogue. Monitoring our communication characteristics and balancing the White Talk and Color Commentary in the conversation will ensure fuller participation.

> **REFLECTION**
>
> Have you ever been in an interracial conversation that was unbalanced in terms of communication style? How did it feel? In terms of White Talk and Color Commentary, how might you have helped bring greater balance to that conversation?

Educators are challenged in interracial dialogue by the fact that power is usually located in White Talk. Consider once again the commentary of Lisa Delpit (1988/1995b) on this culture of power, where power is data and power is impersonal:

> Either by virtue of their position, their numbers, or their access to that particular code of power of calling upon research to validate one's position, the White educators [have] the authority to establish what [is] to be considered "truth" regardless of the opinions of the people of color, and the latter [are] well aware of that fact. (p. 26)

Given this consolidation of racial power through communication style, Delpit (1995a) clearly identifies how and why the authority to focus efforts primarily on accomplishing the tasks of school restructuring easily overshadows the need for educators to examine emotional issues related to personal relationships and overall culture and climate of the institution.

Educators have much "to do," but schools also need "to be" developed as places where people of all races are valued, appreciated, and heard. Schooling as a process is difficult enough without depersonalizing the experience and leaving educators, students, and their families emotionally disconnected.

Regarding the role that racial power plays in interracial communication, Delpit (1995a) further explains,

> The worldviews of those with privileged positions are taken as the only reality, while the worldviews of those less powerful are dismissed as inconsequential. Indeed, in the educational institutions of this country, the possibilities for poor people and for people of color to define themselves, to determine the self each should be, involve a power that lies outside of the self. It is others who determine how they should act, how they are to be judged. When one "we" gets to determine standards for all "wes," then some "wes" are in trouble! (p. xv)

Empowering Communication

It is particularly challenging for administrators of color and indigenous administrators to lead their primarily White staff in conversing openly and honestly about race. Andy Garcia, formerly principal at Christopher Elementary in the Oak Grove School District in San José, California, explains,

> I think it's hard for someone who is not of color to understand that there is a difference being a person of color coming into a building where you don't see staff of color there. It's a little bit more intimidating to give your voice, to give your point of view, to give your understanding. (Singleton, 2002)

Despite the conflicting racial communication styles and the imbalance of racial power in the institution, Courageous Conversation is a surmountable hurdle for all administrators, including administrators of color and indigenous administrators. The Oak Grove School District leadership team participated in Courageous Conversation for several years. As part of the district's practice with the Fourth Condition of Courageous Conversation, Manny Barbara, the White, former superintendent in the Oak Grove School District, established an advisory panel of African American and Latino administrators, known as ALLIED (African Americans and Latinos In Equity Development), who met together to share their perspectives, develop insights, and explore ways to effectively engage their White colleagues, staff members, and families in Courageous Conversation.

The support of ALLIED administrators demonstrates the Oak Grove School District's commitment to developing leadership of color to engage and sustain multiple points of view and critical perspective. Courageous Conversation is an essential foundation for districts that want to examine the inequitable ways power is traditionally determined and distributed. Andy Garcia continues,

> Through the process of learning, I've seen my fellow administrators who are not of color begin to say things that have really fascinated me. Things like, wow, I'm not feeling comfortable with these conversations. And I thought, wow, these are the conversations that we have to deal with every day. All of a sudden these guys are saying they're not feeling comfortable

in these conversations. To a certain extent, that's strength, because suddenly they're not feeling comfortable. All of a sudden I'm able to share because of the power of [ALLIED], because of the support of my superintendent. I'm able to really share my struggle and what it's like. That's been very empowering. (Singleton, 2002)

> In your experience, what takes place when you engage in interracial discussions about race or racism with other educators? In what ways have the conversations been successful or unsuccessful?
>
> **REFLECTION**

CREATING SAFETY

As a society is governed by laws to ensure safety for its citizenry, Courageous Conversation offers a protocol that maximizes safer engagement around the "third rail" issue of race. Although educators must experience discomfort when discussing race, if leaders utilize the protocol proficiently, an environment can be created that provides relative safety for educators of all races to effectively participate in Courageous Conversation. Working together as an adult learning community fortified and sustained by a shared commitment to meet the needs of all children, educators can lay the essential foundation for honest and open conversations about race.

> Good intentions and hard work are not sufficient for eliminating racism in schools. Neither will excellent curriculum and pedagogy in and of themselves be enough to eradicate the achievement gap. We need communities where it is safe enough for the invisible to be made visible, where Whites can listen to people of color talk about how they and their ancestors have experienced racism, and where people of color can listen to Whites talk about how they saw racial prejudice in operation and how it affected them. Listening to one another's stories and emotions helps people identify what needs to change within their institutions, their colleagues, and themselves. Being listened to helps us heal. (Weissglass, 2001)

The Fourth Condition of Courageous Conversation guides us in the development of strategies and tools that challenge the culture of silence surrounding racial matters. Specifically, we break the silence that prohibits educators from exploring deep-seated, unexamined beliefs and attitudes related to student learning as well as to teacher ability and behavior. Many educators of color feel it is unsafe or futile to give voice to their inner thoughts regarding the impact of race on learning and teaching. This phenomenon illustrates Lisa Delpit's (1988/1995b) "silenced dialogue," in which learning does not occur among educators, because a high level of racial tension and division exists.

In typical discussions, White educators fill the room with ideas for improving the achievement of students of color and indigenous students, but their ideas often are not welcomed or supported by their colleagues of color. This is because such ideas often reflect the distance between the White educators' racial experience and that of their colleagues, students, and families of color. As Lena Williams suggests in *It's the Little Things* (2000), White educators may also resort to silence in fear that their comments will be misconstrued as evidence of racist thinking.

The result of these converging phenomena is what we refer to as the *culture of silence*, making race "a nondiscussable," as described by Roland Barth (2004):

> Nondiscussables are subjects sufficiently important that they are talked about frequently but are so laden with anxiety and fearfulness that these conversations take place only in the parking lot, the rest rooms, the playground, the car pool, or the dinner table at home. Fear abounds that open discussion of these incendiary issues—at a faculty meeting, for example—will cause meltdown. . . . Schools are full of these land mines from which trip wires emanate. We walk about carefully, trying not to detonate them. Yet by giving these nondiscussables this incredible power over us, by avoiding them at all cost, we . . . condemn ourselves to live with all the debilitating tensions that surround race. (p. 8)

Dr. Neil G. Pedersen, a White former superintendent, and Dr. Nettie Collins-Hart, a Black former assistant superintendent, both in Chapel Hill–Carrboro City Schools (CHCCS) in North Carolina, worked to develop the skills necessary to move past the culture of silence toward effective interracial conversations about how race impacts student achievement throughout their school system. According to Dr. Collins-Hart,

> We really had to begin to look at the things we hadn't talked about, and race, in a very sensitive and direct way, was the one thing we hadn't dealt with. . . . I think at first the biggest challenge for me personally was getting used to the idea that we were actually going to talk candidly about race. But the next hurdle was developing some skills to talk about it, such as having the same basis of vocabulary and having a similar understanding of race, because it is not something people do naturally, and in interracial groups particularly. (Singleton, 2002)

This conversation was equally uncomfortable for Superintendent Pedersen; not only is he the image of our White-dominated education system, but also he previously embraced the culture that implicitly encouraged silence around issues of race, racial identity development, and institutional racism. He says,

It is uncomfortable being the superintendent of a district and to talk about the issue of institutional racism knowing that you are the leader of that organization and what that may say about you personally. That makes me uncomfortable, because I have to reflect on what role I have in perpetuating policies and practices that need to be changed. (Singleton, 2002)

To counteract their inhibitions and fear of discussing race openly and honestly, Drs. Pedersen and Collins-Hart worked to formally and informally establish and monitor the parameters surrounding their discourse, and doing so ultimately assisted them in engaging in Courageous Conversation.

Context and Conditions

The backdrop for the Courageous Conversation matters, especially if the school system has a history of division between educators of color or indigenous educators and White educators. This context, representing how the community has experienced racial matters in the past, has tremendous impact on educators' ability and willingness to engage in the conversation.

Some thought and effort on the part of educators are required to determine how, when, and where the subject of race is presented. For example, examining how race impacts schooling after a long day of testing, or as the final agenda item at a faculty meeting, does not usually facilitate Courageous Conversation. I have found in our work that springing the topic of race on unsuspecting educators typically does not provide the kind of safer environment required for deep and personal inquiry. Let educators know up front what to expect and when to expect it, and then work to guarantee that the timing as well as the physical environment are conducive to effective dialogue. Certainly, giving advance notice allows some people to find excuses for not being present. On the other hand, a well-planned and well-timed Courageous Conversation is always designed to promote maximum participation and to carry on beyond a single scheduled meeting. Needless to say, if a staff is already suffering from strained relations in general, and is not having any substantive conversation about any matters, launching into a Courageous Conversation about race will be an even bigger stretch for these educators.

For school leaders, however, the subject of race may arise unexpectedly. In these cases, leaders should determine whether a response, action, or solution is required in the moment. In many cases, the situation affords leaders at least a few hours to collect their personal thoughts and gather racially diverse viewpoints. In a school or district that lacks a culture in which racial issues are confronted spontaneously, educators should recognize that spontaneously jumping into interracial conversations about race with other educators, students, parents, or even friends can be quite unproductive and even explosive. I continue to hear from educators how much they appreciate leaders who take time to thoroughly examine the school's, district's, or university's current racial context, climate, and culture as a way of ensuring that more effective dialogue can take place.

Establishing the proper parameters includes reestablishing commitment to the Four Agreements of Courageous Conversation. I have found it effective to post the Four Agreements, Six Conditions, and Compass in the spaces where educators practice Courageous Conversation with each other. If they strategically place posters on the walls or tents on the tables, leaders can refer to the Courageous Conversation protocol at various stages of the interaction, especially when educators stray from the topic, limit participation of some members of the community, or completely withdraw from the dialogue at a moment of heightened discomfort. Eventually, educators will no longer need these reminders, as the institutional culture will have shifted into one that examines race consistently, effectively, and courageously.

Because they began to establish parameters for a safer, albeit uncomfortable conversation about race five years ago, educators throughout the Chapel Hill school system today use a common vocabulary as a way of developing common and deeper understandings about the impact of race on student achievement. Not only was the silence in the superintendent's office broken, but other administrators, equity coaches, and eventually school-based equity teams in each building soon replaced silence with Courageous Conversation. Many of the tools and exercises that Chapel Hill found effective in shifting the racial culture and climate of their district are found in the chapters of this book.

According to Dr. Collins-Hart,

> It really gave us the shared courage to look at issues through the race lens. It equipped us with the skills for looking at schools through a racial lens without attacking or being attacked, but still being critical and honest while reflecting upon race. (Singleton, 2002)

With this safety net in place to catch them, participants began the real work of closing their school system's racial achievement gap.

As guided by the Fourth Condition of Courageous Conversation, CHCCS ventured into the difficulty of sharing power with all stakeholders and intentionally creating formal and informal space for previously marginalized voices of color to influence policy design and instructional practice. According to Dr. Pedersen,

> The work that we have done has really provided an environment in which people can have conversations that simply don't take place on a day-to-day basis. And our success is measured to some extent by the degree to which those conversations now take place outside of the formal workshops. (Singleton, 2002)

Furthermore, the very nature of the conversations has changed dramatically over time. Dr. Pedersen continues,

> We are able to be more direct with each other and more honest with each other rather than being circumspect. It helps us get to the point, and it also helps us to not miss the point. We are not talking around things, and I am able to understand what [educators of color] are saying more accurately than I would have. (Singleton, 2002)

Parameters

The Fourth Condition of Courageous Conversation draws our attention to the complexity of White Talk and Color Commentary and the need for parameters in the conversation. By creating parameters, we create established guidelines for exactly what participants speak about, how long they speak and listen, and who is and is not speaking or listening. In essence, parameters help participants to pay attention to the voices, time, subject or themes, and communication styles present in the conversation. Monitoring the parameters means focusing on how time in the conversation is allocated equitably and how nontraditional ways of communicating are encouraged and valued. As I have observed time and time again, conversations about race are rarely successful when they occur haphazardly or in a highly unstructured fashion. Courageous Conversation initially requires tremendous preparation, and this will continue to be necessary until the culture of the school embraces such dialogue. Then, as witnessed in Chapel Hill as well as other districts, these conversations happen as a natural and normal part of the school's interactions.

> What are some of the necessary parameters that you believe may have allowed the leadership in Chapel Hill to have successful Courageous Conversation? To what degree do these same parameters already exist in your system?
>
> REFLECTION

People

I have discovered that the very way in which educators are seated or grouped dramatically impacts the quality of the conversation about race. This conversation is best held in heterogeneous groups that are just large enough to offer multiple points of view and diverse enough to prevent cultural domination in terms of a preferred communication style.

In large high schools and university settings, facilitators of Courageous Conversation have found value in mixing up the academic departments. In elementary schools, upper grade-level teachers have been grouped with primary grade-level teachers. Initially, small groups might spend a little less time addressing the topic and more time reflecting on the quality of conversation so that members can be aware not only of the content contributions but also of the process evolution. When educators are more practiced in Courageous Conversation, they can talk for longer periods and will naturally monitor the process, thus adjusting the parameters accordingly as they go along.

Whenever possible, the most important consideration is that each dialogue group be multiracial; but keep in mind that just because a group looks racially diverse does not mean that multiple racial perspectives will surface. Thus, leaders should take care to avoid the propensity to isolate people of color and indigenous people in mostly White groups, as this makes it difficult for critical perspective to surface. Ideally, a group should consist of White people, people of color, and indigenous people in relatively equal numbers. We recognize that many school systems have yet to attract and maintain a sizable number of educators of color or indigenous staff, but an effort to bring voices from nonteaching roles in the broader school community into each conversation and to acknowledge missing voices usually provides a sufficiently divergent perspective to carry the group forward.

After the initial conversations, aimed at simply getting every participant to speak, the size of groups should ideally be slightly larger than the three to four participants that research typically suggests (Marzano, Pickering, & Pollock, 2001). Creating two-person groups, or dyads, makes for more manageable and inviting dialogue, but this may leave White educators to generalize the experience and perspective of one person of color over an entire racial group. Considering that people of color and indigenous people are constantly and continuously interacting with White people, there is less of a chance that one interracial conversation will have the same impact on an educator of color's perception of White culture.

It is important to distinguish between *racial stereotypes* and *racial patterns*. A stereotype exists when a relatively isolated characteristic is assumed to be representative of the entire group. In contrast, a racial pattern reveals a characteristic or experience that many or most members of a racial group have been documented to actually share. When several dyads merge together after some initial conversation, participants now in a newly formed, larger group are more likely to be able to differentiate whether information and insight attained in dyad discussions represented racial stereotype or racial pattern.

Explicit and Focused Prompts

Organizing the dialogue around specific, racialized prompts enables educators to delve in deeper and more effectively uncover a critical racial perspective. When trying to develop understanding about the intersection of race and schooling, educators must not hide behind protective, politically charged, and vague language such as *diversity, culture, multiculturalism,* or *differences.* Being explicit means using the words *race, racism, racial discrimination, racial prejudice,* and *institutionalized racism.* In addition, it is important to use the racial terms that speak to color, such as *Asian, Black, Brown, Indigenous, Multiracial,* and *White,* except where the color term is generally viewed as offensive or unacceptable among the identified groups, which is the case of *Yellow* and *Red.* When protective terms such as *African American* and *European American* are used, the conversation is more likely to stray away from race. The next chapter, which introduces the Fifth Condition of Courageous Conversation, provides greater insight into these critical distinctions and explains how the interchangeable use of labels related to race, ethnicity, and nationality can lead to heightened confusion and escalating tensions.

When educators are called to examine racially disaggregated student achievement data, it is helpful to use prompts that explicitly drive their thinking and response to race. For example, if the goal is to better understand why Black, Brown, and Indigenous students are not excelling in reading, the questions should be, How does this particular reading program support the improved achievement of Black, Brown, and Indigenous students? It is insufficient to say "all students" when the data point to an achievement pattern of a particular racial group.

The long history of circumventing the conversation on race is connected to the use of "low-impact" language to address a "high-impact" phenomenon: Low-impact language is too vague and insufficiently honest to get to the root of the problem. Because of this, traditional conversations about diversity have not eradicated racial achievement disparities. Consequently, educators need to create a professional learning climate and culture that supports the development of honest dialogue about race, wherein educators can say what they mean and mean what they say. Table 8.2 shows examples of explicit language substitutes in which more traditional low-impact language is replaced with high-impact language that supports Courageous Conversation.

Table 8.2 Using Explicit Language Substitutes

Traditional Conversation	*Courageous Conversation*
Our school is becoming more and more diverse each year.	We are noticing an annual increase in our populations of students of color and indigenous students.
It is not their culture to disagree with the teacher.	Brown families, more than Black and White families, are likely to view the teacher as a knowledgeable authority figure.
The data show that some children did not meet proficiency goals.	The data show that Southeast Asian students are failing.
The teaching population is not reflective of our student population.	All of our teachers are White, while 90% of our students are Black and Brown.

Time

A powerful and productive conversation requires a high level of thinking and an equally high level of emotional investment. For this reason, a Courageous Conversation about race that substantially influences the way in which school leaders examine educational philosophies, policies, programs, and practices requires not only high level intellectual and emotional investment but also a significant amount of time. Rather than rushing through the dialogue, effective leaders allow all participants to share their feelings, which often means continuing the discussion in the next meeting. Allocating sufficient time enables all participants to feel listened to and validated. The Courageous Conversation safeguard for negotiating this precious commodity of time—of which nobody ever has enough—is to recall one important agreement: *Expect and accept non-closure.*

It is also important to notice who does and does not occupy the time allotted to talking. Leaders may determine a signal that alerts educators when the extent of their contributions might be preventing others from having an opportunity to speak or the desire to listen. Although highly structured conversations that specify how long and how often one may speak can stifle some participants, limited structure invites greater participation by those educators who are reticent or more reserved. Being specific at the outset of the conversation about the amount of time allotted for speaking, listening, and reflecting allows all participants to feel included and respected.

REFLECTION

Reflect on a previous interracial conversation about race. Describe the context and parameters that you believe contributed to its success or lack of success:

- Backdrop/location
- Topic/prompts
- People
- Time and space

THE COURAGEOUS CONVERSATION COMPASS

Linda Darling-Hammond (1997) writes, "In order to create a cohesive community and a consensus on how to proceed, school people must have the occasion to engage in democratic discourse about the real stuff of teaching and learning" (p. 336). Democratic discourse means providing time and space in the Courageous Conversation for every educator's perspective and experience to be listened to and affirmed. When this occurs, everyone at the table feels validated and respected. With personal validation comes a greater willingness to honor the opinions and views of others, no matter how different they may be. Affirmation also enables us to enter into conversation less rigid and more willing to challenge a tightly held personal belief, entertain a different perspective, and transform an unproductive behavior. Affirming differences, however, is an extremely difficult habit for many of us.

For this reason, I developed the Courageous Conversation Compass as a personal navigational tool, which you may recall from a previous chapter, that guides educators through these conversations about race. It helps participants to know where they are personally as well as to understand the place from which others' contributions come; the result is an expansion and deepening of beliefs and opinions for all participants.

Figure 8.1   The Courageous Conversation Compass

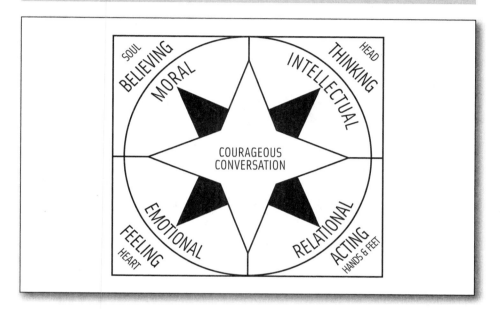

On this compass, we have identified four primary ways that people process racial information, events, or issues: moral, intellectual, emotional, and relational. These are the four points or cardinal directions of our compass:

Those positioned in the *moral* quadrant develop a deep-seated *belief* related to the racial information or event. This belief has to do with the "rightness" or "wrongness" of any given issue. One's justifications for a moral viewpoint are often located in the "gut," and articulating them verbally may not be possible. On an *intellectual* level, the primary response to a racial issue or information is characterized by a personal disconnect from the subject or a steadfast search for additional information or data. The intellectual response is often verbal and based in one's *thinking*. In the *emotional* arena, educators respond to information through *feelings* in the sense that a racial issue strikes them at a physical level causing an internal sensation such as anger, sadness, joy, or embarrassment. Finally, a view positioned in the *relational* zone of the compass reveals one's connection and response to racial information through *acting*, as defined by specific behaviors and actions. In a sense, moral responses reside in the soul, intellectual in the mind, emotional in the heart, and relational in our hands and feet.

The Courageous Conversation Compass resembles a Chinese compass, which has five coordinates: east, west, north, south, and center. On our compass, the four cardinal points are moral, intellectual, relational, and emotional, while the fifth point is where the coordinates symbolically converge in effective and productive interracial dialogue about race: Courageous Conversation. Through *practice,* increasingly we are able to enter the conversation with a racial perspective or response that demonstrates balance of all four quadrants. I name such an entrance as getting or being *centered.*

REFLECTION

For the purposes of understanding and personalizing the Courageous Conversation Compass, reconsider the following issues from Chapter 2:*

- Affirmative Action
- Emergent Bilingualism
- The United States of America's first Black President
- Tribal Sovereignty of Indigenous Nations in the United States

As you say each of the aforementioned phrases, where on the compass do you locate yourself in terms of your initial response? As you ponder the issue for a longer period of time, where do you travel to on the compass?

* Readers outside of the United States should feel free to substitute here four context-specific, current racial topics before engaging in this reflective exercise.

As I wrote this book, I pushed myself to examine numerous racial matters from the multiple positions on the compass and various intersections such as the moral/emotional border. To address the racial inequities in schooling, I believe educators must first recognize the existence of the foundational issue of race as experienced through the four cardinal positions of engagement. This recognition permits educators to move beyond misunderstanding and differing viewpoints toward a much deeper understanding of their own and each other's racial viewpoints.

As participants develop greater will, skill, knowledge, and capacity for Courageous Conversation, they will find themselves centered on the compass, with a deeper understanding of all four positions. Typically, discussions about race end unfavorably, because people struggle to locate themselves or understand the many places others are positioned around a particular racial issue. For example, a White person may speak from an intellectual place when arguing against Affirmative Action, whereas a Brown person may try to convey emotionally how such a policy provided a much needed personal opportunity to attend college. Without understanding how others are positioned, participants in this dialogue would walk away frustrated, believing others had little understanding of or respect for their perspective. When educators attempt to discuss race without considering all four positions and without recognizing the goal of getting centered on the compass for any given racial issue, the result is typically unfavorable.

By using the Courageous Conversation Compass, educators can transform predictable land mines of interracial dialogue about race into fertile grounds for understanding and healing. Guided by the compass, a White teacher can recognize the limits of the typical presentation of data from the relational and intellectual position. Also, the compass enables many Black parents, for example, to recognize how their entrance to the conversation and response from an emotional or a moral position can create a challenge for the teacher to truly understand the reasons for their child's achievement decline. By working together, teacher and parents can center their Courageous Conversation on the compass and discover each other as essential partners in improving student learning.

This process brings balance, openness, honesty, and understanding to interracial dialogue about race. The most transformative Courageous Conversation, which occurs in the center of the compass where all four positions converge, is authentic and fulfilling. Like the pivot point on a navigational compass, the center of the Courageous Conversation Compass is the position from which educators can understand and articulate four distinct viewpoints of a racial issue. In moving toward the center on any given issue, a person's location on the compass, and thus awareness of the topic, will change. By exploring their own racial ideas and those of others, participants achieve a deeper understanding of race and racialized problems like achievement disparity. Doing this, educators also develop an acceptance of and respect for each other's positions, even when they differ.

As an example of how to use the compass to guide interracial discourse, consider the following scenario.

A White history teacher strongly believes that all students, regardless of their racial identity, should meet the same requirements for enrollment in honors or advanced placement classes. In exploring the teacher's opinion, it is clear that his *belief* in equal opportunity drives his perspective. Hence, the arrow is pointing toward the moral position on the compass.

To more critically examine the issue, the aforementioned teacher suggests to his colleagues that they use the compass to examine each other's viewpoints. First, they consider the relational quadrant by talking with teachers of color about their own experiences in advanced level coursework and the impact enrollment trends in such courses had on their performance. Next, the educators explore the intellectual position by studying the disaggregated data, which specifically show how many students of color are enrolled in these courses and what their achievement record has been when compared to the record of White students. Finally, to investigate the emotional position, they listen to students of color share what it feels like to be denied access to higher-level coursework or perhaps to be the only student of color in the entire class.

After engaging with the compass to this degree, the White teacher who prompted the Courageous Conversation has developed in the following ways: He has broader perspective about why access to honors classes may need to be expanded, a deeper understanding of racial injustice, and clear knowledge of the experiences of students who have been denied access to or have felt isolated in the courses.

The compass illustrates my belief that when engaging in Courageous Conversation, the viewpoint of participants typically moves and shifts. Participants find themselves tuned in to some positions and oblivious to others. But, as they intentionally move about the compass, they experience continuous growth in their racial awareness.

REFLECTION

Reflect on your own conversations with colleagues and students who are racially different than you. In what ways have your discussions been limited due to a difference of point of view? How could your familiarity with the Courageous Conversation Compass help you to clarify your own position and better understand the positioning of others?

Talking about race interracially is clearly difficult and can even be threatening, scary, or frightening. I believe this is why people so often resort to silence. Silence among educators when it comes to addressing racial achievement disparities only results in wider gaps and diminished engagement in the process of schooling by students of color, indigenous students, and their families. Paying attention to the Fourth Condition of Courageous Conversation is the best assurance that safety and authenticity will be maximized. I imagine a time when educators will not need to establish parameters simply to have an everyday conversation about race. But until such a time, the carefully determined parameters and the Courageous Conversation Compass will help participants to better understand their various racial positions and how they can begin to navigate toward the common center at which all students, as W. E. B. Dubois suggested in 1949, will have the "freedom to learn."

PERSONAL ACTIVITY: PART 1

INTERRACIAL DYAD

Figure 8.2 is a transcript of an actual conversation on race that took place in one of our Courageous Conversation seminars. The moderator used a process of constructivist listening to guide three people through an exercise called *15-Minute*

Race. Participants use specific prompts and parameters to investigate their own racial perspective in contrast to their partner's. The participants included one White female educator and one Brown male educator, respectively Person A and Person B, and one White female observer. Person A and Person B responded to prompts given by the facilitator. The observer's directive was to listen and, at the conclusion of the conversation, help Person A and Person B recognize their differing styles of conversation known as White Talk and Color Commentary.

Study this Courageous Conversation closely, and identify the process that takes place by following the directions at the top of each column:

- Underline any prompts, parameters, or directions that you find.
- Identify and describe all examples of White Talk or Color Commentary.
- After studying this conversation, respond to the prompts that follow.

Figure 8.2 15-Minute Race Dialogue

Participant [Describe actions of participants]	Dialogue [Underline prompts, parameters, and directions]	White Talk Versus Color Commentary [Describe the White Talk or Color Commentary]
Moderator:	This process is called constructivist listening and is made up of pairs of one White person and one person of color. We are going to give timing and prompts. When A is speaking I'll say, "A, you have so many minutes to talk on . . ." and I will give you the prompt. When A is speaking, B is completely silent. This isn't a conversation in a normal way. B completely listens. Then I'll give B a prompt and a time, and A completely listens. There is no exchange. This is called constructivist listening, and it is designed with a purpose. So A, you are going to have one minute to share the first words that come to mind when you think about race. A, one minute, go.	
Person A: (White woman)	The communities people live in, how communities deal with difference. I think about school, how school deals with differences. I think about color, did I say that? I do think about people's color, and how that makes people see them. That's about all I can think of.	

(Continued)

Figure 8.2 (Continued)

Participant [Describe actions of participants]	Dialogue [Underline prompts, parameters, and directions]	White Talk Versus Color Commentary [Describe the White Talk or Color Commentary]
Moderator:	Stop. B, you have one minute to say to your partner how you define racism. B, one minute, go.	
Person B: (Black man)	The institutionalized practices of a particular racial group to disenfranchise, discriminate against, or in various other ways marginalize another racial group based solely upon that person's race. And, I'd have to add that there is a certain power component to racism. You can have the subordinate disenfranchise and marginalize the dominant group, but it's not racism. It's something else, because that power component's missing.	
Moderator:	Stop. Take 30 seconds for silent reflection. Think about what A said, think about what B said . . . A, you get to start again. This time you'll have two minutes, and you are going to share with your partner one experience you have had with racism and how you responded. Two minutes, go.	
Person A: (White woman)	Well, fortunately—or unfortunately—I haven't had too many. We were kind of talking about one eating with somebody who's another ethnicity at lunch. But that is not so much my experience. But I would say for me, ah, two Black women were having a conversation about their children, and I was . . . it was at the end of a meeting, and it was kind of naturally, we were standing there, and definitely I was not included in this conversation. And it was made really clear by body language that they wanted to have the conversation without me. It was kind of a freeze-out kind of a thing. So, I can't think of many experiences which tell me much, you know, about this whole conversation for us. I haven't always lived, I mean, I have lived in a lot of different places and been in a lot of different areas and still I can't think of any.	

Participant [Describe actions of participants]	Dialogue [Underline prompts, parameters, and directions]	White Talk Versus Color Commentary [Describe the White Talk or Color Commentary]
Person B: (Black man) *Interjecting outside of the prompt while time is still available.*	Well, I think the definition that I gave doesn't allow for that. I'm talking about race and power. If we are all African American in this closed group, it doesn't work. Could you have discrimination based on something else or marginalization within the community, oh certainly! We can go on for a while about that. But, it's the dyad. You have two different ethnic groups, and one is the "dominant" one in society. That's what is kind of driving that.	
Moderator:	B, you have the same prompt, one experience you have had with racism and how you handled it. Also two minutes, go.	
Person B: (Black man)	All right, oh, it's a bad one. It's really kind of small, it's minor, it's petty, but that is the definition of them. I went to a department store at the Sun Crest Mall. I guess I wanted to buy some shirts and—I mean, you've heard the stories—well, there's someone following you around to see if you're going to steal anything. Well, I could not get someone to help me.	
Person A: (White woman) *Interjecting*	Oh, you had the opposite experience of me.	
Person B: (Black man)	Yes, I had to literally confront a salesperson to help me on finding sizes, and she was very reluctant to help me.	
Person A: (White woman) *Interjecting*	Do you think she thought you weren't going to buy something? You have no idea.	
Person B: (Black man)	The impression that I got was that she really couldn' t be bothered. On the other hand, last Christmas in the same department store, I was looking for some jewelry for my wife. I'm walking down the display case and the salesperson—who happened to be British—wouldn't even greet me. These two guys come in from the street, they walk up to the display case, and she's greeting them.	

(Continued)

Figure 8.2 (Continued)

Participant [Describe actions of participants]	Dialogue [Underline prompts, parameters, and directions]	White Talk Versus Color Commentary [Describe the White Talk or Color Commentary]
Person A: (White woman) *Interjecting*	Different race?	
Person B: (Black man)	Yeah, OK.	
Person A: (White woman) *Interjecting*	So then what do you do? What do you say?	
Person B: (Black man)	Ah, two things: Do you want to fight over it and confront the person? Or, you can say, "OK, fine, this is how you are. I will do something else."	
Person A: (White woman) *Interjecting*	(Referring to earlier discussion): So, when we talked about those micro-aggressions?	
Person B: (Black man)	Yeah.	
Person A: (White woman) *Interjecting*	That is definitely . . .	
Person B: (Black man)	You can always point to one or two of them every day. I mean . . .	
Person A: (White woman) *Interjecting*	Every day, seriously?	
Person B: (Black man)	Every couple of days.	
Moderator:	Stop. I want you to think about the observation. I want you to think about how hard it is to stay just a listener. I want you to reflect on what A said and what B said, and on how hard it is to be the listener. 30 seconds . . . B, you are going to start this time and you are going to have two minutes to share one feeling you have about dealing with racism. One feeling, two minutes. B, go.	

Participant [Describe actions of participants]	Dialogue [Underline prompts, parameters, and directions]	White Talk Versus Color Commentary [Describe the White Talk or Color Commentary]
Person B: (Black man)	I expect it. At some point every couple of days, I expect to have some sort of a thing where I am, you know, kind of shaking my head saying, "Well, what was that all about?" And again, every so often my wife and I will be leaving some place and I'll look at her and say, "What was that?" And she'll look at me and say, "I don't know." Or she'll say sometimes, "You know what it was." You expect it; you deal with it as best as you possibly can. Also, it's kind of hard to figure out—at least for me—is this person just being really, really rude? Or is it that they are rude to everybody? Or is it that they are just rude to me? And, if it is just me, it's a very short step to go from that to, "Oh, it's because of race." I don't know, it slows down how I react to it. I am kind of looking for ways to say, "Well, if it is based on race, do I have to do something, respond in some way?" I don't know.	
Observer: (White woman) Interjecting	How often is it that the thoughts come to you, "Is it just that this person is rude and ignorant, or is it just me?"	
Person B: (Black man)	Well, whenever it happens.	
Observer: (White woman) Interjecting	Every time?	
Person A: (White woman) Answering for the Black man	Every time.	
Person B: (Black man)	That is the first thing.	
Moderator:	Stop. B, stop. A, you have the same prompt. You have two minutes. Share one feeling you have about dealing with racism. A, go.	

(Continued)

Figure 8.2 (Continued)

Participant [Describe actions of participants]	Dialogue [Underline prompts, parameters, and directions]	White Talk Versus Color Commentary [Describe the White Talk or Color Commentary]
Person A: (White woman)	I don't expect it. When you said that, it makes me sad because I just assume that they are rude or a jerk, you know. I mean, I never, I don't expect it at all, even if the person is another race than me. I don't expect that it has anything to do with it. You know, I just think they have had a bad day. I don't personalize it. And I can't think of a time that I have even gone back over it and thought, "Gee, what was that about?" You know, I assume more that it's maybe my age, or that I'm a woman, or, I don't know what. But I never go there, never, really. I really don't. Not with me personally, my own personal experience. Sometimes with students I do. Sometimes with students I definitely feel like that they're looking at me as the White teacher, you know? And they don't see me as a person. Especially near the beginning of the year. But, usually that disappears fairly quickly for me. I think for them I'd have to ask them. But, you know what I mean? I can't assume that just ever completely disappears because we are just such a power, you know, in the classroom. But, yeah, when it says, if we're talking about keeping it personal and I'm not getting into the racism of the world, um, I don't expect it at all. I don't get into the car and think, "OK, what's going to happen today?"	
Moderator:	Thirty seconds to silently reflect. What did A say? What did B say? All right, observers, we are going to ask you to share what you heard.	
Observer: (White woman)	The person that was not of color mentioned her experiences as far as racism which was directed at her because she was not of color. I thought it was interesting, she was not of color, but she had a circumstance that she felt uncomfortable in because it was two Black women that excluded her from a conversation. And the person of color said	

Participant [Describe actions of participants]	Dialogue [Underline prompts, parameters, and directions]	White Talk Versus Color Commentary [Describe the White Talk or Color Commentary]
	that he expected racism to happen every day. And the person not of color never expected it, never. You know, it wasn't that they got in the car and expected it to happen that day. I had a hard time with my own personal experiences popping up in my head, and I wanted to talk.	
Moderator: *Commenting to entire group*	Now, one of the things that's clear is that A and B are engaged, OK. And you all are going off on your conversations now. You had a systematic input into the conversation, which we don't typically suggest is so structured and rigid since it is really hard. But, what we do suggest is that you monitor the real parameters or conditions of the conversation. That is to say that you don't just walk out into US society and find people just breaking out into effective racial conversation. You know, it just doesn't happen for us yet, OK? Maybe one day we will see that, but it's not now.	

PERSONAL ACTIVITY: PART 2

INTERRACIAL DYAD

The purpose of the preceding dialogue was to listen, build trust, and believe the stories that another person shared, even if that person's experience was different from one's own. This conversation stands as an example of what typically happens in interracial dialogue around race. It was hard for the White woman to stick to the rules of the conversation and not interrupt; the protocol reinforces the necessity of having strong guidance during the dialogue. This is why there is such a need for the established time allotments, designations for speaking and listening, and closely monitored prompts. Without these, the conversation typically becomes imbalanced.

Nevertheless, notice how powerful the structure became in this conversation. Despite the interjections and the rule breaking, the structure was strong enough to allow both the Black man and the White woman to speak honestly about their respective feelings, experiences, and insights. Effective dialogue took place, and each educator gained a heightened understanding of the other's experiences.

To reflect on this conversation, answer the following questions:

Parameters

- What does the moderator do to ensure effective dialogue?
- What parameters exist to guarantee equity in the conversation?
- In what ways could this conversation be better managed and run?

White Talk Versus Color Commentary

- Give examples of White Talk and Color Commentary that occur in this dialogue.
- Where was the power in the conversation?
- What could be done to create a better balance between the White Talk and the Color Commentary?
- What did you learn about your own communication style as a result of this dialogue?

IMPLEMENTATION EXERCISE: PART 1

INTERRACIAL DYAD

Time required: 45 minutes

Materials required: For each participant, Courageous Conversation Journal and a copy of the worksheet that follows

1. Present the Fourth Condition of Courageous Conversation:

   Monitor the parameters of the conversation by being explicit and intentional about the number of participants, prompts for discussion, and time allotted for listening, speaking, and reflecting. Use the Courageous Conversation Compass to gauge where you and other participants are in terms of your emotional, intellectual, moral, and relational proximity and connection to a given racial topic.

2. Introduce the concept of White Talk versus Color Commentary. Explain that this does not mean that all White people use White Talk and all people of color and indigenous people use Color Commentary. Rather, we need to recognize both as styles of communication that can create difficulty if they are not understood and are imbalanced.

3. Describe the following contrasting traits:

White Talk	*Color Commentary*
• Verbal	• Nonverbal
• Impersonal	• Personal
• Intellectual	• Emotional
• Task oriented	• Process oriented

4. Divide the participants into interracial groups of three to five people and have them fill out the chart on the worksheet by identifying traits that characterize White Talk and Color Commentary. Have the entire group discuss these traits.

5. Create as many interracial pairings or dyads among your group as possible. Those who are not paired can observe the interracial pairings.

6. Identify two or three racial issues that relate to your school or school system. Give the participants one of these at a time as prompts for discussion.

7. Instruct the participants that they will have two minutes to discuss each prompt. Rather than questioning each other's opinion, have the listeners explain where they heard examples of White Talk and Color Commentary.

8. If desired, the observer can trade places with one member of the dyad for the next prompt, as long as the dyad remains interracial.

9. Bring the group back together and debrief the experience. In what ways did the observers hear White Talk and/or Color Commentary? Who primarily used each style of conversation? Was their use balanced in the dialogue?

10. Have all participants reflect on this conversation in their Courageous Conversation Journal.

WHITE TALK VERSUS COLOR COMMENTARY

FOURTH CONDITION OF COURAGEOUS CONVERSATION

Monitor the parameters of the conversation by being explicit and intentional about the number of participants, prompts for discussion, and time allotted for listening, speaking, and reflecting. Use the Courageous Conversation Compass to gauge where you and other participants are in terms of your emotional, intellectual, moral, and relational proximity and connection to a given racial topic.

PRACTICE: THE FOUNDATION OF RACIAL EQUITY LEADERSHIP

White Talk	*Color Commentary*
Verbal	**Nonverbal**
Traits:	Traits:
Example:	Example:
Impersonal	**Personal**
Traits:	Traits:
Example:	Example:
Intellectual	**Emotional**
Traits:	Traits:
Example:	Example:
Task oriented	**Process oriented**
Traits:	Traits:
Example:	Example:

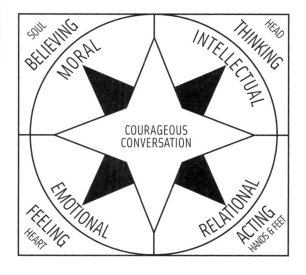

IMPLEMENTATION EXERCISE: PART 2

GETTING CENTERED

Time required: 45 minutes

Materials required: Courageous Conversation Journal for each participant and the worksheet that follows

1. Before introducing the Courageous Conversation Compass, pass out the accompanying sheet to each member of your group.

2. Have each participant describe in writing his or her basic opinion in the following areas: Affirmative Action, race riots, immigration laws, and welfare.

3. Present the concept of the Courageous Conversation Compass to the group.

4. Have participants identify where on the compass their four opinions from Step 2 (above) are located. Have them write on the compass on the worksheet where each of their opinions is located.

5. Instruct the participants to mingle with one another and listen to at least three others whose opinions on these subjects are located at different points on the compass. For example, someone who has an intellectual opinion concerning Affirmative Action should talk to three others who have relational, emotional, and moral opinions on Affirmative Action.

   It is important to note, however, that there should be no discussion or debate after hearing another's opinion—this is meant only as an exercise in listening to and hearing different points of view.

6. Bring the group back together, and reflect on the experience. Could you find people whose opinions were positioned differently on the compass? Was it difficult just to listen to the multiple perspectives without commenting?

7. Have each person personally reflect on the differing opinions for each of the four subjects and keep this exercise in his or her Courageous Conversation Journal.

GETTING CENTERED

Affirmative Action

My Personal Reflection:

My Personal Location on the Compass:

Multiple Perspective(s) From Others:

Brown v. Board of Education Supreme Court Decision 60th Anniversary

My Personal Reflection:

My Personal Location on the Compass:

Multiple Perspective(s) From Others:

Immigration Reform

My Personal Reflection:

My Personal Location on the Compass:

Multiple Perspective(s) From Others:

Trayvon Martin Killing

My Personal Reflection:

My Personal Location on the Compass:

Multiple Perspective(s) From Others:

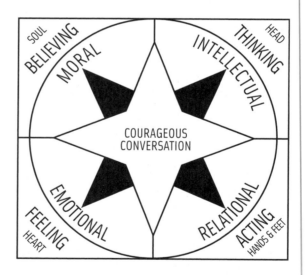

ANDREA JOHNSON

I am a proud *Sista girl* from Detroit. I was born and raised in one of the many middle-class neighborhoods of northwest Detroit. Mine was a staunch, White Catholic community in the 1940s and early 1950s and then became a largely White Jewish community in the late 1950s and early 1960s. By 1965, redlining waned, and Black families like mine peppered each block, one or two families at a time. Our home was a beautiful three-bedroom brick Tudor with a fireplace, a breakfast nook, and a screened back porch. In Detroit, in a pattern that differed from that of many cities across the country, when the Black folks moved in, the White people did not move out—at least not right away. Throughout most of my formative years, I lived in a *real* integrated neighborhood.

The Black middle class was alive and well throughout my youth. We had a Black mayor, Black accountants, Black doctors, and Black lawyers. The superintendent of schools was Black, as were many of the school board members, police officers, and a growing number of fire fighters. The people who worked on the assembly lines in the auto factories made a middle-class wage and lived right beside us in beautiful single-family brick homes with a backyard and a two-car garage. Everyone in my peer group was college bound, and most of our friends' parents had gone to college.

Our elementary school had a Black principal and both Black and White teachers. One of my teachers, Catherine Blackwell, had a profound impact on me during those formative years. Mrs. Blackwell was Black. She travelled frequently to various countries in West Africa and brought back artifacts to share with her students. Some students, Black and White, including me, would wrap her brilliant fabrics on our bodies and heads in traditional style and learn African dance, while others of us played rhythms on her authentic African drums. Mrs. Blackwell had all of us memorize and recite the poetry of Langston Hughes, Margaret Walker, and other Black poets as well as the poems of White poets such as Robert Frost and T. S. Eliot. She taught us about American jazz and European classical music. We listened to and had to identify "great" composers like Coltrane, Ellington, and Miles Davis as well as Mozart, Haydn, and Tchaikovsky. She took us on field trips to jazz concerts, plays, the symphony, and the ballet. We were taught to sing the national anthem, "The Star Spangled Banner," and the Negro national anthem, "Lift Every Voice and Sing," in her class. Mrs. Blackwell continues to be a force in my life. She attended my wedding celebration and we still exchange cards during the holidays.

Each time I have reached into my memory in an effort to recall my first experiences with racism, my recollections have gone deeper into my younger self. At first, I dusted off an incident from my early 30s. I accepted this memory as a "first," because it was the first time I'd lived in a predominately White community in a white-collar suburb of Detroit. I was followed by the police while driving our very suburban-looking minivan to the bank. As I pulled into the parking lot, a second police car arrived as "reinforcement," and I was given a ticket, because although my driver's license had an expiration month of September (and it was September 9th), my actual birth date was the 4th, and therefore the officers determined that I was

(Continued)

(Continued)

driving with an expired license. The officers also questioned me about how long I had lived "way out here" and wanted to know what I did for a living. The traffic stop, the reinforcements, the charges on the ticket, and the questioning were all pretty bogus. As a Black woman who'd lived most of her life as a member of the "majority race" in Detroit, I had never experienced such racism before—or maybe I had.

Next, I remembered experiencing racism as a 13-year-old when a White ballet teacher told me that my body wasn't "suited" for classical ballet. As humiliating as that was for me, the memory allowed me to begin delving further into my psyche to explore the deeper nuances of the ways in which race and racism have impacted my life. I'd always accepted the narratives of my family that positioned us as property owners, thus able to leverage accumulated wealth, buy our way into the middle class, and acquire education and additional property.

My parents met as college students at Wayne State University in Detroit. Both of them came from families who had financial means. My dad's family owned farmland and businesses in a little town near Tallassee, Alabama. Education was very important to the family, and my grandmother, the lightest complexioned of her siblings, was sent to boarding school, where she completed the 10th grade in 1925. My mom's family owned land in Warrenton, Georgia. Her parents moved to Detroit in 1924 and bought a four-bedroom home with an indoor toilet on the city's near west side. Eventually they had a two-bedroom addition built onto the house, and during some rough times, they rented out one of the additional rooms for extra income. As impactful as this narrative is, it doesn't explain the price that was paid for this entry into the "greater society." Each time I would ask my grandparents to tell me about the generations that came before them, they would say "we don't talk about that."

Recently my aunt (the family matriarch) passed away. My mother handed me a binder that held the key to the missing annals of our family's story. There were primary source documents in the binder: pictures, letters, deeds, and other artifacts that connected our family to the white slave masters who owned them. I learned about my great-great-grandmother, Nancy Roberts, who was a blind cook on the Roberts family plantation. Mr. Roberts frequently raped her, resulting in the birth of my mixed-race, fair-skinned great-grandmother Annie. According to the documents, Mr. Roberts left a parcel of land to Nancy and Annie when he died. This began a legacy of landownership in our family. This also illustrates the legacy of racism in our family, a legacy composed of truths that were held as secrets, intraracial racism that comes with light skin and light eyes, shame passed on to my grandparents, and a price paid for our progeny to prosper. My memories are forever changed as I honor and share this painful reality, so the next generation will not be shackled by it. Today, I ponder which of these stories am I sharing and which secrets am I, perhaps unconsciously, withholding from my three children, my nieces and nephews, and other family members of the millennial generation.

With so much genealogy information available to us through scientific and anthropological advances, how does your family's multigenerational racial past inform your understanding of your current racial reality?

NINE

The Fifth Condition

What Do You Mean By "Race"?

Race is an artificial barrier that defines us. Race makes me feel proud but it also makes me feel cautious. I try to go through my day without focusing on it, but I am constantly aware of it. If I am in a place where no one looks like me, I am self-conscious. When I am surrounded by racial diversity, I feel comfortable. Race makes me feel good when I think of my ancestry, but it makes me feel bad when I think of division. It is the package that we come in, but it does affect our interactions with others. Race plays a big role in our lives and we have to get beyond those barriers.

—Jackie Thompson, Professional Staff
Developer, Davis School District, Farmington, Utah

What is race? To this Black educator, race is very real. To others, race might be abstract, a label, a box to check, a history, an ethnicity, a memory, a nonentity, a judgment. Despite how differently people may view race, the truth is that race is quite real. Certainly, race is a constant reality for Jackie Thompson, a professional staff developer in the Davis School District in a suburb of Salt Lake City. Whereas Jackie is Black, most of the staff in her school system are White—and at the same time, the student of color population in her district is doubling every few years. One of Jackie's responsibilities is to train teachers in REACH, which stands for Respect Ethnic and Cultural Heritage. The purpose of this program is to help the primarily White educators in her system begin to understand the racial differences that exist between them and their students of color. Her work begins with helping the largely White staff understand race.

First and foremost, race in the United States is the social and political meaning that we individually and collectively affix to the color of our skin and other visible physical traits. Although technically race means little more than this, it is arguably the reason for more national unrest, misunderstanding, and terror than any other aspect of our diversity. Because race is so tightly linked to our personal and collective identity, an insufficient understanding of race stirs predictable emotions. Feelings and deep-seated beliefs connected to race are strong and polarizing; they trigger denial for some and life-defining acceptance for others. Such intensity and polarity makes having conversations about race even more difficult.

To reach some shared understanding of what race is, the Fifth Condition of Courageous Conversation guides participants to

> establish agreement around a contemporary working definition of race that clearly differentiates it from ethnicity and nationality.

Biologically, race is nothing more than the color of our skin, texture of our hair, and shape, color, and dimension of physical features such as eyes and lips. So much social and political meaning has been attached to these physical determinations of race, however, that the simplicity has given way to a complex phenomenon in this country over the past four centuries.

REFLECTION

What is your own working definition of race? Do you feel that your definition is sufficient? In what ways do you differentiate race from ethnicity and nationality?

A BRIEF HISTORY OF RACE

Racial differences are a social construct rather than a biological reality; science has found far more genetic differences within individuals of the same so-called race than among those of different races (Adelman, 2003). The very term *race* is problematic, as described by Henze et al. (2002): "It has been used to describe physical differences of populations which are then erroneously associated with mental capacities and the ability to achieve a high level of civilization" (p. 8). Furthermore, in addressing the socially constructed realities manifested by race, "it is precisely because racial discrimination has been real, even though race is not, that we have to continue to monitor inequities by examining data across racial and ethnic categories" (p. 8).

Both social and natural scientists will undoubtedly continue to debate the true meaning of race in universities, governments, and corporations around the world. In the meantime, what does not seem to change is the fact that race is lived in patterned and predictable ways, regardless of how we may intellectually construct it. It is precisely this notion of how we live race, rather than what race means, that deepens the conversation about race for educators. Examining and understanding how race is lived differently by White people and by people of color or indigenous people today in the United States of America and in various other parts of the world is what the Fifth Condition of Courageous Conversation refers to as the "working definition of race."

To establish a working definition of race, we first need to briefly explore the historical and contemporary evolution of race. We also must investigate how and why people tend to collectively redefine race by using descriptions based on ethnicity and nationality rather than skin color. Developing a clearer understanding of race allows for more effective dialogue about race, racism, and resulting racial disparities.

Race in American Society

Speaking about the history of race in the United States and the way racial determination has been justified scientifically, Evelynn Hammonds, a historian of science, once wrote,

> If we just take African Americans as an example, there is not a single body part that hasn't been subjected to [scientific] analysis. You'll find articles in the medical literature about the Negro ear, and the Negro nose, and the Negro leg, and the Negro heart, and the Negro eye, and the Negro foot, and it's every single body part. They're constantly looking for some organ that might be so fundamentally different in size and character that you can say this is something specific to the Negro versus Whites and other groups. Scientists are a part of their social context. Their ideas about what race is are not simply scientific ones, are not simply driven by the data that they are working with. They are also informed by the societies in which they live. (quoted in Adelman, 2003)

The history of race in the United States is both long and complex, and it is not our goal to retell it, even though we firmly believe that exploring non-White historical perspectives can support the development of critical thought about the impact of race on schooling. Instead, I will simply highlight a few key and well-documented moments that shape the arc of the American, and in many ways, contemporary Western civilization, collective racial reality. Since publication of the first edition of *Courageous Conversations About Race,* the appeal of my racial equity work has crossed international borders. Most notably, my work with educators, government officials, clergy, and community leaders in Canada, Australia, and New Zealand has revealed racial histories and current conditions remarkably similar to ours in the United States. I say this not to diminish the cultural uniqueness of these and other English-speaking countries where Courageous Conversation is practiced, but rather to invite our international racial equity leaders to consider how their own national racial narrative, and counternarratives, given our similar origins, offers some thematic overlap with respect to how we live race currently.

American Racial Binary

It begins with the arrival of Northern and Western European settlers in the Americas in the 1600s, a period marked by the extermination of indigenous peoples and the enslavement of Africans. Both of these occurrences establish in this country the racial hierarchy in which Whites position themselves over people of color and indigenous people, and institutionalize the American racial binary of White to Black, or, as I am beginning to think about it now, as nonindigenous to indigenous. While it is the former binary construct of White to Black that gets deconstructed in much of the United States and in the Western civilization racial narrative, this same White to Black narrative can render indigenous people invisible, in this country and many other locations around the world, particularly when the term *Black* references people of African ancestry. For this reason, I challenge myself to augment each part of our racial anthology with inquiry into the plight and treatment of indigenous people (American Indian, First Nations, Aboriginal, Maori, etc.), and particularly the experience and perspective of Black-skin indigenous people, at each critical and historic milestone.

In this emerging racial caste system, later immigrants to the Americas from Eastern and Southern Europe suffered initial domination at the hands of the Northern and Western Europeans who had become the established nobility class of those who owned property, not only land but also people whom they enslaved. Whether they worked out their term of indentured servitude or relinquished their language, religion, or customs, White-skinned, primarily European ethnic newcomers were encouraged, if not pressured economically, to "melt" into what was already forming as the dominant White American race.

By the time immigrants from Asia and Middle Eastern countries began to arrive in the late 1800s, it was clear that the meaningful American racial classifications were White and Black. Whiteness or Blackness determined whether or not people received the full rights of citizenship. This blatant social, political, and economic racial hierarchy prompted most of these groups—Chinese, Japanese, Arabs, and Armenians, to name a few—to strive for the White label and accompanying status. Some even asked that their request for Whiteness be adjudicated by the highest courts in the land.

Thomas Jefferson, as one example, gave tremendous support to the emerging Black and White racial caste system by advocating the development of a US Census. His beliefs regarding Black inferiority and White superiority are clearly stated in his seminal work, *Notes on the State of Virginia* (1781/1996). Jefferson also characterized the racial ambiguity for groups existing between Black and White on the continuum, which he referred to as *mulatto*. In his writings, he posits that mulattos could—with care—eventually become White. In Jefferson's influential eyes, however, Black people lacked the intelligence and other genetic properties ever to be White.

Although today his beliefs seem radical and even offensive to many people, Jefferson's thoughts on scientific racial determination, also called *eugenics,* resurface every so often in popular films like D. W. Griffith's *Birth of a Nation* in 1915 and recently in Richard Herrnstein and Charles Murray's (1994) best-selling book, *The Bell Curve: Intelligence and Class Structure in American Life.* As I have participated in Courageous Conversations about race, I have discovered these Jeffersonian ideas about race are still deeply embedded in the attitudes and practices of a surprising number of educators today.

A reifying of the racial "color line" and pronounced division of White and Black America continued into the 20th century. The return home of World War II veterans marked a time when greater permanence in second-class citizen status of various groups of people of color and indigenous people occurred, while innovative government-sponsored privileges for White Americans were being implemented. The rapid influx of Latino immigrants, which also characterized the 20th century, boosted White Americans' fear that they would soon miss out on limited resources. Political efforts in the late 1990s and early 2000s in California and Florida to promote English-only legislation, restrict the issuance of drivers' licenses to legal citizens only, and even make public education and health care unavailable to "undocumented" people all may be reflective of this ongoing fear of "non-White" immigrant takeover.

Although the "scientifically reasoned" ideologies of eugenics have been categorically disproved, whispered beliefs about superiority and inferiority based on race have in many ways led schools to unconsciously support institutional policies, programs, and practices that favor White students over students of color and indigenous students. Such education trajectories continue to support the escalating racial achievement disparities we witness today.

When the United States swelled with pride and confidence as a young industrial nation, the image of wealth, success, and power was unfailingly White by design. Indeed, he was the "all-American boy" that this nation celebrated as her symbol of both physical beauty and economic prosperity. Contrasting with images of hope, wealth, and prosperity or rags-to-riches fables was the poverty and despair experienced by many people of color and indigenous people as a result of social bigotry and government-supported racism, for example, Indian sovereignty laws, Jim Crow segregation, and "fair" housing laws. White Americans—now a culture into which the once-hated Eastern and Southern European ethnics had "melted"—assumed that their refined culture and wealth was, according to Evelynn Hammonds, a "preordained natural order" (quoted in Adelman, 2003). This contemporary perspective was grounded in White society's preexisting beliefs in social Darwinism, the idea that only the fittest and most talented race deserves to survive in society, accumulate riches, and gain power. Hammonds continues,

Those that [believed in] White racial superiority wanted to confirm what they saw, which is to say that the proper place of the Negro, or in other regions of the country the Native American or the Chinese, was at the bottom of the social and political hierarchy. And if you can say that they are fundamentally biologically different, then it's natural for them to be at the bottom of our social hierarchy.

Racial purification was one of the primary aims of the 20th century eugenics movement. Consequently, global practitioners of the movement focused on propagating a White race that was more physically fit, intelligent, and capable than people of other races. The inverse of this objective was to orchestrate a well-planned genocide of the weak and infirm—the "colored" of society. To this aim, eugenicists proposed a number of unthinkable measures, including lifelong segregation, sterilization, restrictive marriage, eugenic education, forced breeding, and even euthanasia. Despite their extreme nature, these proposals were actually adopted both inside and outside of the United States, eventually giving justification to the 20th century's greatest horror, the Holocaust. According to Joseph Graves, "The Nazi propaganda machine pointed out that their eugenic policies were entirely consistent with and in fact derived from ideas of American race scientists" (Adelman, 2003).

The triumph of Black athlete Jesse Owens at the 1936 Berlin Olympics in Nazi Germany began a slow shift in racial beliefs toward the more prevalent thoughts of today. These games were supposed to serve as concrete proof of White supremacy and legitimize the global domination of Hitler's Aryan nation. Yet, Jesse Owens won four gold medals in competition against White athletes. The United States and much of the Western world were faced with a quandary: How could a society that believed in White racial dominance come to terms with the Black athlete's success? Ever since, the belief in Black physical dominance and athletic superiority has persisted, although in some circles, Black people are still thought to lack the same mental capacity and other more common White civilized traits; evidence of the power of this belief is shown in the fact that the number of athletic coaches of color is significantly smaller than the number of professional athletes of color. At the time of Owens's victory, Dean Cromwell, his coach, said the Negro athlete excelled because he was "closer to the primitive. It was not so long ago that his ability to sprint and jump was a life and death matter to him in the jungle" (quoted in Adelman, 2003). Such beliefs indicate how tightly views about racial supremacy can be held. Today, belief in the athletic dominance of Black people and their lack of so-called civilized traits persists within White culture—and unfortunately, within our schools. Comments like "We can't teach those kids," "It's not our fault they don't learn," and even "You are a role model for your race" communicate the persisting White cultural belief that people of color and indigenous people are inherently inferior.

It is naïve to assume that such an influential movement as eugenics has no lasting impact, both within the White community in terms of lingering beliefs and within communities of color, which bear the brunt of such degrading and debilitating "scientific reasoning." This "lack of opportunities to heal from hurt," as Weissglass (2001, p. 50) says, is a primary reason that racism persists today. Weissglass continues,

It is obvious to most people that it is hurtful to be the target of racism (or any form of bias). It is less obvious that any oppressive attitude is harmful to the individual who holds it. Oppressive attitudes limit one's potential, actions, relationships, and emotional health. (p. 50)

Beliefs in racial superiority inhibit not only the person of color who is the victim but the holder of that belief as well.

White Flight

Despite the history of extermination, enslavement, internment, colonization, and annexation of indigenous people and subsequent groups of people of color; despite the racist foundations of this country; despite eugenics; and despite the Supreme Court rulings on schooling; some argue that the most dramatic racial impact on education continues to stem from the government's housing policies of the 1940s. Specifically, the GI Bill and the Federal Housing Authority (FHA) provided the conditions that led to suburban expansion, urban renewal, "White flight," ghettoization, and the so-called inner-city problems that exist today.

As military personnel returned from World War II, the US government aimed to support some veterans in achieving the American dream of home ownership. Consequently, the government spent billions of dollars to stimulate suburban housing developments and to make available low-interest mortgage loans. For the first time in history, men and women who had served their country could purchase a new home with a down payment of as little as 10% of the selling price and a low-interest mortgage loan for the remaining 90%. To guarantee that its investment in property would appreciate in value over the life of the loan, the US government instituted a system of determining investment growth potential. Government-determined redlining became the way in which real estate developers and mortgage lenders identified and thus, determined communities. Still grounded in beliefs about racial supremacy and inferiority, property value seemed to be based as much on the race of the owner as it was on the physical structure or location and size of land.

In the sophisticated system of color coding, communities where high concentrations of Black people lived were red-lined, whereas areas that were integrated or becoming more Black or mixed neighborhoods were, respectively yellow- or green-lined, and areas that were all White were blue-lined. This federal assessment encouraged bankers to expedite loans to those who could bring racial value to an area, while it also encouraged developers to place "White Only" clauses in community association bylaws and charters to ensure White racial permanence and increasingly higher yields on the investments, or growing (capital) equity.

Today, as postindustrial cities undergo urban renewal, once red-lined neighborhoods where Black, Brown, and Indigenous families find themselves in alarming numbers are now being regentrified for White ownership. Poor families of color increasingly have nowhere to move except into the remaining housing projects that the government financed for people of color as an alternative to the White suburban expansion.

Not only did White people actualize White flight from their once loved suburbs back into a regentrified city or to an ever-farther away suburb, but they took with them their property values. This, in turn, affected the resources available for municipal services, such as schools and law enforcement, in the communities they fled. Many Americans seemed to think the new residents of color willingly allowed the neighborhood to deteriorate after they moved in. However, what might be more accurate is that our entire society, including the government, contributed to the devaluation and eventual demise of communities of color by assigning and perpetuating a cultural belief that greater value is attached to Whiteness.

History of Race in Education

Racial inequity in American education—and frustration with it—has a long history dating back to the founding of the nation. While the Declaration of Independence holds that "all men are created equal," the historian James Horton has said,

> We are a society based on principles literally to die for, principles that are so wonderful that it brings tears to your eyes. But we are a society that so often allows itself to ignore those principles. We live in a kind of heightened state of anxiety because we know we are not what we could be or what we say we are. (quoted in Adelman, 2003)

This perpetual anxiety about schools has resulted in extensive efforts to criticize, change, and use public education as a means to some other political end.

As it stands, the American public school system has never quite lived up to expectations. As Linda Darling-Hammond (1997) states, "Through decades of separate and unequal schooling that continue to the present, the right to learn in ways that develop both competence and community has been a myth rather than a reality" (p. 7).

This myth of effective education began with the creation of public schools, originally intended only for the White people and the well-to-do. During the first half of the 19th century, it was a crime in the southern states to teach an enslaved person how to read, and school funding for the rich and the poor in the northern states was purposely unequal.

As the Industrial Revolution came into full gear after the Civil War and segregation was officially instituted, public education came to be seen as a factory system to create the nation's workers. There was always a constant divide, however, between the rich and poor, the White and Black. According to Darling-Hammond (1997),

> Large impersonal factory-model schools with rigid tracking systems were created to teach rudimentary skills and unwavering compliance to the children of the poor. The more affluent and advantaged were taught in small elite private and public schools or carefully insulated special tracks within comprehensive schools, where they were offered a stimulating curriculum, personalized attention, high-quality teaching, and a wealth of intellectual resources. (p. 7)

There was never any intention to create equitable institutions of education, and thus, schools attended by children of color and indigenous children predominantly were so chronically underfunded and inadequately supported that they could never rise above mediocrity.

The Color Line

Aside from the sociopolitical struggles around racial determination of citizenship and American ethnicity, the public education of all school-age children and the manner in which the history of the United States would be taught have required generations of legal action and public advocacy. Initially, legislators barred non-White children from schools, but the underground education process and the work of missionaries had provided well-established schooling for Black children by the time of Emancipation. As the schooling of Black children moved into the public sector, segregation was the norm. This was officially upheld in 1896 by the US Supreme Court decision, *Plessy v. Ferguson,* which legalized separate schooling for White children and children of color in the United States.

In 1903, W. E. B. DuBois, among the first African Americans to receive a PhD from Harvard, described the problem of the color line and illustrated the "relations of the darker to the lighter races of men" (1903/1996, p. 15). DuBois and other prominent scholars recognized that despite efforts to educate non-White children in this country, ideas and practices connected to race would create a lasting achievement gap.

It took more than 50 years for the Supreme Court to acknowledge, in 1954, that the unleveled social playing field for White people provided educational advantage as well. The *Brown v. Board of Education* decision also led to scrutiny of other racially segregated institutions and is widely viewed as the turning point in American civil rights. Although *Brown* made racially segregated schooling illegal in the United States, the implementation of this decision "with all deliberate speed" led to some desegregation efforts that are in and of themselves cause for the persisting racial achievement disparity that exist today. As I write this second edition of *Courageous Conversations About Race,* we mark the 60th anniversary of the landmark *Brown* decision. In Topeka, Kansas, and a majority of other places around this nation, segregated preK–12 education continues to be the norm, if not by school building, then certainly by classrooms within a building.

It is not my intention to debate the merits and effectiveness the Court's decision and laws. Nor will I offer the detailed historical perspective surrounding the many other events that have brought permanence to our racial challenges in the United States. I am primarily interested in assisting educators in having a Courageous Conversation as it relates to the impact of race on schooling today. At the same time, I suggest that educators take the necessary time to deepen their understanding of how the history of race is inextricably linked to modern education. Some may want to pause here and review some primary source documents and historical artifacts. Remember to search for multiple racial perspectives, as the Third Condition suggests, as this will help flesh out some critical understandings. In your research, undoubtedly you will come across issues such as IQ (standardized) testing, busing, redistricting, academic tracking, and special education, to name only a few. Each of these topics has not only a historical foundation but also racial implications for contemporary schooling.

> **REFLECTION**
>
> In your own school or school system, what evidence suggests that the history of race still impacts institutional philosophy, policies, programs, and/or practices? Does your system still experience academic tracking, course and activities enrollment, intelligence/aptitude testing, and remedial education, which stratify students, unintentionally perhaps, by race? How are these unintended racial outcomes being addressed?

A WORKING DEFINITION OF RACE

Race continues to create confusing and often polarizing relationships between people of all racial groups. For example, on a school or university faculty, race—as a sociopolitical phenomenon—can be embraced by a few who wish to exploit it, upheld by some who have come to accept its reality, denied by others who don't understand it, and avoided by those who are shamed by it. It is clear, however, that as suggested in Dr. Ladson-Billing's foreword to this book, few people of color and indigenous people have been able to or allowed to fully transcend a deficit racial identity imposed by society. Even Oprah Winfrey—one of the wealthiest and best-known women in the world—recently has talked about being followed by suspicious sales clerks in stores, when she was not recognized, simply because she is Black. In addition, I struggle to find White Americans who have not benefited, to some degree, by having White skin. At the least, they have not had to think about race, much less constantly worry about being marginalized or mistreated because of it.

Defining Racial Identity

As a way of defining race and racial identity, I choose to initially examine the racial experience and commentary of someone who figures prominently in the public's eye: Barack Obama. Born in Hawaii to a White American mother and Black Kenyan father, Obama attended the prestigious Punahou School and later graduated from Columbia University and Harvard Law School. As the first Black president of the *Harvard Law Review,* Obama brushed arms with then-professor Derrick Bell, also known as the father of critical race theory, on his way to becoming a civil rights attorney and professor of constitutional law at the University of Chicago. After spending several years in the Illinois House of Representatives, Obama, at age 43, was elected to the US Senate in 2004, the same year he was selected to give a speech at the Democratic National Convention. In 2007, Obama beat out Hillary Rodham Clinton to become the democratic nominee for president. Elected to the highest United States office in 2008 and again in 2012, President Barack Obama became the first person of color to occupy the Oval Office. In 2009, President Obama was the recipient of the Nobel Peace Prize.

Because of this public description, Obama is said to have broken the color barrier. But is Obama Black? Or is he African American? Could he be biracial? What is Barack Obama's race, and who gets to decide?

President Obama represents a classic case of racial complexity and confusion for people living in the United States. Ethnically, he represents multiple cultures due to the honored traditions and backgrounds of his parents, and publicly, he acknowledges this fact. But the public, for a variety of reasons, often struggles to accept the Black visual or racial identity that society frequently uses to describe him. For our President, despite his multiracial parentage, considers himself to be Black and only Black.

In the first edition of *Courageous Conversations About Race,* I introduced this notion of racial complexity by sharing a narrative about professional golfer Tiger Woods. Since that time, Woods publicly fell from grace on and off the green, receiving a high level of global scrutiny that many people of color believed revealed some unexamined racism within the golfing community and broader society. Still, the fact remains that Woods is an extraordinary golfer, and it can be said that he is the greatest Black golfer that ever lived. Because of this public description, Woods is said to have broken the color barrier in a sport that, until recently, has been largely White. For this, he is compared to the likes of Jackie Robinson, Althea Gibson, Arthur Ashe, and other sporting firsts. But is Woods Black? Or is he African Thai American? Could he be *Cablasian*—a term he used to define himself when answering the persistent public questions about his racial identity? What race is Tiger Woods, and who gets to decide?

Tiger Woods also represents a classic case of racial complexity and confusion for people living in the United States. But Woods, unlike President Obama, struggles to accept the Black visual or racial identity that society frequently uses to describe him. In his own statement regarding his identity, Tiger Woods (1997) writes,

I am the product of two great cultures—one African American and the other Asian.

On my father's side, I am African American. On my mother's side, I am Thai. Truthfully, I feel very fortunate, and *equally proud,* to be both African American and Asian!

The critical and fundamental point is that ethnic background and or composition should NOT make a difference. It does NOT make a difference to me. The bottom line is that I am an American . . . and proud of it!

Without question, Tiger Woods has the right to be proud of his multiethnic heritage as well as his national identity. He also has the choice as to whether he claims his own racial identity. But despite his intention to control public claims about his race, much of society will box him in with other Black people due to his obvious appearance, while they attempt to recognize and understand his more subtle ethnicities. In truth and in accordance with how race is lived in the United States of America, Tiger Woods can claim to be part Asian and part African American, but most will continue to see him, as they do our President, as "just Black."

In 1997, when Woods won his first PGA Master's Tournament, he was widely heralded and embraced as the first "Black man" ever to win that competition and don the "green Master's jacket," the traditional symbol of the tournament winner. Because Woods saw himself as just a golfer and not a "Black" golfer, he appeared unprepared for this "breaking the color barrier" experience in what was virtually a White-only sport. The onslaught of praise, empathy, rejoicing, anger, and even racial slurs that resulted from Woods's triumph illustrates what is meant by the working definition of race in the United States. Unfortunately, heated public discourse did not center on Woods as a golfer or Woods as a young man born to an African American father and Thai mother. Woods was called the first Black man to win the Master's. In accepting this distinction, Woods was from then on to be celebrated, owned, defended, and even chastised by the Black community. Equally fascinating were the reactions from appropriation to guilt and disgust that circulated throughout White America. Certainly, the lack of public response from Asian communities only adds additional layers to an already complex tapestry known as the American racial experience.

REFLECTION

How does the story of Barack Obama reinforce and/or challenge your current beliefs about racial identity development?
How does the story of Tiger Woods reinforce and/or challenge your current beliefs about racial identity development?

President Obama's and Woods's stories reveal the power of race. Race outweighs or *trumps* other identities, because through race, American society initially identifies and defines people living both here and abroad. How we individually and personally view ourselves may have little to do with how our race is determined by society collectively. With all due respect to Tiger Woods's rich ethnicity, the fact remains that he is viewed as Black, and many of the children and adults he inspires—and attracts to golf—are Black. Recently, Woods himself indicated that he relates personally with other great Black athletes, such as Michael Jordan. Furthermore, his charitable work is focused around helping children of color enjoy golf. For someone who began his career having little public regard for the meaning of race, Woods has illustrated just how powerful and overwhelming racial socialization in the United States can be.

Three C's of Identity

The Fifth Condition of Courageous Conversation encourages us to establish and use a working definition for race. Racial labeling in the United States has traditionally confounded and confused the Three C's of Identity: Corner, Culture, and Color. Although intense debate still occurs in our society about the meaning and functionality of one's nationality, ethnicity, and race, it is essential that we agree on a workable definition of each of these three characteristics. The criteria offered here focus us on how each of these phenomena is lived by people in the United States and various other parts of the world.

Corner

To provide a clearer explanation of some often confusing terms, I am reintroducing Curtis Linton, who coauthored with me the first edition of the *Courageous Conversations About Race*. Curtis and I share the same US origin or nationality. *Corner* designates citizenship, either by birth or naturalization, as specified on a government-issued passport. A person must be able to locate his or her nationality on a globe and name it as such. Curtis and I are both citizens of the United States of America.

Culture

The word *American* reflects another factor, our ethnicity. While both Curtis and I are US citizens, our racial biographies illustrate that our *culture* or ethnicity varies considerably and significantly. My culture is African American or, as I prefer, Black American; it includes Black English language, Black Baptist and Methodist religions; jazz, soul, rap, house, and R&B music; and soul food. Additionally, many of my icons are Black American, such as Martin Luther King, Bobby Seal, James Baldwin, and Barack Obama. I am greatly influenced by Black American writers like Phyllis Wheatley, Ralph Ellison, and Toni Morrison. Black American educators Barbara Sizemore, Asa Hilliard, James Comer, and Gloria Ladson-Billings have greatly informed my perspectives. Curtis's cultural affiliation is White American; it includes White English language, the Mormon religion, White rock and roll, and the food and lifestyle of the American West. As you have probably surmised from reading his racial autobiography in Chapter 3, Curtis's culture, or ethnicity, has shifted significantly with his more recent adoption and raising of two Black American children.

Our culture describes how we live on a daily basis in terms of our language, ancestry, religion, food, dress, musical tastes, traditions, values, political and social affiliations, recreation, and so on. When compound descriptions are used to describe ethnicity, the two words represent the balance between the two cultures or perhaps an emerging third culture or cultural hybrid. For example, a student of Mexican ancestry who was born in the United States, speaks English in public but Spanish with relatives, and occasionally partakes in celebrations recognizing the traditions of Mexico most definitely exists in a culture best described as between American and Mexican and thus is ethnically Mexican American. However, a Black student whose ancestors are a tribe of former Ghanaians, captured and enslaved in the United States in the 1600s, today has an experience and perspective that is different than that of contemporary White Americans and of Ghanaians. Thus, ethnically speaking, he is African American or Black American. The former describes a student who is actively bridging cultures, whereas the latter is not active in bridging cultures, even though many of the primary Ghanaian cultural precepts are alive and well through what is known as ancestral memory. Both examples, however, illustrate a third culture or cultural hybrid that not only reflects distinctive aspects of each individual ethnicity but also offers a unique history, language, music, religion, food, fashion, and values representing the intersection of two (or more) distinct cultures.

Color

The final C of identity denotes *color* characteristics, or race. According to these terms, I am Black, and Curtis is White. For the most part, race is the meaning affixed to the noticeable melanin content seen in the skin, hair, and eyes. Those who are rich in melanin are said to be "of color" or indigenous, whereas those who have the least amount of visible melanin are defined as White.

REFLECTION

Identify your own personal three C's of Corner, Culture, and Color. Can you identify the three C's of your closest friends? To what degree do your friends represent national, ethnic, and/or racial diversity?

The Fifth Condition of Courageous Conversation helps us to avoid the tendency to use identity terms interchangeably. For example, to isolate race—which the Second Condition guides Courageous Conversation participants to do—one must recognize and understand exactly what race is and how it is lived. Too often in the United States, we blend the three C's of our nationality, ethnicity, and race, even though when we reference any of these three, race is typically the operative in our minds and actions. This is why the Courageous Conversation strategy posits that race typically trumps ethnicity and nationality in our interactions.

Racializing Culture

Another way of viewing the interplay of the three C's is to recognize that we racialize our culture and corner. For example, specific color images are conjured up when we say *all-American, rap, country, Salt Lake City,* and *NASCAR,* even though no racial terms are specifically fixed to these ethnic traditions. Similarly, some people may decide "who belongs in this country" and "who doesn't" by the way they look, without ever actually considering the person's actual country of birth, naturalization, or current legal citizenship.

The Fifth Condition of Courageous Conversation encourages participants to deepen the discourse by being intentional and explicit about their own racial identity. When examining race, aside from the notion of racial culture, ethnicity and nationality are of less importance. Specifically, Brown people who hail from various Latin American countries but all have dark skin will have similar experiences in the United States, even when they don't share the Spanish language. Their common experience is racial despite their ethnic and nationality differences. Even more interesting is how our society will predictably look on these darker Latinos with expectations that they have limited English skills and, if in California or Texas, are of Mexican ancestry; if in Florida, are Cuban; or if in New York, are Puerto Rican or Dominican. For these reasons, ethnicity and nationality need to be clearly differentiated so that race can gain our focus.

Ethnic Versus Racial Experiences

In the discussion of race and ethnicity, race as it relates to color begins to affect and even overshadow ethnicity. For example, music and food originate in a place or with an ethnic group and are not inherently racial, yet we may make references to Black music or Asian food. Ultimately, ethnic markers become racialized in the United States except when they reference the behaviors, attitudes, beliefs, and traditions of White American culture. For example, it is likely and acceptable to hear a group of White people say, "Let's visit a Black church and have some soul (i.e., Black) food," but they wouldn't say, "Let's visit a White church and then have some White food." *White* is the ethnic description often left out of the conversation, even though White American is the dominating ethnicity in the United States. Does "country western" mean White music, and if so, why is it offensive to many if we refer to it as such? Why is it that when the phrase "all-American boy" conjures up an image of a White boy, White is not a part of the description, and yet it is part of our collective expectation? Interestingly, I have found this same phenomenon of assuming White as a defining yet unspoken racial description to occur among Australians when they determine who are the Aussies in the room. Typically African, Asian, and Indian Australians, born and raised in Australia, are overlooked.

This process of racializing ethnic experience also happens with individuals. Sandra Cisneros is considered a Brown or Hispanic author, Gwendolyn Brooks and

Maya Angelou are seen as Black authors, and Amy Tan is an Asian author. But F. Scott Fitzgerald and John Grisham are identified simply as American authors—not White authors. This is how race enters the conversation discreetly when referencing Whiteness and boldly when referencing color.

Assimilation Versus Acculturation

A person's ethnicity is indeed fluid, and changes to it occur through the process of assimilation or acculturation. Through assimilation, people are required or encouraged to sacrifice their primary culture or relinquish their ethnic traits in exchange for new and different traits. For example, although they hear Spanish spoken at home, Brown students may lose their fluency because of pressures from educators, peers, and perhaps parents to speak English only.

Through acculturation, people integrate their primary ethnic characteristics into the new culture they are adopting. For example, our adopted "Tex-Mex" food fuses the cuisines of Mexico and the American Southwest. The process of acculturation can also enable students to continue developing in their own primary cultural traditions while sampling or even immersing themselves in a new and different school culture. Specifically, Chinese American students can enjoy a hamburger in the school cafeteria, eat Chinese American food in a predominantly White suburban mall food court, and still crave authentic Chinese cuisine prepared at home using spices, produce, and seafood purchased at the Chinese grocery. These blended cultures stem primarily from desired acculturation but can also be born out of a purposeful but unsuccessful resistance to assimilation. In the face of dominant White culture, many people of color and indigenous people fail in their attempts to maintain their own ethnic culture, while others wish to assimilate into Whiteness but feel unwelcome due to their identifiable non-White physical racial characteristics.

Defined by Race

Distinguishing between ethnicity and nationality helps us to understand the labels we place on others and that others place on us. As stated previously, race denotes the social meaning affixed to skin color, whereas ethnicity defines cultural markers, such as language, religion, and food; nationality describes only country of origin or naturalization and is a matter of official and legal documentation. The working definition of race, however, recognizes that these three identifiers do not operate with equal force and familiarity in US society. As a result of our racialized culture, people's color tends to define much of their culture, as well as determine whether they should gain full access to the benefits of US citizenship.

When Curtis Linton enters the room, he is seen as a White male first and Mormon later, should he choose to reveal this latter part of his ethnicity. If he publicly identifies as Mormon, few would question the validity of his affiliation with the Church of Jesus Christ of Latter Day Saints, because it is seen traditionally as a White institution in the United States, even though its racial membership may be more diverse around the world.

When I enter a room, I am viewed as a Black man. When I speak, some will question my Blackness, because I have spent much of my formal education and professional life in and around White culture. That is to say that my references and phraseology are familiar to White people. The fact that I attend a Black Methodist church, appreciate Black music, and favor soul food is not questioned. But, if he were to say I was Mormon, many would experience dissonance and perhaps have trouble believing me. This is because Mormonism has traditionally not been viewed as a part of the Black American experience.

When it comes to nationality, however, neither of us is questioned on our US citizenship, because racially, we both fit the look of an American citizen, even though Curtis appears "all American." Our US-born Latino and Asian American friends, however, are often required to prove their national identity. They may not be asked to show their passports, but they are commonly asked where they are from. This is one way in which race is lived in the United States of America.

Unfortunately, the conversation about ethnicity is often short-circuited, because race enters so quickly into the dialogue. People may believe that they are talking about ethnicity when they address differences, but in fact, they are talking about race. Educators purport to be looking at student achievement data disaggregated by ethnicity, when they are actually examining data more closely linked to the races of their students. By separating race from nationality and ethnicity, we can better practice conversations that focus on race.

REFLECTION

Answer the following statements:

Racially speaking,

the "me" I see is _____.

the "me" you see is _____.

the "me" I think you see is _____.

Are all three responses the same? If not, how are they different? How do some of your closest colleagues and/or older students answer these questions? Do you or they experience struggle or conflict as they complete the sentences? What do you believe to be the reason for this dissonance?

IMPLEMENTATION EXERCISE

THREE C'S OF IDENTITY

Time required: 45 minutes

Materials required: For each participant, Courageous Conversation Journal and the worksheet that follows

1. Present the Fifth Condition of Courageous Conversation:

   Establish agreement around a contemporary working definition for race that is clearly differentiated from that of ethnicity and nationality.

2. Introduce and differentiate between the Three C's of Identity:

   Corner: Nationality

   Culture: Ethnicity

   Color: Race

3. Describe the intersection of race, ethnicity, and nationality, as shown in the following diagram. Explain that the star symbolizes the working definition of race or a clear understanding of one's racial identity or racial culture.

4. Have each participant define and identify his or her own personal Corner, Culture, and Color on the worksheet. Emphasize the need to differentiate among the Three C's. Remind participants that race is not the same as ethnicity or nationality.

5. Divide participants into small interracial groups of three to four people. Have them share with the group their Three C's.

6. After this discussion, have each participant create his or her own working definition of race, one that represents a clear understanding of racial identity or racial culture.

7. Address the following prompts within the small groups:

   - What is the identity with which you feel most comfortable?
   - How does your Corner identity differ from your Culture identity?
   - What connections exist between your Culture and Color identities?
   - Of the three identities, which do you believe others see in you?
   - Do you feel comfortable explaining how you derived your working definition of race?

8. Share small-group observations with the larger group, and have participants reflect in their journals.

THREE C'S OF IDENTITY

FIFTH CONDITION OF COURAGEOUS CONVERSATION

Establish agreement around a contemporary working definition of race that is clearly differentiated from that of ethnicity and nationality.

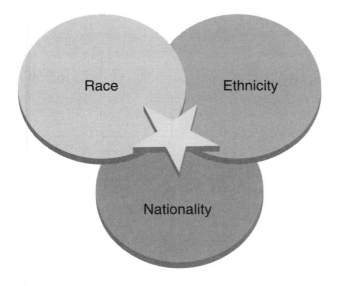

➢ Corner

My nationality is . . .

_____

_____

_____

➢ Culture

My ethnicity is . . .

_____

_____

_____

➢ Color

My race is . . .

_____

_____

_____

★ My working definition of race is . . .

_____

_____

_____

RACIAL AUTOBIOGRAPHY

LUIS VERSALLES

I dedicate this narrative to my late father, Lazaro Versalles Sr., who modeled for me what it means to live your life in a manner that is consistently present to that which carries heart and meaning each and every day.

Never has an examination of the presence and role of race in my life taken on greater significance than in the final six months of my father's life, shortly after his terminal lung cancer diagnosis. This racial autobiography highlights some poignant moments in our story.

I cannot begin to explain how difficult it was when I received the news, in the winter of 2012, that my father had only a few months left with us due to his condition. Such insight provided me clarity in those final months and a deep desire to leave nothing unsaid, to convey to him my eternal gratitude for all he had taught me about life and fatherhood.

Through his example, dad demonstrated the importance of empowering your children to embrace their racial identity. He would often tell me how proud he was of the work I was doing in leading school systems toward racial equity. Simultaneously, he always reminded me of the importance of affirming the racial and cultural identities of my own two biracial children, Lucia (5) and Rio (4). My father shared memories of racial strife between him and his father, Zoilo Sr., a dark-skinned Black Cuban male (*negro* in the lexicon of race in Cuba), because my father lived his racial life as a *trigueño* according to Cuban society, which roughly translates to "dark-brown." He spoke of how his father and other Black Cuban men of his age would engage in *chistes* or *refranes*, jokes or old sayings, that reified the racist foundations of Cuban society. These "good natured" exchanges deeply impacted him, and it took great resolve on my father's part to not internalize these anti-Black messages at a young age.

To get centered, dad and I talked at great length about the role of intraracial White racism in Cuba and the United States, alike. Having come to the United States from Cuba in the early 1960s, dad quickly learned that White US Americans, or in his language, *los americanos*, cared not about racial designations made in Cuba that made distinctions between *negros* and *trigueños:* In Bloomington, Minnesota, in the 1960s, his lived racial experience was clearly that of a Black man, and his strong Spanish accent only intensified the discrimination he would face in many instances.

My father's lessons taught me that combating internalized racism in myself and for my children would require a two-part ongoing process. The first part of this process consists of learning about the manifestations of White supremacy, based on the colonial histories of their countries of origin, that have followed Latinos to the United States. Second, my process for combatting internalized Whiteness required that I make sense of the racist context of the United States that works to problematize a Latino racial identity. We discussed how there is hardly an awareness of the reality of Black Latinos; such a social construction is only recently finding it's way into the racial lexicon of the United States today. For

(Continued)

(Continued)

example, during the global slave trade, ten times as many Africans were enslaved in Spanish and Portuguese colonies in central and South America as were enslaved in North America. Yet, the systemic racism that permeates Latin America, impacting access and opportunities for Afro-Latinos, is rarely illuminated. Such omissions leave the powerful connections existing between Black people in the United States and Latin America invisible and thus unrecognizable and misunderstood, resulting in the perpetuation of systemic racism on a larger scale.

As I unpack how this theme of Black Latino racial invisibility has impacted me, personally, I see my first memory of race—the experience of having my name, Luis, interchangeably used with *javao* by my family. You see, *javao* is a Cuban racial term that roughly translates to "light-skinned." The unspoken part of that description, "Black" is frequently omitted from the Cuban racial consciousness due principally to Cuba's historical construction of race. This is unlike the US context, where a person with "one drop" of Black blood was commonly understood to be "Black." In Cuban society, where White Spaniards were the minority in relation to the much larger representation of enslaved Black Africans and a much smaller indigenous population, just the inverse is "true": Even Cubans who visually present as light-skinned Black frequently identify as "*blanco.*" This subtle yet powerful reminder of my standing in the racial hierarchy of my family stayed with me for some time—that I was *javao,* and therefore somehow "better" than other members of my family who were darker complected than I.

Through our Courageous Conversations in the final months of my father's life, a renewed hope emerged in me: By giving voice to these experiences, my father and I collectively healed from them. I sensed that I had in some small way reciprocated, giving one gift to the man who had selflessly given his family so much over his lifetime: the gift of knowing that his son would be dedicated to leading the rest of his life free from the psychological entrapments of racism in our society. I saw a weight lifted from him, even in these most difficult days of his life. Indeed, in his final days on this Earth, he would repeat that he was *contento,* pleased with what he had accomplished in his life and ready to face what needed to be faced.

As I write this narrative I too find myself in a place of deep reflection, wondering how different my racial identity development process as a youth might have been had I understood *javao* to be what it truly is: "light-skinned Black." I write this narrative at a time in our history when my experiences across the nation show me there is a dearth of understanding of how Black people in this country of various ethnicities and nationalities struggle to see the commonality in our quest for racial equity. I write this at a time when many White Latinos I encounter have little consciousness of the impact of their White skin, despite their Latino cultural affinity. I write this narrative from an authentic place of non-closure, as I still grapple with what it means that Latinos will soon become the largest racial group in our nation. I am discomforted that so many of us (myself included) are still sifting through the meaning of our racial experience. Are you?

TEN

The Sixth Condition

Let's Talk About Whiteness

The virtual invisibility that Whiteness affords those of us who have it is like psychological money in the bank, the proceeds of which we cash in everyday while others are in a perpetual state of overdraft.

—Tim Wise (2000, p. 2)

C onversations about race often prove difficult, and shining light on White as a color, culture, and consciousness is the most challenging aspect of these interactions. Not only does White define the dominant race, but also it represents the standard by which our racial awareness, experiences, and perspectives are judged.

At the foundation of all race relations in the United States of America and in other parts of the world to which I have traveled is the presence of White people sharing a somewhat common level of understanding—or misunderstanding— about their own racial roles and experiences. Also at this racial core, White people are prominent in interpreting the experience and perspective of the racial "other" through their White lens. In other words, the way in which the dominant racial group collectively determines what is and is not *White, Black, Indigenous,* or *Asian,* for example, determines how each of us will be included and excluded in conversations. Equally significant is that many White educators, as Tim Wise suggests in the preceding quote, fail to recognize that White is a race or color, much less that Whiteness represents a culture and consciousness that is shared by White people.

The Sixth Condition provides guidance as educators venture into this deepest and most essential dimension of and challenge to racial dialogue:

Examine the presence and role of Whiteness, its impact on the conversation, and the problem being addressed.

In this chapter, I will shine the light on racial dominance to uncover how Whiteness challenges the performance of students of color and indigenous students while shaping and reinforcing the racial perspective of White children. Initially, we must explore White as a color, culture, and consciousness. Second, we will revisit the previous five conditions, only this time with the explicit purpose of understanding how they are each impacted by Whiteness. Finally, we will examine how White racial identity is formed and developed as well as explore how White cultural identity influences learning and teaching.

WHITE IS A COLOR

Video

Whiteness
*www.corwin.com/
CCAR*

I was faced with a reality I had never anticipated. I began to realize that despite my activism, despite my good intentions, despite how "down" I perceived myself to be with the cause of justice, I was still part of the problem. I was actively receiving the perks of Whiteness, and collaborating with the system of White supremacy, whether I liked it or not.

—Tim Wise (2002, p. 227)

These feelings captured the racial predicament of Tim Wise, a White social justice activist from Nashville, Tennessee, as he faced for the first time the uncomfortable reality that—even though he fought for racial justice—he still partook daily in the benefits of being White. Despite his good intentions to be a racial equity leader, what Wise discovered was that his existence was made much more pleasant and less complicated because he was White. Without ever choosing it, he had received racial privilege his entire life. Wise (2002) continues, "It wasn't just the privileges and advantages that I remembered, but the silences as well; the times I had sat back and said nothing despite knowing that I was surrounded by racial injustice—injustice that was operating to my benefit" (p. 232).

When examining racial privilege in our system of education, the experience of White students is just as informative as that of students of color and indigenous students. Consider Tim Wise's (2002) experience in school: Even though he admits he was not a very serious student, the system still encouraged his eventual success. Wise now recognizes that, from the earliest days of kindergarten, his peers of color were not offered the same wonderful opportunity, high expectations, or encouragement to excel. As Wise finally realized, the privileges he received were primarily due to the color of his skin: White. Educators cannot truly understand the challenges faced by students of color and indigenous students—challenges that result in lowered achievement—until we all develop a deeper understanding of what it means to be White.

WHITE PRIVILEGE

We often hear people referred to as being privileged, which usually is a comment pertaining to the individual's financial or economic status. To be privileged, indeed, means to be of elevated economic means. To have a privileged background means that one's family had material wealth. In Courageous Conversation, however, privilege takes on a different meaning: it refers to the amount of melanin in a person's skin, hair, and eyes. Ironically, the more melanin a person has, the less *privilege* or racial advantage he or she receives.

For those who have not examined their lives through the lens of race, the mere suggestion that they are privileged might evoke strong emotions, particularly if they see themselves as hard-working or from challenged economic circumstances. It may be difficult to grasp the fact that White privilege has little to do with a person's economic status. It refers to the advantages that White people receive simply by virtue of their appearance and, to a lesser degree, the privilege lighter-skinned people of color and indigenous people garner as compared to darker members of the same or different non-White racial groups.

Consider the following thoughts about White privilege by Wellesley College professor Peggy McIntosh (1989):

> I think Whites are carefully taught not to recognize White privilege, as males are taught not to recognize male privilege. So I have begun in an untutored way to ask what it is like to have White privilege. I have come to see White privilege as an invisible package of unearned assets that I can count on cashing in each day, but about which I was "meant" to remain oblivious. White privilege is like an invisible weightless knapsack of special provisions, maps, passports, codebooks, visas, clothes, tools, and blank checks.
>
> Describing White privilege makes one newly accountable. As we in women's studies work to reveal male privilege and ask men to give up some of their power, so one who writes about having white privilege must ask, "Having described it, what will I do to lessen or end it?"
>
> After I realized the extent to which men work from a base of unacknowledged privilege, I understood that much of their oppressiveness was unconscious. Then I remembered the frequent charges from women of color that White women whom they encounter are oppressive. I began to understand why we are justly seen as oppressive, even when we don't see ourselves that way. I began to count the ways in which I enjoy unearned skin privilege and have been conditioned into oblivion about its existence. (p. 10)

What is your reaction to the concept of White privilege? If you are White, does this challenge your self-identification in society? If you are a person of color, how do you cope with the daily injustices triggered by White privilege?

REFLECTION

Educators must acknowledge White skin privilege and work to develop a deeper understanding of this reality in order to fully examine the cultural implications of Whiteness in schools. By completing the following exercise, entitled "White Privilege: The Color Line Exercise," educators can develop a clearer understanding of the ways in which skin color, and specifically Whiteness, impacts their daily experiences.

Although the directions call for you to conduct the exercise with a large group such as a faculty or staff, we suggest you first complete the exercise on your own and then do it again with a friend of a race different than your own. Once you have finished reading *Courageous Conversations About Race* and guided your colleagues through some understanding of the Four Agreements and five previous Conditions, you may then choose to guide your colleagues through the color-line exercise.

IMPLEMENTATION EXERCISE

WHITE PRIVILEGE: THE COLOR LINE EXERCISE

I developed the following exercise after reading Dubois's *The Souls of Black Folk* (1903/1996) and then participating in SEED (Seeking Educational Equity and Diversity) training with Peggy McIntosh in 2002. As a part of our training, we read McIntosh's article "White Privilege" (1989), which is autobiographical; in it, she compared her circumstances only to those of a small group of African American women in her building and in her line of work. She did not claim that her examples of privilege applied to all White people in all times and places relative to all people of color. Many people, including me, have found, however, that McIntosh's observations on her life have some bearing on our own experiences. The point of my exercise is to think about racial privilege as a corollary of racial discrimination and to see whether and how any of the points on McIntosh's list apply to you.

Time required: 60 minutes

Materials required: For each participant, Courageous Conversation Journal and a copy of the exercise in Table 10.1

Review the Four Agreements and the first five Conditions of Courageous Conversations.

Prepare the group by introducing the Sixth Condition:

> *Examine the presence and role of Whiteness, its impact on the conversation, and the problem being addressed.*

1. Invite participants to make personal sense of Whiteness. Offer them an explanation of White as a color. If the color-line exercise is to be effective, you must be working with a racially diverse group.

2. Have each participant complete the color-line exercise in Table 10.1, which is adapted from the work of Peggy McIntosh (1989) and uses the scale it provides. Reiterate to the group that they must answer all questions and may enter only a 5, 3, or 0; that is, they may not enter 1, 2, or 4 in response to any question.

3. Have participants total their scores and then line up in an arc, with the persons who had the lowest scores to the right and those with the highest scores to the left.

4. With the group arranged in this arc, pose the probing questions in the box that follows. With each question, have appropriate members take a step forward into the center of the arc. Once the group has noted the response, have those who stepped forward return to their original places.

PROBING QUESTIONS

- Would all women step forward?
  What you see is how race impacts women.

- Would all women with an advanced degree step forward?
  What you see is how race impacts women with higher-level education.

- Would men with an advanced degree step forward to join the women with advanced degrees?
  What you see is how race impacts people with advanced degrees.

- Would all White people step forward?
  What you see is White privilege and the color line.

---

5. Now read to the group the following excerpt from *The Souls of Black Folk,* published in 1903 by W. E. B. DuBois, a Black man who had a PhD from Harvard:

   The problem of the twentieth century is the problem of the color line, the relation of the darker to the lighter races of men in Asia, Africa, America and the Islands of the Sea. . . . Curious it was, too, how this deeper question [of the color line] ever forced itself to the surface despite effort and disclaimer.

   Then ask the group, Where is our color line between the lighter and darker races?

6. Following the series of probing questions and the reading, allow the entire group some time to process the exercise together in the arc.

7. Finally, have the participants return to their tables, where they will continue conversations in smaller multiracial groups. Recognize that the

patterns revealed by the probing questions above may be upsetting and even shocking to some participants.

8. You may wish to have each educator complete the exercise in Table 10.1 with a friend of a different race and report on this at your next meeting.

Recognize that some White participants may not know anyone of a different race whom they consider a friend. These educators might reflect on why their friendships include only people of the same race.

Table 10.1   White Privilege: The Color-Line Exercise

Respond to each question using one of the following scores:

5   if the statement is mostly true for you
3   if the statement is sometimes true for you
0   if the statement is seldom true for you

Because of my race or color . . .	*My response*	*Friend's response*
If I wish, I can arrange to be in the company of people of my race most of the time.		
If I should need to move, I can be pretty sure of renting or purchasing housing in an area which I can afford and in which I would want to live.		
I can be pretty sure that my neighbors in such a location will be neutral or pleasant to me.		
I can go shopping alone most of the time, pretty well assured that I will not be followed or harassed.		
I can turn on the television or open to the front page of the newspaper and see people of my race widely represented.		
When I am told about our national heritage or about "civilization," I am shown that people of my color made it what it is.		
I can be sure that my children will be given curricular materials that testify to the existence of their race.		
I can go into supermarkets and find the staple foods that fit with my cultural traditions; I can go into a music shop and count on finding the music of my race represented; I can go into any hairdresser's shop and find someone who can cut my hair.		

Because of my race or color . . .	*My response*	*Friend's response*
Whether I use checks, credit cards, or cash, I can count on my skin color not to work against the appearance of financial reliability.		
I can arrange to protect my children most of the time from people who might not like them.		
I can swear, or dress in secondhand clothes, or not answer letters, without having people attribute these choices to the bad morals, the poverty, or the illiteracy of my race.		
I can speak in public to a powerful male group without putting my race on trial.		
I can do well in a challenging situation without being called a credit to my race.		
I am never asked to speak for all the people of my racial group.		
I can remain oblivious to the language and customs of persons of color who constitute the world's majority without feeling, in my culture, any penalty for such oblivion.		
I can criticize our government and talk about how much I fear its policies and behavior without being seen as a cultural outsider.		
I can be pretty sure that if I ask to talk to "the person in charge," I will be facing a person of my race.		
If a traffic cop pulls me over, or if the IRS audits my tax return, I can be sure I haven't been singled out because of my race.		
I can easily buy posters, postcards, picture books, greeting cards, and children's magazines featuring the people of my race.		
I can go home from most meetings of the organizations I belong to feeling somewhat tied in, rather than isolated, out of place, outnumbered, unheard, held at a distance, feared, or hated.		
I can take a job with an affirmative action employer without having co-workers on the job suspect that I got it because of race.		

(Continued)

Table 10.1 (Continued)

Because of my race or color . . .	My response	Friend's response
I can choose public accommodations without fearing that people of my race cannot get in or will be mistreated in the places I have chosen.		
I can be sure that if I need legal or medical help, my race will not work against me.		
If my day, week, or year is going badly, I need not ask of each negative episode or situation whether it has racial overtones.		
I can choose blemish cover or bandages in "flesh" color and have them more or less match my skin.		
TOTAL SCORE		

WHITE IS A CULTURE

Although shocking and disturbing to many of us, White privilege is often a difficult phenomenon for White people to acknowledge and own. Sometimes, a sophisticated level of understanding occurs, but White educators feel challenged in mustering the will and finding the skill to confront their privilege or the corresponding oppression experienced by people of color.

Even Peggy McIntosh (1988), the White scholar whose writings made the concept of White privilege accessible to many White people, says,

> I repeatedly forgot each of the realizations on this list until I wrote it down. For me, White privilege has turned out to be an elusive and fugitive subject. The pressure to avoid it is great, for in facing it I must give up the myth of meritocracy. If these things are true, this is not such a free country; one's life is not what one makes it; many doors open for certain people through no virtues of their own. (p. 9)

Entitlement

Beyond skin color privilege exists a racial culture that is defined by the behaviors of White people, who often function unaware that they live a privileged existence. When White people are unconscious of their privilege, these skin color benefits are viewed as entitlements. Therefore, when people of color and indigenous people question these privileges, they are viewed as aggressive and seen as encroaching on the lifestyle that White people believe to be their legitimate right.

Furthermore, when people of color and indigenous people—not having these racial benefits or advantages—are unable to reach the same life goals as White people, they often are viewed by the privileged race as weak, unskilled, unintelligent, and even lazy. In a protected enclave of Whiteness, be it a suburban neighborhood or a faculty meeting room, White people are buffered from encroachments on their privilege. Sharing perspective about what is hard work and what are the appropriate ways to behave within protected environments of unacknowledged privilege, White people define the right way to do school and live a productive life. This forthrightness in determining the "right" way to do things could also be seen as determining for people of color and indigenous people the "White" way to function in life and specifically in school.

Understanding White Culture

Even though much of a school's decision making occurs on an intellectual level in White majority enclaves, White people tend to understand little about what it means to be White. Conversely, because deriving material success in our schools and society most often involves negotiating White culture, people of color and indigenous people can define multiple characteristics of White culture with relative ease.

When teachers venture into their classrooms, most teach their own personal culture first and the subject matter or standards second. Similarly, when educators assess student performance, much of the process and content of the assessment has more to do with the teacher's culture than the student's culture. To what degree, then, do students need to be proficient in White culture to achieve in schools where most teachers are White females?

Likewise, what happens when the culture of our Black and Brown male students does not correspond to the White female teachers' culture in the classroom? Can effective learning and teaching take place when there is cultural incongruence and conflict in the classroom and throughout the school? Racial conflict among educators and between educators and students cannot be resolved when White educators are unaware of their racial culture and people of color and indigenous people feel unsafe to reveal the prevailing characteristics of Whiteness. Thus, to what degree might Black (Brown, Indigenous) male students' lack of proficiency in White (female) culture be a reason that they persistently and disproportionately occupy the lowest achievement categories?

Defining White Culture

From the work of Elise Trumbull, Carrie Rothstein-Fisch, Patricia M. Greenfield, and Blanca Quiroz (2000), we have learned that *White culture* is characterized by individualism, whereas *cultures of color* are more often characterized by collectivism. In their research entitled *Bridging Cultures,* they studied the classroom and home behaviors of Latino and Southeast Asian American students in Southern California and compared them to behaviors of White students. These two differing sets of characteristics impact the actions and interactions of both groups. Understanding these differences is critical if White people and people of color are to engage in more effective dialogue. The cultural differences based on race are detailed in Table 10.2.

Table 10.2 Cultural Differences

White Individualism (Representative of prevailing US culture)	Color Group Collectivism (Representative of many immigrant cultures)
• Fostering independence and individual achievement	• Fostering interdependence and group success
• Promoting self-expression, individual thinking, and personal choice	• Promoting adherence to norms, respect for authority/elders, and group consensus
• Associated with egalitarian relationships and flexibility in roles (e.g., upward mobility)	• Associated with stable, hierarchical roles (dependent on gender, family background, age)
• Understanding the physical world as knowable apart from its meaning for human life	• Understanding the physical world in the context of its meaning for human life
• Associated with private property, individual ownership	• Associated with shared property, group ownership

From a cultural standpoint, examining the presence and role of Whiteness is the most critical condition for innovating and differentiating instruction in such a way that all students achieve in a rigorous curriculum. This same examination, however, often triggers defensiveness in White people, particularly those challenged to embrace the concept of White privilege.

Nonetheless, as certain as we are about the existence of Black culture, indigenous culture, and Latino culture, White culture must also exist, simply by virtue of the number of White people in American schools and society. It is White culture that primarily establishes the standards for all intraracial and interracial group interactions. Thus, White culture dictates to some degree how, when, and where other racial groups determine, develop, and honor their own cultures.

REFLECTION

How have you observed White individualism and/or color group collectivism in your personal life? Your professional life? In the school system where you work? Can you describe a personal or professional situation in which there was balance between White individualism and color group collectivism?

WHITE CONSCIOUSNESS

Given their position in terms of racial privilege and cultural dominance and power, White educators are apt to develop a certain way of thinking or a consciousness about specific educational and societal challenges that is often not aligned with the perspectives of educators of color and indigenous educators. Many White people do not consider how their lives are impacted by their own Whiteness. Conversely, people of color and indigenous people feel, consciously or not, that they often must determine and declare what is the proper White behavior and operating White perspective in any given situation.

For example, many people of color and indigenous people feel the need to be cautious in mixed racial groups to not offend or disturb White people's disconnect from their own racial beliefs and behaviors. When more than two people of color or indigenous people gather together, it reminds White people that race, in fact, exists. As the number of people of color or indigenous people in a room or on a committee increases, many caring White educators' greatest fear surfaces—that of being labeled a racist. People of color and indigenous people are required to be aware of White icons, fashions, and follies to participate appropriately in interracial professional and social interactions. Furthermore, White people tend to dominate conversation by setting the tone for how everyone must talk and which words should be used. All of these "White ways" must be recognized, internalized, and then silently acted on by people of color and indigenous people as a way of avoiding marginalization or retaliation by White people. People of color and indigenous people must become proficient in balancing their primary culture with White culture, or they run the risk of being consumed by it, which is also known as the burden of "acting White" or being "whitewashed."

The aforementioned White cultural characteristics, such as individualism, blur into the consciousness of Whiteness, which becomes not only a way of behaving but also a way of thinking and believing. Throughout my Courageous Conversation research and practice, four distinct and yet overlapping ideals emerge as defining elements of White consciousness: universal perspective, individualism, avoidance, and decontextualization.

I acknowledge that these characteristics could be linked to other diversity phenomena apart from race. What I am suggesting, however, is that White privilege and entitlement lead White people to develop perspectives and reach intellectual conclusions that are unique to their race and at times create conflict for people of color and indigenous people.

Universal Perspective

The notion of a universal perspective begs the question, "Doesn't everybody experience life the way that White people have experienced it?" In my article "White Is a Color!" (Singleton, 1997) I coined the term *Whiteism* and defined it as (1) not recognizing White as a dominating color, nor recognizing the unearned power and privileges associated with having white skin and (2) having a sense of

(White) entitlement but lacking awareness of the experiences and perspectives of non-White-skinned people.

Because White people are rarely forced to acknowledge or address the reality of their skin color privilege, there is little or no collective recognition or empathy for the struggle experienced by people of color who, by definition, lack these privileges. Thus, when the notion of racial privilege and the corresponding oppression is brought to the attention of White people, they often struggle to see it as real or valid. Consequently, White people and indigenous people embrace the cultural conclusion that people of color use race as an excuse for their individual failures and shortcomings. Because White people so often see personal effort as the only source of success in life, they believe that people of color use a "race card" to avoid hard work. Although it is true that hard work will lead to better results for all students, given the racial imbalances discussed earlier, effort and rewards do not always align for people of color and indigenous people, simply because they do not receive White privilege.

Individualism

Individualism claims that "I earned this," making the "effort equals reward" perspective a deeply embedded ideology within White culture. Because of this, White people often fail to make the connection between themselves and the many other White people in any given situation who reinforce White cultural values and thus ensure maintenance of the systemic delivery of White privilege.

For example, when White teachers make references to White icons, to events or places that White people visit, and to issues that draw the interest of largely White audiences, White children are more likely to make the critical connections because of their White cultural upbringing. The school day consists of multiple opportunities for students to connect with or disconnect from the teacher. Depending on the educator's attention to this intercultural relationship based in race, his or her students will succeed or fail.

To assert that White people are individualistic disregards to some degree this backdrop of White racial bonding. That is, White people depend on the overwhelming presence of other White people in positions of power and influence to maintain a system of racial advantage. Rarely do White people enter into, much less thrive, in environments or situations where they exist as the racial minority among similarly educated, skilled, resourced, and accomplished people of color or indigenous people. At the same time, many White educators believe that gains in school, as in their own lives, come from individual effort and accomplishment rather than from the presence and support they demand from other, similarly situated White people.

Peggy McIntosh (1988) speaks to the White cultural disposition surrounding individualism in the following way:

> My schooling gave me no training in seeing myself as an oppressor, as an unfairly advantaged person, or as a participant in a damaged culture. I was taught to see myself as an individual whose moral state depended on her individual moral will. My schooling followed the pattern my

colleague Elizabeth Minnich has pointed out: Whites are taught to think of their lives as morally neutral, normative, and average, and also ideal, so that when we work to benefit others, this is seen as work which will allow "them" to be more like "us." (p. 4)

For these reasons, schools and classrooms are organized in many ways around the idea of individual effort; this includes the way we test, call on children for responses one at a time, and provide individualized work spaces and personal supplies. Although group work has become more acceptable, students often strive to differentiate themselves, their own personal effort, and their individual high level of understanding from that of the group.

Beverly Daniel Tatum (1997) titled her book, *"Why Are All the Black Kids Sitting Together in the Cafeteria?"* partly to attract the attention of White educators who struggle to understand why students of color and indigenous students behave the way they do. We have heard many White educators express curiosity and concern about students of color congregating in racial affinity groups. This is evidence of White individualism as it represents an unspoken belief that members of a given racial group do not need one another for fellowship, safety, or survival.

Tatum could just have easily named her book, *"Why Are All the White Kids Sitting Together in the Cafeteria?"* or in the classroom, on the swim team, or in the National Honor Society. But this concept would be foreign and even insulting to White people who choose not to notice their own need for White racial collectivity. It is ironic, however, that the cultural demand for racial dominance coexists with a White cultural belief in individualism. This incongruence is often troubling for people of color and indigenous people.

Avoidance

"This isn't my problem" represents the attitude of avoidance. Many White people have developed and embraced sophisticated ways to avoid thinking and conversing about their own positions of racial privilege and power. In his book, *Uprooting Racism,* Paul Kivel (2002) explores stages of avoidance, which begins with denying the entire notion of racial dominance and progresses to a counterattack that posits a competing victimization—a claim that society is out to persecute White men.

Recent conversations about "reverse racism," which traveled as far as the US Supreme Court in 2014, show the power of White people to defend their perceived entitlement and racial dominance. Since the 1970s, the Court has not acknowledged the escalating images of Whiteness at the highest levels of government and industry in relation to the dramatic demographic shifts in favor of people of color. Again, McIntosh's comments (1988) add insight:

In proportion as my racial group was being made confident, comfortable, and oblivious, other groups were likely being made unconfident, uncomfortable, and alienated. Whiteness protected me from many kinds of hostility, distress, and violence, which I was being subtly trained to visit in turn upon people of color. For this reason, the word "privilege" now seems to me misleading. . . .

I want, then, to distinguish between earned strength and unearned power. (p. 12)

Decontextualization

Decontextualization is evidenced in the oft-heard question, How does this particular situation have anything to do with race? Given that so many White people have trouble seeing themselves as part of a dominating racial group endowed with privilege and power, they also tend not to see how this context of Whiteness has connections to events and outcomes at home and abroad. The moment-to-moment impact and influence that White thinking has on the lives of people of color create a web of racial cause and effect that is invisible to many White people. Because of this virtual invisibility, White people tend to focus on only one part of the event and forgo analysis of a larger historical racial dimension or its present impact and future implications.

For example, as White educators wonder why Black and Brown boys are disproportionately prone to fighting in school, they criticize Black and Brown culture and question why violence is taught in homes of color. Missing from their inquiry and analysis, however, is how these boys might be affected by growing up in a White-governed country, which threatens young men of color at will, distrusts their ability to succeed and follow laws, and allows daily racial stress to mount in neighborhoods, schools, and classrooms. As long as police officers shoot and kill young, unarmed males of color for merely being present, or disproportionately deploy Brown males to fight wars in countries of color abroad, aggression in these communities will continue to be demanded, reinforced, and rewarded. That is, there is a cause/effect relationship between societies defined by White dominance and control and the outcomes achieved by White people and thus by people of color and indigenous people. In her book, *It's the Little Things* (2000), Lena Williams writes, "My actions . . . are the results of the cumulative effect of a lifetime of racial slights and injustices suffered because of my color" (p. 10). Because the privilege of Whiteness is to not suffer these microaggressions, the White consciousness does not incorporate race as a topic into its reasoning and analysis of local, state, national, and world events.

REFLECTION

What personal connections can you make to the universal perspective, individualism, avoidance, and decontextualization of White consciousness? As a White person, how do these characteristics of consciousness impact your relations with others? As a person of color, how do you handle White people who unconsciously exhibit these characteristics?

WHITENESS AS EXAMINED IN THE FIVE CONDITIONS

When conversing about race, we ultimately must speak to Whiteness directly and candidly. Our most significant interaction revolves around our ability to inquire into Whiteness at all three levels: color, culture, and consciousness. To summarize our discussion on race, we will now review the first Five Conditions of Courageous Conversation through the lens of Whiteness. By merely substituting *White, Whiteness,* and *Whiteism* for all references to race, we will arrive at the deeper examination and understanding that the Sixth Condition offers.

Remember that according to the definition of Courageous Conversation, the first two conditions are about *engaging,* the second two conditions are about *sustaining,* and the last two conditions are about *deepening* our interracial dialogue and understanding. The most difficult and most discomforting of the conditions is the Sixth Condition—examining the presence and role of Whiteness. Personalizing (First Condition) Whiteness (Sixth Condition) is the essential progression that enables educators to attain a workable understanding of how race impacts schooling in general and, specifically, the achievement of all students.

Whiteness in the First Condition

To examine Whiteness within the First Condition is to *establish a White racial context that is personal, local, and immediate.* Traditionally, White Americans have failed to view White as a race. Consider once again the exercise that asks, "How much does race impact my life?"

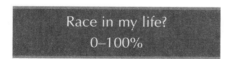

Race in my life?
0–100%

Typically, when White people consider this question for the first time, they do not count their time spent with other White people as having racial impact. Consequently, they often see race as being synonymous with color, but colors other than White. To view the First Condition through Whiteness is to ask the degree to which White, Whiteness, and Whiteism impact my life. With this phrasing, it is virtually impossible to leave White privilege, positioning, and power out of the equation. Until educators acknowledge White to be a race, it is impossible to recognize the full impact of racism on student learning. Our deeper level of analysis points us toward understanding how neighborhoods that are all White, clubs that are all White, and the advanced placement or honors classes that are virtually all White impact *all* students' perspectives and performance.

Whiteness in the Second Condition

Once we have acknowledged that White is a race and Whiteness impacts each of us personally, locally, and immediately, we can then *isolate Whiteness* and determine how it impacts a given racial situation.

Consider the reactions of White educators to the Volkswagen advertisement presented in Chapter 6. Because White people can grow into maturity in this society without ever authentically interacting with a person of color, be it in their neighborhood, workplace, church, or the media, a White perspective on such negative representations of color is often lacking. Because the media in our society does not demonize White people in the same way it poorly represents people of color, the impact of a negative advertisement is minimized by White people. Typically, *white* is portrayed as the standard of beauty, intelligence, and moral correctness. Whiteness is indeed presented as the social, political, and economic yardstick by which everything and everyone is measured. When educators isolate these omnipresent occasions of racial standardization, they notice in their schools the pervasiveness of Whiteness and the overwhelming number of circumstances in which White cultural adaptation is required of students of color.

Whiteness in the Third Condition

We need to *normalize the social construction of Whiteness* to engage multiple White points of view and *surface critical perspective*. Once Whiteness is made visible and examined as a distinct and pervasive racial experience, White people will still offer a multitude of interpretations as to why Whiteness dominates in discourse and other interactions. Clearly, some White people adamantly and forcefully subscribe to beliefs of White supremacy passed on from previous generations. Although most educators would never admit to these beliefs, their low expectations and doubts about the ability of their students of color are revealing. For me, growing up in a thriving Black working-class community and attending all-Black schools, churches, and social gatherings, notions of Black excellence were unquestioned. It was not until I attended the predominately White Park School that I began to consciously embrace color inferiority and White supremacy. Today, many of my former teachers at Park would be heartbroken to discover that they helped instill these beliefs in their beloved student. Unfortunately, intention is not necessary to faithfully practice Whiteism and promote Whiteness.

A more sophisticated understanding of the social construction of knowledge prompts us to investigate how this phenomenon of Whiteness has been and continues to be constructed. Such inquiry leads us into developing critical perspective about Whiteness and how it plays out in curricular and instructional designs and decisions.

Establish Parameters

The Fourth Condition requires that we monitor the elements of the Courageous Conversation Protocol, paying attention to which parameters we establish to advance the dialogue toward a deeper, transformative space. Given Whiteness often dictates rules and regulations for interracial discourse, the Sixth Condition guides us in dismantling such White rules of engagement, which serve as barriers that prevent people of color and indigenous people from entering into the conversation authentically.

The Contemporary Social and Political Construction of Whiteness

In the Fifth Condition, we explored the historic progression of race in the United States. A sophisticated analysis of how Whiteness is socially and politically constructed today points us to conversations surrounding the sociology of a diminishing yet still dominating White population and the politics employed to maintain White power. The question of who merits White status remains a centerpiece discussion. Contemporary census takers struggle with finding the exact racial language to describe immigrants from Mexico, Latin America, and the Pacific Islands. White government officials and their supporters will embrace Latinos as part of the new White race, just as long as there are no requirements for Spanish-language acquisition or other non-White cultural adaptations. But if Latinos push for greater protections for and use of Spanish, or intensify demands for federal immigration policy reform to result in laws consistent with those facing Europeans, they become racially Brown.

Contemporary Whiteness, as a sociopolitical construction, is far more focused right now on the movements of Latinos than on the traditional gauge of Blackness. Some suggest that this might be a way of avoiding the unresolved racial tensions between and among Black and White people. Others squarely see the new focus as the way White people can hold on to power and gain political insurance through forging alliances and granting a modicum of power to Latinos and other non-Black people of color. The 2010 census document—which essentially forces Latinos to classify themselves as White, Black, or Indigenous, because *Latino, Hispanic,* and other familiar ethnic terms do not qualify as racial descriptions—creates a de facto White majority. How the growing population of Latinos racially identify themselves and are racially identified by the US government will determine whether this nation recognizes its inevitable people of color majority status or further institutionalizes policies, programs, and practices that racially misrepresent, silence, and confuse our populace. Institutionalized *White supremacy*—not the radical elements of the KKK, Aryan Nations, and other white supremacist groups—governs mainstream social institutions and is at the heart of exploring how Whiteness gets constructed in the current political and social contexts.

Multiple Points of View and Critical Perspective About Whiteness

After examining how we socially construct Whiteness, the challenge is to unleash multiple viewpoints to surface critical perspective. In doing so, what we discover is that White people tend not to be aware of who they are as *White* people.

In addition, we have come to realize that people of color have discovered aspects connected to White culture and ways of being White that many White people themselves have never recognized or fully understood.

The analysis of what it means to be White has traditionally been done only in contrast to what it means to be Black, Brown, Asian, or Indigenous. The challenge here is that Whiteness needs to be analyzed and understood on its own merits and not simply as a result of dissecting or diminishing other racial groups. What does it mean to be White, and what are the characteristics of Whiteness? These questions provoke our critical thought and are worthy of educators' time and focus.

REFLECTION

What does it mean to be White, and how has Whiteness been socially constructed in your own life? Without comparing White to other races, what are the characteristics of Whiteness? How does Whiteness impact you?

Whiteness in the Fourth Condition

The Fourth Condition invites us to monitor the parameters of the conversation and to use the Courageous Conversation Compass to determine how we are positioned intellectually, relationally, emotionally, and morally with respect to issues of Whiteness. We need to determine the optimal parameters for examining and understanding Whiteness. Exactly how we determine groupings, prompts, and time allocations will have a great impact on how all people, but especially how White people speak, listen, and reflect on Whiteness. Given the predictable discomfort of such a process for many White people, all participants need to be prepared, supported, and continuously reminded to stay focused on Whiteness and stay engaged.

Consider again White Talk and Color Commentary:

White Talk

- Verbal: Focused on talking and offering racial meaning through word choice, voice tone, and intonation

- Impersonal: Focused on the sharing of racial perspectives or experiences of someone not immediately present or involved in the conversation

Color Commentary

- Nonverbal: Focused on offering racial meaning through facial expressions, body movements, and physical gestures

- Personal: Focused on sharing one's own personal racial narrative, perspectives, or experiences

- Intellectual: Focused on what one thinks (or has read) with respect to race

- Emotional: Focused on what one feels (or has experienced) with respect to race

- Task oriented: Focused on engaging in dialogue for the purposes of solving a problem or getting something accomplished

- Process oriented: Focused on engaging in dialogue for the purposes of feeling present, connected, or heard

In the conversation on Whiteness, an understanding of these contrasting characteristics is necessary so that all participants can monitor their own engagement in the conversation. Typically, Whiteness is talked about only when it is threatened, for example, during conflict arising from school desegregation and affirmative action in college admissions or teacher of color hiring. White people tend to exempt themselves from having the characteristics of Whiteness rather than view Whiteness as a constant—a natural characteristic of themselves based on their personal membership in the White racial group.

While a high degree of emotional disconnectedness from Whiteness exists for many White people, examining the presence and role of Whiteness, rather than launching into the typical dissection of color experiences, seems to stir deep emotional engagement among White people. Specifically, publicly naming White as a culture and challenging White educators to examine underlying desires to maintain racial privilege or advantage prompt feelings that are unusual and uncomfortable for most participants of Courageous Conversation.

If everyone is to travel deeper into this conversation and integrate White Talk with Color Commentary, it is important that White people get emotional about Whiteness and invest in challenging White cultural domination. Until White educators experience lasting emotions related to Whiteness, they will struggle to understand why their students of color and indigenous students exhibit such strong emotions around and connections to race.

The extreme emotions experienced in the Courageous Conversation are normal and necessary. The universal presence of these emotions signals to people of color and indigenous people that White people are willing to authentically engage in the conversation. Anger, guilt, and shame are just a few of the emotions experienced by participants as they move toward greater understanding of Whiteness. We have found that this full engagement and the difficult management of emotions eventually give way to feelings of liberation that come only with deeper racial understanding and clarity.

To fully understand Whiteness, White racial dominance needs to be intentionally and explicitly explored. To do this, however, White people need to listen to people of color and indigenous people describe the ways in which Whiteness is manifested and experienced. Likewise, White people should engage in a self-assessment of when and how Whiteness has benefited them in schooling, the community, the workplace, and their social interactions. This thorough and honest assessment helps White people feel less threatened by the presence and behaviors of people of color and indigenous people. When White educators no longer feel compelled to defend their racial privilege and power, they are more likely to address the racial inequities that exist in the school philosophy, structures, policies, and practices.

After working with me for a couple of years and becoming more aware of his own Whiteness, Curtis Linton, coauthor of the first edition of *Courageous Conversations About Race,* was faced with the opportunity to embrace his newfound awareness of racial inequity or to retreat back into the arena of White privilege. Standing in line at John F. Kennedy Airport, Curtis was thrust into a situation where he could easily have engaged in the "silence dialogue." A White man at the counter next to him was demanding that the Latina agent check an additional bag at no extra charge. He badgered her incessantly, claiming that other agents had done it for him. As the agent continued to refuse, the man became increasingly upset. Eventually, the agent threatened to call over a security agent. In response, the man muttered, "Spanish bitch!"

With strong justification, the agent became quite upset and called over both security and a supervisor. Agitated, the man asked what he had done. In response, the agent said that she was proud of her heritage and that what he had said was racist and offensive. Shocked and surprised, the man said, "I'm not a racist—I'm Jewish!" What he did not realize is that before he is Jewish in this highly racialized society, he is White, and he was acting as such.

Curtis was the nearest White person, so the man turned to him and asked, "What did I do?" This was a moment of truth for Curtis. Fighting the urge to retreat within White privilege and remain silent, Curtis responded, "That was racist and very offensive." The man responded, "She wasn't showing me any respect!" Once again having to go beyond his comfort zone, Curtis said, "You are the one who showed no respect, and you were out of line."

After this, the man no longer wanted to speak with Curtis and turned to press his case—unsuccessfully—with the supervisor, another Latina. Curtis concluded this experience of having to move beyond the privilege of Whiteness by reassuring the supervisor that the agent was justified and that the man was out of line.

REFLECTION

Curtis described the aforementioned scenario as an act of racism. How do you see it?

As easy as it might be to redefine this situation in which Curtis engaged as one of gender or class discrimination, what if racism was the sole motive?

White privilege allows White people to decide when and where not to address racial issues. White dominance allows them to continue to receive the benefits and opportunities associated with Whiteness, whether or not they acknowledge this additional assistance. For Curtis, race at this moment became personal, local, and immediate. He could easily have let the situation pass without saying anything, but the reality for the Latina agent is that race is always personal, local, and immediate. So, why should it be any different for Curtis? In this situation, White privilege became White responsibility. This response occurred, however, because of Curtis's continuous examination of White privilege and White cultural dominance.

Whiteness in the Fifth Condition

So much of this chapter has been focused on how Whiteness is lived—the "working definition of Whiteness." By virtue of the Fifth Condition, we can better understand how White skin signals cultural correctness and national legitimacy. In terms of nationality, White Americans often feel a unique sense of entitlement to "Americanism," partly because many never travel beyond the borders of the United States. Based on the number of passports issued, some demographers estimate that less than 34% of all Americans ever travel outside of this country ("The Unfriendly Border," 2005), and this fosters ethnocentrism and an expectation that others will observe and honor "our" cultural ways. Likewise, many White Americans are nearly oblivious to other national norms, cultural beliefs, and racial lifestyles. Domestically, this explains why White Americans rarely assimilate into another culture—they always exist and always expect to exist within the standard of American Whiteness.

Even more important, however, is acknowledging that many White people have a hard time dealing with the dominance of Whiteness because of White privilege. Consequently, the belief that White people are accorded advantage just based on skin color is foreign and threatening to their strongly held notion that White people achieved their superior status because they "earned it" exclusively through hard work. These tendencies are embedded in the White racial culture and perspective.

In terms of color, White people are seen as being White regardless of what their national or ethnic origin might be. People are identified as White before they are acknowledged as Jewish, Italian, or Scandinavian. This reality of being White in the United States today must be acknowledged, especially by White people, in order for any of us to gain a possibility of authentically transcending race.

Likewise, although it is often redefined as mainstream American culture or middle-class values, White culture is as racially distinct as Black, Brown, Indigenous, or Asian culture. Whiteness is also the dominant culture that governs the American school system. Rather than being defined as a separate and equal culture, it is most often understood as the "correct" culture or the "right" way of learning.

WHITE RACIAL IDENTITY DEVELOPMENT

The Sixth Condition of Courageous Conversation, examining the presence and role of Whiteness, enables us to discover the context in which all racial matters are judged. In this very specific investigation, we come to see how White functions not only as a color but also as a culture and a consciousness. But to deepen our inquiry into Whiteness, we can also look at how White identity development occurs and progresses for members of the dominant race and how this identity, at its various stages, might impact people of color.

Although several race scholars have attempted to explain the process of White racial identity development, no one has yet had significant impact on shifting the way White Americans think about their own raciality. This is partly due to White privilege and the ability of those who have it to simply avoid, ignore, or minimize the impact of race on their lives. Given that White people generally have difficulty seeing themselves as racial beings, it is no wonder that the notion of a psychosociological depiction of the White racial experience has been overlooked or diminished by so-called scholars, executives, governors, and everyday White folks. Even so, I believe that understanding how White educators experience their own Whiteness, as well as how they view other White people, people of color, and indigenous people through the lens of Whiteness, is critical to improving schooling. In short, until White educators understand their own racial experience, their interpretation of the racial experience of children of color and indigenous children will be distorted.

Janet Helms (1990) offers one such model for understanding White racial identity (see Table 10.3). Helms suggests that White people experience a progression from essential "color blindness" to a non-dominating stage of Whiteness.

Of course, no theoretical framework can precisely define the many complex and unique aspects of individual identity. What this model can do is affix language to some of the common racial experiences that many White people share. As they would with any developmental scale, White people might see aspects of their current experience in more than one stage on the continuum. This is an indication that people are probably not stationary or fixed in their racial identity.

Table 10.3   Helms Model of White Identity Development

Contact: Whites pay little attention to the significance of their racial identity; "I'm just normal"; perceive themselves as colorblind and completely free of prejudice.

Disintegration: Growing awareness of racism and White privilege as a result of personal encounters. This new awareness is characterized by discomfort.

Reintegration: Feelings of guilt or denial may be transformed into fear and anger directed toward people of color. Whites may be frustrated if seen as a group rather than as individuals.

Pseudoindependent: The individual gains an intellectual understanding of racism as a system of advantage but doesn't quite know what to do about it.

Immersion/Emersion: Marked by a recognized need to find more positive self-definition. Whites need to seek new ways of thinking about Whiteness, ways that take them beyond the role of victimizer.

Autonomy: Represents the culmination of the White racial development process. A person incorporates the newly defined view of Whiteness as part of a personal identity. The process is marked by an increased effectiveness in multiracial settings.

REFLECTION

If you are White, where do you locate yourself on the Helms Model of White Identity Development? Has your position changed over the last few years? If so, how and why? If not, what might have prevented your development?

If you are a person of color or an indigenous person, where do you believe your White colleagues—who believe themselves to be most racially conscious—are located on the Helms Model of White Identity Development? In the past year, have you seen evidence of their progress according to the Helms model? How might you share your observation about their racial identity development with them?

An emerging consciousness surrounding Whiteness is critical to building racial equity. This is the purpose of Courageous Conversation—to engage, sustain, and deepen interracial dialogue about race, and especially about Whiteness. By acknowledging and understanding Whiteness, White people begin to see the way in which their culture subordinates other cultures. With consciousness comes action, and with action comes transformation.

IMPLEMENTATION EXERCISE

DECENTERING WHITENESS

Time required: 45 minutes

Materials required: For each participant, Courageous Conversation Journal and a copy of the worksheet that follows

1. Present the Sixth Condition of Courageous Conversation:

   Examine the presence and role of Whiteness, its impact on the conversation, and the problem being addressed.

   Based on your reading, define Whiteness according to

   Color

   Culture

   Consciousness

2. Divide participants into small groups of three to four, and distribute a copy of the worksheet to each group.

3. Have groups work on defining, unpacking, applying, and decentering: *Defining* means to arrive at a common definition for the characteristic. *Unpacking* invites the group to explore how the concept plays out in each member's personal life. *Applying* is to find the connections between the characteristic of Whiteness and schooling. *Decentering* is to identify ways in which group members challenge or replace the characteristics of Whiteness with other contrasting ideals.

4. Based on each group's level of readiness, have group members construct the meanings of the terms listed below on their own, or ask them to refer back to meanings presented in this chapter.

   Universal perspective

   Individualism

   Avoidance

   Decontextualization

5. Bring the groups back together and debrief the experience.

6. Have participants reflect in their Courageous Conversation Journal on the concept of Whiteness and how it informs their understanding of race and their own personal racial identity.

SIXTH CONDITION OF COURAGEOUS CONVERSATION

Examine the presence and role of Whiteness, its impact on the conversation, and the problem being addressed.

DECENTERING WHITENESS

This exercise assists educators in defining, unpacking, applying, and decentering Whiteness. Participants should complete each column in the table to develop a fuller understanding of how White consciousness impacts teaching and learning.

DECENTERING WHITENESS

Whiteness	Defining: What does it mean?	Unpacking: What does it mean in my life?	Applying: What does it look like in my work?	Decentering: How do I challenge it in my work?
Universal perspective				
Individualism				
Avoidance				
Decontextualization				

REV HILLSTROM

RACIAL AUTOBIOGRAPHY

I have shared my racial autobiography with thousands of people; however I have never been asked to write it. As a person who places great value in oral tradition, I find this exercise to be quite difficult, as it seems to limit my adaptive response to the people with whom I am sharing. My hope is that somehow my story finds its life and frees itself from the printed page and into the heart of the reader.

As a person of both indigenous and European descent, I am often confronted with the reality that I do not have the right to claim membership in either racial group, as I simply am not White enough for the one, and I am too White for the other. As I explore Whiteness and racial identity, I have come to know that my racial identity lies often between how I perceive myself, how others perceive me, and how the three main characteristics of race (color, culture, consciousness) impact me and others in attempts to classify me racially.

I was born Michael Crowley in October of 1965 in a small sleepy town in southern Iowa. My family relocated to the western suburbs of Minneapolis, Minnesota, where I live today. Though the timeline is uncertain, it was shortly thereafter that my mother (white) and father (mixed) divorced, leaving me no access to my father, who moved to Coldwater, Kansas, where he spent the majority of his remaining days.

My mother, a beautiful, industrious, resourceful woman, remarried a white male of Finnish descent while I was still preschool age. Based upon this union, an agreement was made that my father would remain out of my life and that I would be raised as the child of this man. This led to a formal adoption in which my name and, arguably, my racial identity changed. My father's name was also Michael Crowley, and everything he was, in one stroke of a pen, was removed from me.

This new family structure provided my first memorable racial experience. I remember one bright summer day playing with my new cousins when my would-be grandmother asked me and the other children, "Why is that boy so brown?" Until then I never gave it much thought, but looking at my cousins and other relatives, I realized she was right: In comparison, I was much darker than they were, and to be honest, I liked it. I liked the way I looked and felt that I was the fortunate one who did not need greasy lotions to avoid sunburn and that I did not have to deal with the pain and discomfort of the consequences of it wearing off. These utopian dreams of family eventually dissipated, and by the time I was 7 years old, I lived in an environment of severe physical and psychological abuse. By age 10, I had had enough, and I convinced my mother that I needed my father back in my life, so a trip was planned to Coldwater, Kansas, for me to meet him.

That weekend was foundational in my development as an indigenous person. It may be hard to imagine, but as a young boy who had lived through what I had, I had developed a belief that if only my absent father had been present, much of my trauma could have been avoided. He would have addressed all my lifelong questions about why I wasn't loved and accepted by others, especially my family, and why I was browner than most children, and even more complex questions like my unique relationship with spirits and animals. I entered the weekend with high expectations of my father, and to be honest, every word he spoke might as well have been the gospel truth, because I needed a savior.

I could go on and on about that weekend, but for the purpose of this story I want to share one life-changing conversation between my father and me. During this conversation, my father gave me four things:

The first was a belt: I asked "Daddy what is this for?" to which he responded, "to think twice before I take my pants off." At age 10, I failed to see the wisdom in that statement, however as I grew older, this directive has proven invaluable, and to this day I wear a belt daily.

The second item my father gave me was a pocket "Buck" knife. I remember asking him "Daddy what is this for?" His response was "It is a tool that if used properly will serve you well and if needed can be used to protect yourself." This advice has shown itself to be true too as my father suggested. I remember being an adult in my 30s attending Augsburg College as an undergrad. I was in the chemistry lab doing an experiment that required the use of a Bunsen burner and a paper filter. I noticed that many of my classmates had failed to keep their paper filters from starting on fire, thus producing inaccurate results from their experiments due the fact that the end mass measurement was compromised, because the paper filter had been destroyed by fire. Seeing this, I chose to pull my knife out from my pocket and use it move around my paper filter and keep it from burning. Much to my surprise, a young white female classmate yelled at the top of her lungs "weapon!" This triggered the response from me, "I can protect us!" Fortunately the professor, who was chair of the department, pulled me aside and advised me that a knife like mine was considered a weapon and that the school had a zero tolerance policy with respect to weapons, which in theory required that I be expelled permanently. But due to his cultural sensitivity, knowledge of this incident never went past his office, and because of that I was able to stay in college; I became the first indigenous person to graduate from Augsburg summa cum laude with a double major. Eventually I went on to get a masters degree and a doctorate. Without that chemistry professor's effective cultural lens, none of this would have happened; I would have been expelled.

The third item my father gave me was a single shot .410 shotgun. After receiving this gift, as before, I asked him "Daddy what is this for?" This time he replied, "If you learn how to use this, you will never go hungry, and you will be able to provide for your family." Never was there a comment about using it as a weapon.

The fourth and last item my father gave me was a hat. As my Daddy placed the hat on my head I asked again, "What is this for? " He paused and said, "This is a little different. You know you're an Indian." I said, "Yes, I have always known." He went on to say this hat would help and protect me. I learned from him that

(Continued)

(Continued)

the hat would help me to think twice before I let things in or out of my head. He told me stories of how our relatives used a head covering when dealing with the White man as a form of protection. This lesson taught me to be cautious of White society, and I had already experienced the need for this caution countless times. I have worn a hat every day of my life since then. Today, my father's advice reminds me both to be proud of my Indian heritage and to heed the lessons of it.

Twenty years went by after that one and only miracle weekend before I met my father again at age 30. Unfortunately the pages of this and a hundred other books could not contain the gifts of knowledge that have been shared with me surrounding my own indigenous identity. Suffice to say that my racial development was first sparked by a consciousness that led to my cultural development in a way that affirms my indigenous identity. This racial development occurred in spite of the way I appear to many people, which is as a White person.

That weekend illuminated my understanding and set me on a lifetime pathway of studying indigenous epistemology and pedagogy. From that weekend forward, I became a different type of learner who has come to recognize that we are all relatives, truly interconnected on countless levels, and over the years through both my dominant-culture education and my indigenous holistic approach to learning, I have begun to internalize that all knowledge that is, has been, and ever will be has always existed. And that real, meaningful learning occurs through developing a relationship with the knowledge at its indigenous source—not in the arrogant misconception that I in my own humanity (Whiteness) can create or discover knowledge.

As I attempt to put this all in context of my racial autobiography, I am reminded of an intense ceremonial time in my life, where I had been placed on a hill to pray and fast. At this life-changing time, I was given the name "Tall Staff." The medicine man who placed me on the hill shared many things with me regarding my name and said that with time my understanding would grow regarding my name and the responsibilities that my name carried. This name has shaped every aspect of my being both personally and professionally. I now understand that as Tall Staff I am obvious for all to see, and that like a staff, which serves as the place in an altar to have things tied to and from, I now too must serve as that place to make connections to and from.

PART 3 PERSISTENCE
The Key to Racial Equity Leadership

In US education, our beliefs have perpetually conflicted with our reality. For example, educators say we believe that *all* children *can* learn, but reality shows that many are not learning. The perennial racial achievement disparities between White students and most students of color and indigenous student groups have been among the more persistent and reliable education statistics. Perhaps we have not expended sufficient time, effort, or resources necessary to eliminate these gaps. Even clearer, however, is the fact that we have not maintained explicit focus on the way in which race impacts achievement. Thus, *persistence* is the third characteristic of racial equity leadership.

Persistence in this work means staying the course in pursuit of equity. Persistent educators consistently and collectively push forward with their transformation strategies. They take the time to learn what is needed to improve instructional effectiveness, and they commit to achieving the necessary results, no matter how difficult the challenges may be. Persistent educators acknowledge and confront the real fears that arise when challenging status quo policies, programs, and practices. We lead the way to equity as if there were no tomorrow, ever mindful of the fact that powerful resistance and systemic retaliation can line our pathway to justice.

With the passage of the No Child Left Behind Act in 2000, Race to the Top in 2009, and other related legislation, educators are now held to a higher standard and greater accountability—that *all* children *must* learn. The No Child Left Behind Act's statement of purpose explicitly requires schools to engage in "closing the achievement gap between high- and low-performing children, especially the achievement gaps between White students and students of color or indigenous students, and between economically disadvantaged children and their more advantaged peers." The Obama administration reified this central focus on equity in Race to the Top legislation. For more than a decade, federal legislation has mandated that educators be persistent in their efforts to eliminate racial achievement disparities, affording *all* students the opportunity to meet rigorous standards.

Key to addressing and eliminating racial achievement disparities is increasing teacher effectiveness with students of color and indigenous students in the classroom. Studies have shown the dramatic long-term effect on achievement when students consistently have effective versus ineffective teachers (The Education Trust, 2009). Educators have little control over students' background or the challenging experiences their students will bring with them to school. What school systems can impact, however, is the quality and preparation of teachers. Educators can also make decisions about class size, access to resources, and opportunities for academic enrichment, each judged through the lens of equity. When educators fail to provide an effective in-school learning environment for students, the uncontrollable, external mitigating factors have a more devastating impact on student achievement.

Some educators have been informed about the various types of reforms needed to eliminate racial achievement disparity. Unfortunately, systemic transformation is often thought of as simply a technical challenge that requires structural changes throughout the system. In other words, educators often believe that by implementing some "silver bullet" strategies and perhaps a redesign in the schedule, program, or personnel, the gap will go away.

However, lasting transformation is not merely technical or structural, nor does it result from a series of random acts of equity or pockets of excellence in the system. It requires that we as educators first imagine a new way of delivering education—and then embrace it. Central to this type of transformation are cultural changes that engage us, first and foremost, in deep, personal, introspection around our beliefs about the impact of race in our own lives. Understanding who we are, racially speaking, both in our perspective as well as in reality, is the initial step to engaging systemic transformation. Next, we must conduct a thoughtful examination of our mental models about the ability of all students, but particularly the ability of students of color and indigenous students, to perform at the highest levels. This will help us minimize the distortion that predictably arises when we think of ourselves as colorblind, an attitude that contributes to our being unconscious of racial differences. To eliminate racial achievement disparities, we must confront our own racial beliefs and attitudes before we can facilitate classroom changes to effectively engage students of color and indigenous students, as well as consider how we teach to the standards and assess mastery of academic subjects.

Maintaining focus along this personal and professional, multilevel course of action is difficult, but persistence is the key to racial equity leadership, precisely because systemic transformation, involving cultural and structural change, is hard to orchestrate; it takes a great deal of time to achieve sustainable results. Without persistence, however, we will continue to drift from one school improvement initiative to the next without developing capacity for lasting, systemic change. *With* persistence, we will have the time and support we need to personally and professionally develop, apply, reflect, revise, and master the necessary knowledge and skills to guarantee success for all students.

ELEVEN

How Racial Equity Leaders Eliminate Systemic Racial Disparities

Adolescents of color really begin to think about their identities during adolescence. That's an important time to explore racial and ethnic identity. While White youth are also exploring their identity at this time, they usually aren't exploring the racial aspects of that identity. So, it's not uncommon to find adolescents of color actively exploring identity, which manifests itself in styles of dress, patterns of speech, music, and who they hang out with in the corridors of their schools.

All of this is happening in the presence of White teachers who have no personal history with that type of identity exploration, nor have they given much thought to their own identities, even in midlife. If one person is having an experience that another has not shared or even thought about, it's easy to see where there can be misunderstanding and conflict. This is particularly true when adults respond by telling youngsters not to do the things associated with their identity exploration: Don't wear those clothes, don't listen to that music, don't talk that way, don't sit together in the cafeteria.

—Beverly Daniel Tatum (quoted in Sparks, 2004, p. 49)

Critical to the academic success of students of color and indigenous students is having quality relationships with their teachers and the other adults in school. As Tatum suggests here, it is important for educators to understand the cultural identity of their students. Likewise, educators need to empathize with where students of color and indigenous students find themselves, racially speaking, and what their experiences are. By offering their students the racial understanding, empathy, and compassion they need, educators begin to develop their effectiveness with students of color and indigenous students.

Now that we have explored the Protocol, Four Agreements, Six Conditions, and Compass of Courageous Conversation, we want to briefly focus on some areas for their application in schools and districts. Although my references in this chapter primarily highlight preK–12 system implementation, my work with institutions of higher education, government agencies, and community-based organizations over the past decade assures me that the Courageous Conversation protocols and framework are both relevant to and applicable in these environments as well. As educators and others utilize and master the Courageous Conversation protocol as their prevailing strategy for discourse, they have opportunities to examine more closely theories and practices aimed at eliminating racial achievement disparities. Courageous Conversation lifts the unconscious veil of colorblindness and silence and requires educators to develop their racial consciousness in a way that is humane and productive.

INVISIBILITY VERSUS HYPERVISIBILITY

Curtis Linton and many educators with whom I work grew up in an almost entirely White environment where they never had to acknowledge their White racial experience. In contrast, at a very young age, my friends of color and I encountered racially unconscious White people, which forced us to acknowledge our race and actively engage in our racial identity development. Most of the time, Curtis is racially invisible—he is rarely labeled or set apart for being White. For the most part, he is required to recognize his Whiteness only when he deliberately places himself in a racially diverse context in which race is acknowledged. On the other hand, I have experienced hypervisibility ever since I ventured out of my nurturing Black community to attend a White independent school. Every day, I am forced to acknowledge my race. Whether I am vacationing, working, worshiping, or socializing, I am defined and responded to, all over the world, first and foremost as a Black man, whether or not I choose to be labeled as such.

To illustrate the hypervisibility I experienced in school, imagine that the black dot in Figure 11.1 is a Black student, and the circle represents his school environment or context. Traditionally, the white space between the circle and the Black student has not been defined; in other words, when asked what surrounds the black dot, most people would say *nothing*. When nothing is noticed within the circle except for the Black student, the White context or White cultural backdrop is neutralized or made invisible, and all dark dots, by virtue of their color contrast, stick out or are hypervisible. This same racial phenomenon can be witnessed in the experience of other student of color groups and indigenous student groups.

Figure 11.1   One Black Student

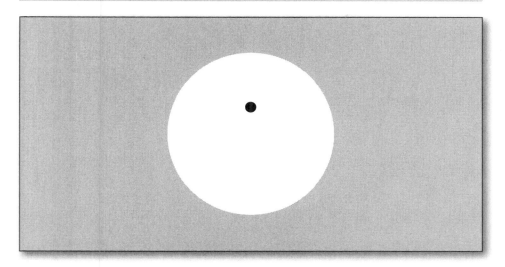

Rather than simply representing an empty circle, this space actually comprises a plethora of white dots—or White students and adults. But their Whiteness is only made apparent by the Black dot—or the student of color or indigenous student. When several students of color are grouped together amid the larger number of White people, they become even more noticeable and may even threaten the White dots' sense of entitlement to the entire space. As described in the book by Beverly Tatum, "*Why Are All the Black Kids Sitting Together in the Cafeteria?*" (1997), Black students grouped together become hypervisible and draw disproportionate attention to themselves, as illustrated in Figure 11.2.

Figure 11.2   Black Students Grouped Together

When only the associations of Black, Brown, Asian, or Indigenous students are recognized or scrutinized, the larger group of White students is left invisible in terms of color, culture, and consciousness. This is not to say that we do not notice the White students' presence, but rather their color, culture, and consciousness are viewed as normal and appropriate. Thus, these factors are not scrutinized or examined.

To authentically understand and address the needs of the students of color, the White students and their culture must also be acknowledged or made visible, as shown in Figure 11.3. Only then can we recognize the ways in which White culture impacts the educational experience of students of color and indigenous students.

Figure 11.3 White Students Made Visible

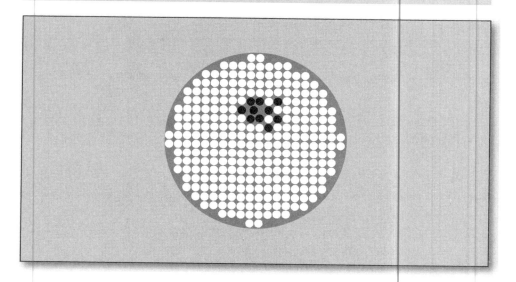

Along with a pursuit of racial equity comes an emerging sense of empathy. A lone White student within a school of Brown or Asian students also becomes hypervisible, as shown in Figure 11.4. As unfair as it seems to single out this White student, it is equally problematic that educators continuously single out the students of color or indigenous students among the larger White student population.

A reality in schools, however, has been that the students of color and indigenous students, but not the White students, tend to be dealt with inequitably, because of their race, racial culture, and racial consciousness. Experience tells me that many White Americans find it painful to see that people of color and indigenous people continue to have it so tough in life due to racism. It is equally uncomfortable to acknowledge that White racial privilege remains a staple ingredient in American culture and that an informal racial support system affords every White person an easier and more humane day.

When White privilege persists in schools without acknowledgment, and when Whiteness in schools remains invisible, White educators may experience difficulty seeing how different life is for students of color and indigenous students, whose

Figure 11.4 One White Student

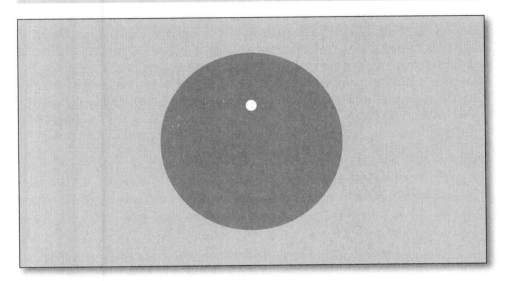

race and racial culture are hypervisible. With White privilege comes an unconscious skepticism about or dismissal of the racial perspective or experience of
people of color and indigenous people, and an insensitivity toward the White racial
backdrop of North American society and of other parts of the Western world.
Understanding the concepts of racial hypervisibility and racial invisibility in
schools is crucial as we build a system of educators who persist in their racial
equity leadership work.

REFLECTION

Have you observed hypervisibility among students of color or indigenous
students in your school? How does recognition and scrutiny of them
compare to the treatment afforded to White students?

UNDERSTANDING STUDENTS OF COLOR AND INDIGENOUS STUDENTS WITHIN A WHITE SCHOOL

People have often posed the question, If race matters in schooling, then why do
Asian students do so well? I believe that expectations play a significant role in
this regard. Asian people have been labeled by the dominant White race as the
"model minority," and they are encouraged and supported by White people to act

accordingly. Whereas White Americans, collectively speaking, use positive racial characteristics—intelligent, hardworking, quiet, and unassuming—to define Asians, Black, Brown, and Indigenous students are often defined as academically at risk, gang-affiliated, and lazy, among other negative descriptions. The key concept, however, is that the achievement of all students is typically measured against White student performance. White students are considered to be the norm, reference group, or standard, and so their performance as a racial group is rarely examined or questioned. To understand why certain groups of students outperform others requires familiarity with phenomena such as *stereotype threat*; such understanding allows us to better interpret achievement disparities existing between and among student racial groupings.

Stereotype Threat

Researcher Joshua Aronson (2004) has stated,

Stereotype threat and the responses it elicits can play a powerful role in the relatively poor achievement of certain students—African Americans, Latinos, and girls in math-oriented domains. . . . Understanding stereotype threat has the potential to help educators narrow persistent achievement gaps. (p. 14)

Through the powerful research that he has done with Claude Steele (2011), Aronson has not only discovered reasons for Black and Brown students' lowered achievement but has also shown how stereotype threat diminishes the achievement of White students when they are placed in direct competition with Asian students.

According to Aronson (2004), students negotiate stereotype threat when they are made aware of any stereotype existing in an academic setting, whether negative or positive, and they will almost always perform accordingly. In their research, Steele and Aronson have administered tests to college students—primarily grouped by race or gender. Before the examination, the researchers announce that they are administering a test that will disprove a stereotype, such as that Asians are better at math than Whites, that Whites perform better than Blacks, that males achieve higher than females in science, and so on. The same tests are administered to a control group, but with no reminder of the stereotype before the exam is taken. Comparing results, Steele and Aronson have repeatedly shown that the contrasted student groups—Asians and Whites, for example—can achieve equally well but will achieve according to the stereotype if they are reminded of its existence in explicit or even unintentional ways.

What their data suggest is that the stereotype threat can trigger acceleration or remediation in student performance; over time, this will determine the level of student engagement and success or the lack thereof. Educators, therefore, need to engage in conversation about how racial stereotypes "in the air" impact student performance and what educators might do to identify and mitigate these harmful messages.

REFLECTION

How have you personally been affected by stereotype threat? Have students with whom you have worked also been affected by stereotype threat? How might educators assist students in overcoming stereotype threat?

Third Culture and Racial Isolation

Indigenous people and other people of color who strive to conform to White culture and or embrace White racial consciousness often find themselves living in what we define as a *Third Culture*—always striving but never succeeding at fitting into Whiteness, and no longer culturally accepted within their own primary racial culture either.

When I first arrived at the predominately White independent school, I realized that for the first time, all of my teachers were White. This was not my typical experience: All but one of my elementary school teachers were Black. When I asked why this was the case, the principal asked, "Why does it matter?" Speaking from their White racial consciousness, the White educators, collectively, had no correlating experience of being the only White person in an institutional context. However, I—a young student who was quite conscious of my racial difference—needed to know who in this school might connect to the culture from which I came. Who would understand my references? Who would be able to accurately read my expressions? And who would be able to effectively communicate with my family? From the dominant White culture, the response "Why does it matter?" essentially puts the question back on the students posing it. This response informs these students that their inquiry is irrelevant, and their search for meaning, no matter how honest or personal, is basically misguided or even inappropriate. Furthermore, I essentially was being told by my principal and teachers that "race doesn't matter," yet, I was constantly reminded of my racial difference: White students would not date me, they told racist jokes around me, they sometimes would not invite me to their parties, and they investigated my culture as though it was foreign and derelict.

By the end of my first year at this school, I learned that I was not supposed to ask racially loaded questions, and eventually, I stopped thinking about race altogether. To accommodate this high-power school setting, I had to redefine my entire life in a White cultural way. What happened to me—and what happens to other students of color in racially isolated situations—is that they begin to see themselves as inadequate. At school, the only Black adults I saw were the custodians, cooks, and bus drivers, further reinforcing and affirming in my mind, as well as in the minds of my White classmates, notions of White supremacy.

Although their situation may not be as extreme as the one I endured, indigenous students and students of color experience racial isolation in a White-dominated school context during the day and often find their own primary culture—say, their primary language, icons, and community affiliations—increasingly foreign and distant. This is what we mean by a Third Culture experience: racially speaking, neither here nor there. I wasn't truly gaining the privileges of those having White skin, but I was losing contact and connection with my Blackness on a daily basis. In essence, I was forced to trade my kinship and alliance with people of color for a possibility of episodic inclusion in the White cultural enclave of high academic achievement and overall scholastic success.

REFLECTION

Can you think of people who have existed in a racial Third Culture? What can you recall about their experience of negotiating two distinct racial cultures? In what ways have they attempted to reconnect with their own culture, or is their struggle to be viewed and accepted as White more pronounced?

UNDERSTANDING SYSTEMIC WHITE RACISM

In order for systemic White racism to persist as the status quo, it must be supported and reinforced or institutionalized. As shown in Figure 11.5, institutionalized White racism can be pictured as a tabletop supported by four legs: internalized White racism, interracial White racism, intraracial White racism, and reverse White racism. Systemic racism can be viewed as the glue and nails that hold the entire table together or those aspects that ultimately yet often discretely assure its functionality. Only at this latter level of racial analysis do we understand race to be something beyond one's individual skin color, culture, and/ or consciousness and to be a system of power afforded to those willing to embrace White, racially dominant beliefs about and behaviors toward people of color and indigenous people.

Internalized White racism presents itself differently in a White person than it does in an indigenous person or person of color, although the result is the same— diminishment of all people who are not White. For White people, internalized White racism may range from the radical White supremacist rhetoric espoused by the Ku Klux Klan to more passive acts of White supremacy exemplified by White people who fail to notice when people of color and indigenous people, their ideas, or their contributions are not present or are not sought after in professional meetings or social gatherings.

For people of color and indigenous people, internalized White racism can appear in active forms of self-hatred as well as a more subtle, perhaps passive form of disapproval of other people of color because they lack White color, culture, or consciousness. For a time in my life, I recall believing that I was not attractive to

Figure 11.5 A View of Systemic White Racism

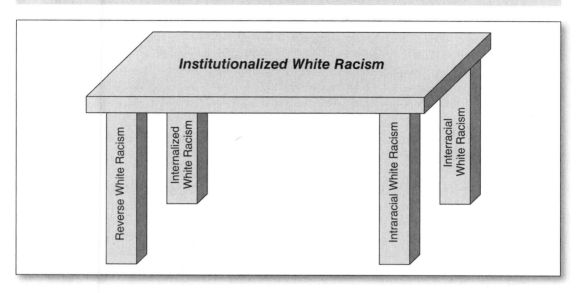

others because of my hair texture and dark skin and eye pigmentation. I wanted to look like the many White icons and images that my school held up as what is perfect, beautiful, and smart. While I never went as far as to surgically reshape my face and features, straighten my hair, or bleach my skin, as many in communities of color have, I was still quite active in embracing and promoting the White cultural norms. Passively, internalized White racism presents itself as an unconscious belief by people of color that White people are superior. In these instances, people of color fail to realize that they do not associate with other people of color and do not feel the need to seek the professional or personal company of members of their own racial group. Ironically, White people who choose not to personally or professionally comingle with people of color often are frowned upon by their progressive White counterparts. However, when persons of color lack any connection or association with other people of color, they are hailed by progressive White people as open, friendly, and desirable. As one who walked this very common racial path for many years, I am edified by the multitudes of White friends who "complimented" me on the fact that they did not think of me as Black.

Interracial White racism occurs when different groups of color are in conflict with one another over their positions relative to the dominant racial culture and their proximity to White racial power, as pictured on top of the table. For example, in the mid to late nineties, California's Black and Brown educators were battling each other for a share of bilingual funding. In the moment, neither disempowered group had time to recognize that several powerful White policymakers and large numbers of voters were quietly working to eliminate all English as a Second Language (ESL) programming and budgets. Interracial struggles between marginalized groups of color only diminish the power of the groups of color and increase White racial power. Thus, people of color and indigenous people who are in racial conflict with one another are promoting or perpetuating White racism even without the presence of White people.

Intraracial White racism typically occurs among members within a particular group of color. For example, some indigenous people predictably will assimilate into the White culture to a larger degree than other native people. These varying levels of assimilation or resistance to Whiteness may result in a clash between different indigenous people, which threatens solidarity among native people as they work to collectively challenge White supremacy. Once again, we observe struggles among Brown and Asian students based on when their families immigrated to the United States. Divisions among Latinos challenge their solidarity when they need to challenge White privilege and White cultural imperialism.

Often, however, the racial implications of these intraracial struggles are masked, because the formative topic seems to be language preservation and acquisition or immigration status, rather than race. The reality is that these issues are important mainly to White Americans, because speaking Spanish challenges the English-only culture that has held in place monolingual White leadership and power. Similarly, federal immigration policy will determine how quickly the United States of America advances to an inevitable Brown majority. The rapid growth of the Latino population carries with it the power of numbers: the ability to vote into political office Brown people and Brown perspective. A racial group divided cannot threaten White privilege, presence, and power to the same degree. Thus, intraracial White racism defines yet another process through which people of color promote and perpetuate White supremacy.

Reverse White racism, which seems to get the greatest attention in this entire construct of systemic White racism, is characterized by strong feelings of discontent, mainly among White people. As I mention in this book's introduction, it is here that White Americans collectively speak out against and target for elimination affirmative action or any programs that would funnel opportunities toward people of color and indigenous people that were once denied to them. Because Whiteness is characterized by a sense of entitlement, White people fail to recognize that White students also gain admission to college not because of individual merit but because they are children of alumni or because of other family connections to the sources of institutional power. Reverse White racism seems to be somewhat a misnomer, because many "qualified" White students do not gain admission to the college of their choice. But why are the relatively few admitted students of color the focus of White American scrutiny rather than the larger number of White students who gain admissions for reasons other than their personal merit or academic accomplishments? What confuses matters even more is the people of color and indigenous people who challenge the legitimacy of affirmative action because of the scrutiny and backlash they endure from their White peers on campus. In my former days as an admissions director at an Ivy League university, I often told the students of color whom I advised, "If a light shined down on the campus and identified all students who did not 'earn' their way into this university through higher than mean tests scores and grades, disproportionately and overwhelmingly illuminated would be White students. So often, the very students who did the least to gain admission to the university feel the most entitled to their coveted place in the class."

Finally, institutionalized White racism can be viewed as the policies, practices, and programs that intentionally or unintentionally perpetuate dominant White racial presence, positioning, and power. In school systems, these aspects are reflected through HR protocols that continuously attract, employ, and promote White educators over people of color and indigenous people. Examples of institutionalized racism are also evident in curricular and instructional choices as well as "zero tolerance" discipline policies. Institutional racism is foundational in the way many school systems have designed attendance boundaries or determined selection criteria for gifted programs or qualification and placement into special education.

While the tabletop sits visibly as the most functional part of the structure, its functionality is supported by the strength of its legs. In short, the table represents the full construct of White racism that is reinforced into a system by an abundance of nails and/or glue for integrity and strength. For many, challenges to racism are often focused on the system as a whole. Unfortunately, such a strategy of naming the systemic racial challenges can often leave otherwise powerful people in the system, both individually and collectively, not understanding exactly what to do to minimize the impact of racism. By addressing how we each, individually, perpetuate white racism in our practices, we can then, collectively, challenge the policies we have created and program we have enacted to guide our institutions. Such a process of advancing from our personal, local, immediate impact of race through our professional engagements truly fosters accelerated organizational transformation. This process of dismantling systemic racism through Courageous Conversation is the hallmark of racial equity leadership.

> Of the five parts of systemic White racism (four legs and table top), which do you identify with most: *reverse, internalized, intraracial, interracial,* or *institutional?* Which do you identify with least? In what ways has your school system specifically addressed or challenged systemic White racism?

REFLECTION

THE INJUSTICE OF GRADUALISM AND INCREMENTAL CHANGE

In recent decades, some people of color and indigenous people have advanced into jobs and moved into neighborhoods where they were once excluded, thus creating a belief that with time and hard work, the North American racial power imbalance will just disappear. This conclusion is challenged by critical race theorists, including Derrick Bell (1992), Gloria Ladson-Billings (2006; Ladson-Billings & Tate, 1994) and Richard Delgado and Jean Stefancic (2012). Their racial critique is grounded in evidence that indicates important shifts in racial power or systemic White racism are not gradual or unintentional. South Africa, for example, had two Black presidents in the first decade after the end of apartheid, whereas only seven senators have populated the US Senate since the passage of the 1964 US Civil Rights Act. It is only in the last six years that the United States of America can boast of having a president who is not a White male. Absent a narrative that speaks to the inherent racism of incremental change, one will be hard pressed to offer a reason why no person of color has before been elected to this highest place of leadership.

Presidents Bill Clinton and George W. Bush both have claimed to have hired the most diverse Cabinets ever assembled, asserting that progress is being made. Critical race theorists ask who is setting the schedule for achieving racial proportionality and balance. Real racial gains are painstakingly slow, both in US government and in our schools. The comparative rarity of Black and Brown superintendents of schools is a prime example of slow transformation. Critical race theorists argue that gradualism or support for incremental racial change is a major reason for the permanence of systemic White supremacy. While people of color and indigenous people are urged to be patient by those in power, access to opportunity, excellence, and leadership remain the property of Whiteness, no matter how much "progress" has been made.

REFLECTION

In what ways has gradualism and a preference for incremental change challenged your own development and progress as well as that of educators and students (indigenous and/or of color) in your school system?

In conversations focused around the themes of this chapter, the actual color of one's skin becomes less of a factor as one's knowledge about race, racial identity, and systemic White racism grows. Understanding how, when, and where race intersects with schooling allows educators to learn from each other and engage their students. Only through this heightened engagement of our students of color and indigenous students will school systems experience transformation that ensures success for all students. The purpose of Courageous Conversation is not to accomplish gradual change in our systems, but to urgently and radically embrace the possibility of eliminating racial achievement disparities. Such disruptive and accelerated racial equity leadership must be our moral and professional imperative.

IMPLEMENTATION EXERCISE

DEFINING THE INTERSECTION OF RACE AND SCHOOLING

Time required: 30 minutes

Materials required: Courageous Conversation Journal for each participant, and chart paper, red and blue markers, and tape for each group

1. Re-create the invisibility and hypervisibility charts at the beginning of this chapter and present the concept to your staff.

2. Divide participants into small multiracial groups.

3. Distribute two pieces of chart paper, one red and one blue marker, and tape to each group.

4. Have groups label one sheet "Staff Barriers" and the other sheet "Student Barriers."

5. Have each group divide into two teams, one being White educators and the other being educators of color and indigenous educators.

6. Ask educators of color, using the red marker, to list staff barriers to closing the racial achievement gap, and ask White educators, using the blue marker, to list student barriers to closing it. Give both groups five minutes to list as many barriers as they can.

7. After five minutes, have the groups switch posters and continue working on the other list for five more minutes. Each piece of chart paper should have entries written in both red and blue.

8. Have the White educators, the educators of color and indigenous educators come back together in their small group and reflect on what was written.

9. Bring all the groups back together and reflect on the experience. What was discovered? What ideas emerged? What are the most common barriers that exist both for staff and for students? How did the race of the work group affect the responses listed?

10. Have the participants personally reflect in their Courageous Conversation Journal.

COURTLANDT BUTTS

RACIAL AUTOBIOGRAPHY

As early as I can remember, I was fascinated with the world itself and how things work. Growing up in Philadelphia, my early years offered very interesting experiences. Everybody in my neighborhood and surrounding community was Black. I saw different "colors" of people on television, and my family would often venture downtown for shopping or business, where a variety of people of different economic statuses, religions, shapes, sizes, and colors were present. But I didn't give it much thought. Based on the religious practices of my parents and grandparents, the first thought I remember having was that's the way God made them. Though I noticed people were different colors, I did not have a significant consciousness or understanding of race until I was four years old in preschool. This was the beginning of my racial life.

My brother and I attended Mrs. Slaughter's preschool in West Philadelphia. Mrs. Slaughter, a brilliant Black woman, was once a teacher in the Philadelphia school system, but then she left to start her own educational institution. As a result of her love and commitment, at four years of age I tested at a third-grade reading level under the Philadelphia Public School System evaluation. (This test had been requested by my mother.) This elevated reading comprehension level was the norm amongst my classmates. Mrs. Slaughter would often say, when our academic performance was praised, "Why should you or I expect anything less?"

In Mrs. Slaughter's class, we were asked what we wanted Santa to bring us for Christmas. When it was my turn, I asked for a Tonka truck. My friend Jennifer asked for a baby doll. My friend Tamera asked for a baby doll as well. Then, in an almost panicked disposition, Tamera raised her hand again and said, "Make sure it's a white baby doll!"

At that time, I did not recognize skin color as significant. I'm innocently looking at Tamera thinking, "Well that's cool, because sometimes I like playing with my brown horse, sometimes my white horse, and sometimes my polka dot horse. Maybe she needs a white doll to complete her collection." Mrs. Slaughter repeatedly asked the dark-skinned Tamera, who was as brown as I was, "Why don't you want a baby doll that looks like you?" Soon Tamera began to cry and looked to me as if I were going to help her. But I was both confused and silent. From that moment on, I perceived my friend Jennifer as my White friend Jennifer. Then I noticed she was the only White girl in class. After school I ran to my best friend J.J.'s house. Hours earlier, I hadn't known his parents were a mixed race couple. Now I asked him, "Did you know your mom was White?"

Since the doll experience, I have applied a new lens when viewing the world, and I am certain I have had countless experiences navigating race and racism. As a Black male in the United States, the older I get, the more intense are these experiences. My personal encounters moved from what I once viewed as isolated occurrences to profound and repeated systemic patterns. By third grade and for all of my elementary schooling across three states, I was taught by White teachers, exclusively.

Reflecting on my experiences through sixth grade, I was fortunate to have supportive and nurturing teachers, none of whom ever broached the topic of race. For me, coming from an educational experience led by Black teacher leaders to several years where all of my teachers were White, there was a noticeable void in racial dialogue. The racial constructs I internalized were learned at the bus stop, in the community centers, and at recess, where often I was forced to confront race. It was as if an entirely different world, of which my teachers were unaware, existed right in front of them. When my family moved from Camden, New Jersey, to Orlando, Florida, I was called "nigger" by hateful White students and adults in the community more times than I can remember. It wasn't that I never heard that word before, but it sounded different when Richard Pryor or my cousins used it. Some of the White people seemed intent on hurting me and attacking my identity. In the South, color lines were drawn, and someone was sure to sound an alarm if they were crossed, as when my mother tried to enroll my brother and me in the nearest elementary school, which was predominantly White. She literally was told, "You live on the wrong side of the street for them to come here." My mother recently shared with me that she did not have a consciousness of how deeply seeded the systemic racism was, even though she was in the middle of it.

As many middle school–aged preteens are searching for identity, race becomes even more significant. I adopted many of the ways of White friends in my neighborhood as well as many from my cousins and neighbors back in Philly, where hip-hop culture had a huge influence on us. "Who am I?" and "how am I going to be?" were the primary questions with which I struggled during middle school. I was eventually able to fuse the two racial cultures; wearing a style of clothing that many of my White classmates wore along with my hip-hop gear provided me access to and acceptance in both White and Black spaces. This way of being continued on through high school, although there were always personal reminders that I had a predetermined inferior place amongst the racially dominant caste.

There were two pivotal moments in my high school experience that brought clarity to my identity and purpose. My algebra teacher, a White female, convinced me to take two additional years of math even though I completed my requirements early. The second was my high school counselor, Mrs. Reed, an African American woman who reminded me that I was Black and that I had a responsibility to go as far as I could in life. She convinced me to apply to Florida A&M University (FAMU), a school I had never heard of and my classmates had not spoken about. Mrs. Reed described what an HBCU was (historically black college/university) and its importance to the Black community. Given none of my White classmates valued the HBCU, how important could it be? Still, I reluctantly filled out the application, as my internalized Whiteness recalled an expression my grandmother often said, "If it ain't White, it ain't right!"

(Continued)

(Continued)

What attending FAMU did for my Black identity and overall development was extraordinary. I immersed myself in a legacy of excellence where all of my professors looked like me. I was introduced to the history of Black pioneers who were critical to the development of this country, the world, and our human dignity as Black people. I believe one must live through the HBCU experience to truly understand it. FAMU academics were important, but more critical was learning to be real about who and what I am as a Black person. This defining experience prepared me to navigate predominantly White environments and to be mindful of the presence and impact of my own Whiteness.

I carried this charge with me as I furthered my education at the University of Northern Iowa (UNI), where I earned a full scholarship. Although this predominantly White institution had incredible facilities, technology, resources, and highly skilled professors, there was something missing. Because I had a clearer sense of my racial identity after my FAMU experience, I joined with other Black HBCU alumni at UNI to form the Minority Graduate Student Association (MGSA), and I was elected president. Beyond graduate school, I taught at UNI for a while and traveled to 11 different countries before returning to the United States and taking up work at Spelman College, an HBCU for women located in Atlanta, Georgia.

I have a passion for truth, justice, and the development of "Knowing Thyself." It is my most sincere hope that our social systems promote this for our children and families. I am called to continue the work of many who have come before me and supported me throughout my development. Currently, I am an international consultant for racial equity and social justice in education employed by a racially conscious Black man. I wonder if my ever-expanding and deepening racial consciousness and expertise in helping educators identify and address racism ever will be recognized by my society not as militarism or defiance, but as an act of love?

TWELVE

Exploring a Systemic Framework for Achieving Equity in Schools

Solving the problem of racism is America's unfinished agenda, and it must be regarded by educators as a moral imperative.

—Gerald Pine and Asa Hilliard (1990, p. 596)

Think back to the schooling circumstances of EJ, my cousin, which were described in the introduction: EJ was a young Black student adrift in a White-dominated school. Yes, even in a school in which the principal, many of the teachers, and over 90% of the students are Black, EJ's schooling is defined as White dominated because of the overwhelming presence of systemic racism in the Baltimore school system. What would EJ's school look like if it were to become anti-racist and truly equitable? For that matter, pause and consider any student, particularly one who is African American, Latino, Southeast Asian, or Indigenous, with whom you have worked personally and who has struggled in school. Why do these students struggle? Is it simply because of the socioeconomic challenges many of them bring with them to school, or can their difficulty also relate to the known barriers that the school system continues to place in the child's footpath to success?

Now reconsider these children as if they were your own students. What would you want for them that exists within the grasp of educators? Is it more than what is available and accessible to them in school now? Does the school—and do you as an educator—have the same level of expectations for these children as you have for other students? Would you want your own children to have the same relationship with you and other adults in the school that your struggling students of color and indigenous students have? Think of your school system in terms of equity, support, expectations, opportunity, access, and acceptance. Now ask yourself, is your school system adequate for your struggling children of color and indigenous children?

REFLECTION

Consider whether or not you feel that your school system is "good enough" for your own child. How many of your colleagues would choose your school system for their own children? How does this discovery impact your passion for, perspective about, and practice toward improving schooling for our most needy student populations?

A VISION OF EQUITY

If your school is truly equitable, all children arrive each day at a clean, well-resourced, and inviting environment in which the educators are sure of their capabilities, excited about teaching *and* learning, and steadfast in their resolve to dismantle the barriers, such as harmful stereotypes and labels, that block children's freedom to learn. As students enter through the front doors, the principal and other members of the administration, faculty, and staff greet them by name and inquire about a recent personal challenge or triumph as well as the well-being of a supportive family member. Children feel safe and secure in this school, not due to locks, metal detectors, and security guards, but due to their understanding that school has their physical, emotional, intellectual, and spiritual safety at heart.

As they continue into their classrooms, students, again, are warmly and enthu-siastically greeted by the teacher. In class, students are exposed to a rigorous and demanding curriculum that challenges them fully. Students need not worry whether this or any other class is advanced or remedial, because all students are placed in classes that push them to excel, regardless of their skin color, linguistic background, or previous learning challenges. This class is not disproportionately White or discernibly Black, Brown, Indigenous, Asian, or Multiracial; it includes proportional representation of all the students in the school so that no student is isolated racially.

In facilitating learning, teachers are well aware of the individual talents of the students and provide the support that every child needs. The curriculum is respect-ful and reflective of the diversity of students' experiences, cultures, and languages, both those that are represented in the classroom and perhaps some others as well. Furthermore, students see themselves in the curriculum and at times in the instructor, and they are encouraged to relate to both personally. Students can rest assured that every teacher will teach to standards and instruct from a common, viable core curriculum that is used throughout the school. Because learning goals and objectives are clear, students know that the teachers' aim is to promote their mastery of the subject matter. Students never worry that they will be shortchanged in terms of expectations, support, or opportunity to try, fail, try, fail, and try again until they achieve mastery.

Teachers have the freedom to use a variety of research-based teaching methods, activities, and materials as they desire, but they also welcome being held accountable for each student achieving the standards on a regular and timely basis. In our racially equitable school system, teachers know that the institution exists to support them in improving their teaching. There is no retribution or condescension directed toward teachers who attempt to take advantage of the support system or who suggest changes and ways of improving it to better serve *all* students. The teachers work closely as a professional learning community, using disaggregated data and action research to determine how best to reach every child. When one teacher succeeds, methods that led to success are shared with the other teachers in an atmosphere of mutual support, void of turf protection and characterized by a passion or will to achieve excellence schoolwide.

The teachers in this racially equitable school know that they have a voice that matters in its governance. The administration is driven by the needs of the teachers, not by hierarchical positional power of "us versus them" or by mandates that overwhelm rather than support. The administration and faculty together set the standards that the teachers work to achieve. Through their collaboration, they experience the freedom, ownership, and accountability they need to accomplish the job. Administrators are not found in the office or behind a desk somewhere but are seen throughout the campus encouraging students, supporting teachers in classrooms, and addressing school-related problems quickly, efficiently, and completely.

Furthermore, the administration leads the effort to reach out to all parents and members of the community. The school sees the community as an asset, and the community sees the school as a center in the neighborhood. As family members enter the building, they know without a doubt that the school welcomes their presence. Parents and other community members do not feel disenfranchised, nor do they feel intimidated due to their own personal educational attainment, English language skills, racial description, economic status, dress, or perceptions of school derived from their own personal experiences. Families know that their voice matters in school affairs. They are invited, encouraged, and expected to participate in parent–teacher councils, teacher assistance, leadership teams, fund-raising efforts, vision creation, school-improvement projects, and afterschool activities. The families and community members feel ownership of the school, and they are affirmed as a vital part of student success.

As children excel in each and every classroom, they discover for themselves that education does indeed serve them. They begin to believe that they will receive every tool they need to succeed beyond the classroom. As they engage in activities after school, they are treated with respect and dignity. Above all else, they are expected to reach high and supported to succeed often. When students graduate, they exit secure in their knowledge and their abilities. They have not been sheltered, coddled, and limited; they have been pushed to excel beyond their own expectations. Education has fulfilled its mandate with these students, and they are prepared to attain all their hearts desire.

For the past 13 years, we believed that EJ Singleton and other students like him deserved nothing less when they went to school each day. In 2014, EJ graduated from the Baltimore County Public School System equipped with far less than we hoped for and possessing much less than what the world demands of him today. For EJ and countless others like him, our call to transform schools into racially equitable institutions must grow louder and stronger.

> **REFLECTION**
>
> Compare your school to this vision of an equitable school. In what ways is your school system approaching, achieving, or straying away from this vision? Where is your school system strongest, and what is your most noticeable deficiency? Given the current beliefs and behaviors of your colleagues, does it seem possible that your school system could be transformed into the envisioned institution? Why or why not?

SYSTEMIC RACIAL EQUITY TRANSFORMATION

Eliminating racial achievement disparities begins with refocusing schooling on the children's educational needs rather than on the personal needs of the adults who inhabit the buildings or on the needs of the most vocal, privileged, and powerful citizens around the country. Next, leaders from inside and outside the school district must cooperatively determine a set of core values that will guide relationships among the staff, students, and families. These values must exist at the heart of the district's educational philosophy, policies, programmatic structures, and instructional practices. The cultural fabric and structural determinations can be reinforced and sustained by Courageous Conversation, which ensures that all people, issues, and perspectives are welcomed and addressed. Continuous improvement becomes a natural and normal state of affairs for all members of the community.

Transforming District and School Culture

The culture of a school system is based in its language—in the styles and processes of communication that take place among its key stakeholders and constituencies. Consequently, the way to transform district and school culture is to transform the language that is used. Racial achievement disparities cannot be eliminated without talking about race, and specifically talking about the opportunity, access, and success gaps existing between White students and most students of color and indigenous students. Similarly, educators must be able to examine the teaching gap, or the propensity for our most needy students of color and indigenous students to be taught by less trained and accomplished teachers. Effectively talking about such racialized teaching, learning, and performance disparities first requires effectively talking about race. This is why the Courageous Conversation protocol—the Four Agreements, Six Conditions, and Compass—provide the structural and strategic foundation for having conversations about race that are truly transformative systemwide.

Although it is transformative in and of itself, simply talking about race effectively is insufficient. Courageous Conversation needs to fit within a larger framework aimed at total district, school, and classroom improvement. Pacific Educational Group's (PEG's) model for *Systemic Racial Equity Transformation* presents three overlapping domains within which Courageous Conversation guides the dialogue. As illustrated in Figure 12.1, the three domains are community, leadership, and learning and teaching. You will also notice four content and process realms—Courageous Conversation Protocol, Critical Race Theory Tenets, Systems Thinking Tools, and Adaptive Leadership Principles—depicted in the model, the first mentioned being the focus of this book. PEG posits that school leaders must understand and be able to guide their practices using all of these to achieve sustainable, systemic equity transformation. The three remaining components of PEG's theory for transformation are explored in detail in *More Courageous Conversations About Race* (Singleton, 2012), my second book, which is focused on advancing and supporting educators in applying the Courageous Conversation protocol at the personal, professional, and organizational levels.

With the educational needs of *all* children at the center, represented by the six hands, and a set of core values surrounding them, Courageous Conversation will launch educators into deep and sustainable improvements focused around community, leadership, and learning and teaching. As you can see in Figure 12.1, Courageous Conversation is the strategy that encapsulates and defines systemic improvement. In addition, each domain is interconnected with the other domains. Consequently, systemic racial equity transformation occurs where it all converges: at the only place that touches the life and learning of *all* our children.

Pacific Educational Group's framework has evolved out of partnering with a variety of districts over the last two decades, districts that are still striving today to eliminate racial achievement disparities. We have learned that addressing only classroom instruction, only leadership, or only community in isolation is insufficient for sustainable reform. Likewise, talking about difficult issues without focused discussions on how those issues impact teacher–student relationships will leave educators with a broadened perspective but little ability to translate meaningful dialogue into effective classroom practices.

Courageous Conversation holds this holistic transformation framework together. As educators develop their ability to participate in and then facilitate the participation of others in Courageous Conversation, they can better recognize and understand the linkages that exist between dialogue and the domains of systemic transformation. Following is a brief introduction to the three domains: leadership,

Figure 12.1 Pacific Educational Group's Systemic Racial Equity
Transformation Framework

learning, and teaching and community. To further illustrate the complete framework in action, Chapter 13 contains a case study of systemic equity work in progress in St. Paul Public Schools in St. Paul, Minnesota.

REFLECTION

What has been your experience with school reform efforts that focused solely on instruction, leadership, or community in isolation? What kind of dialogue took place during the effort, and how effective was it? What were the results of the effort in terms of improved achievement for all students and especially students of color?

Leadership

Systemic Racial Equity Transformation requires *leadership.* When only a few people in a school system are examining race, sustainable changes that impact overall results will not occur. If achievement is to improve for all student groups, school site and district office leadership need to establish a culture in which effective practice with the Four Agreements, Six Conditions, and Compass of Courageous Conversation is eventually internalized by all educators. If a vision for racial equity is embraced only in selected classrooms, departments, or schools, those educators who are disengaged will simply move to places in the district where fear of transformation, resistance, inequity, and racism remain unaddressed. The value for and focus on racial equity must be systemic to buffer underserved and/or struggling students of color and indigenous students throughout the system from educators unwilling to examine their individual and collective roles in perpetuating racial achievement disparity.

Equity Teams

The district- and school-based Equity Teams or E-Teams include emerging leaders who wish to develop their will, skill, knowledge, and capacity to support their colleagues in understanding race and deinstitutionalizing racism. This leadership development process begins with the system leaders addressing their own beliefs or mental models and then continues into careful examination of their instructional practices. Once this phase of development is in motion, the leaders are poised to engage their colleagues in ongoing, job-embedded professional learning.

Members of E-Teams are not necessarily the typical school leaders, as traditional leadership teams are often defined by seniority or popularity. E-Teams are developed using a different set of criteria. E-Team membership is predicated on having the passion for understanding equity and the courage to lead at the system, school site, or classroom level toward anti-racist education. At the school level, the principal always leads the E-Team, just as a superintendent must offer leadership to the district E-Team. The principal draws the members of the E-Team from the various departments or grade levels, paying close attention to those who will bring to the team credibility, courage, confidence, and compassion.

The responsibility of the E-Team is threefold:

1. Engage in a process of investigation to discover how race impacts their personal and professional beliefs and behaviors.

2. Lead the school or central office staff in the examination of individual and institutional culture as it relates to equity and anti-racism.

3. Establish a professional learning community in which adults can effectively develop skills and knowledge necessary to improve student performance and eliminate racial achievement disparities.

District offices and school sites are not always ready to become places for healthy adult learning. In fact, a significant challenge to improving schooling is that some educators are poised not to learn, but rather to posture as though they "know it all." E-Teams, therefore, must create a community in which adults can learn, a community in which professional learning is repositioned as thoughtful, data-based inquiry rather than a source of quick fixes and trick strategies. Most important, the E-Team professional learning environment must invite emerging leaders to begin from a place of "they don't know what they don't know." That is, otherwise-competent school leaders must feel comfortable asking questions about race and equity, no matter how basic the questions may seem, because only then will educators cease to act from the dangerous place of "they don't know, but they think they do."

Racial equity leadership is incubated and practiced by the E-Teams. As an entire district staff begins to engage in developmental exercises and professional learning led by the E-Teams, its members discover ways of transforming institutional culture and appropriately reforming structures that impede student performance. The cultural shift is evidenced by a Courageous Conversation about race and by an engagement of individual and organizational passion for achieving educational equity. This conversation and passion drive the innovative improvements in how educators organize to design and deliver quality instruction. Over time, racial equity leadership becomes the standard throughout the district.

Learning and Teaching

As a system moves toward effectively designing and delivering quality instruction, thus addressing *learning and teaching,* educators begin to examine their classroom practices through the prism of racial equity. Teachers will often say, "Give me a strategy," but there are two inherent problems with this request: (1) Teachers are not situated to be learners, and (2) they do not understand racial equity. If a teacher is just handed a culturally relevant strategy without first establishing the language or ability to talk about race, that strategy will most likely be used ineffectively, if at all, because the teacher does not understand it or necessarily believe in its relevance.

The E-Team can serve as the bridge between teachers' current understanding and skill level and the vision of quality instruction that they need to reach. E-Teams work to support teachers in their preparation to engage in racial equity work at the classroom level. An E-Team's goal is to develop the teachers' understanding of race through practicing Courageous Conversation and to guide their initial transfer of this conversation back to their classroom. This reflective practice or action research is the key component of the learning and teaching domain.

Educators cannot effectively implement a culturally relevant strategy if they believe themselves to be colorblind or are simply unwilling to examine race in their own lives as well as in the lives of their students. The E-Team is charged with moving a cadre of teachers to a level of readiness where they can more thoughtfully examine and change their classroom practice.

CARE Teams

Engaged teachers who demonstrate readiness to explore at a deeper level in the equity learning community are invited to be members of the CARE Team. CARE stands for Collaborative Action Research for Equity. Race impacts not only the lowest performing students—it impacts all students. Through CARE, teachers analyze a focus group of students to learn how best to teach and support them in their learning.

CARE is designed to support teachers in discovering the challenges in their relationships with students of color and indigenous students and then to improve their instructional delivery accordingly. As a part of CARE, each teacher partners with a focus group of students of color and/or indigenous students to better understand aspects of teaching that positively impact student learning. Engaging student voices and examining student work are central in developing CARE teachers' ability to pinpoint how and when their teaching is most and least effective.

CARE teachers meet approximately every six weeks as a district collaborative and even more frequently as a school team to share what they have learned, observe one another's instruction, and talk about the progress or setbacks of various students in their focus group. Together, CARE teachers discuss, plan, and design rigorous, standards-based lessons that intentionally engage their focus students as well as all other students in the classroom. Within CARE, teachers research and develop strategies that enable them to provide students with greater access to the curriculum and opportunities for meaningful learning.

Community

I define *community* as a network of effective and supportive relationships shared by all throughout the system. Although improving relationships between White teachers and families of color and indigenous families are central to this domain, community also incorporates interactions among administrators, teachers, and students. This work begins with everyone acknowledging that the school represents a community in and of itself and is also a part of an established broader community.

Typically, a school district functions apart from its community, especially in systems with large populations of families of color and indigenous families. The educators typically travel in and out of the community for work, but the students and families remain. Consequently, the entire school community as an entity needs to be engaged in conversations about how an appropriate education for the children in that community should be defined and be delivered.

This conversation—focusing on community education, awareness, engagement, and empowerment—must take into account and give value to the resources that the community provides. One resource is that families have tremendous knowledge about how to be successful with their children in ways the school never sees: in the churches, homes, community organizations, and neighborhood—all institutions that are intricate parts of the established community. Another resource the community holds is the humor, contemporary idioms, and oral histories that educators must reference to connect academic disciplines to the students' real experiences. Likewise, the community is present for the joyous celebrations, rituals, and ceremonies that the students know and value. To the degree that their teachers relate to what is happening in the established, broader community, the children can view teachers as another integral part of their community.

PASS Groups

To facilitate the basic goal of developing and strengthening the institutional appreciation for *community,* the professional, school-based educators and the community-based educators (families, clergy, and government and law enforcement officials) initially need to engage in a different kind of conversation that recognizes and values their disparate experiences. As the third branch of Systemic Racial Equity Transformation, leaders formalize the relationship between the institutional and established community members by organizing PASS Teams. Comprising both types of educators, school based and community based, PASS stands for Partnerships for Academically Successful Students.

The PASS Team recognizes that Courageous Conversation fortifies community. Therefore, members work to institutionalize the Four Agreements, Six Conditions, and Compass of Courageous Conversation in the established community, just as it is internalized in the institutional community. School-based PASS Team members help the community-based educators understand the standards by which the children are measured. The community-based educators help school-based educators understand the community standards. Together, they develop standards that go above and beyond those of the district and state to ensure that students grow into respectful, contributing, and proud citizens of the community. The PASS Team focuses on engaging school-based, central-office, and community-based educators together in the best interests of the students. When any one of these constituencies is disengaged, the entire community experiences deficiency.

To build trust, the community needs to see teachers struggling openly with conversations about race rather than avoiding them. Furthermore, White teachers, especially those working largely in communities of color and indigenous communities, need to witness families and clergy improving their effectiveness in the interracial conversation as well. This innovative form of dialogue is important, because with few exceptions, the communities of color and indigenous communities are isolated and have most likely not had favorable interracial interactions with White educators. Through PASS Teams, students ultimately benefit, as deeper understanding and greater trust is built between school-based and community-based educators, leading to authentic support, improved instruction, and higher student achievement.

Role of the Principal

While engaging the passion, practice, and persistence of both community and district leadership is essential to achieving equity, the principal is the key and guiding force behind equity efforts in a school. Without the principal's full and complete commitment, eliminating racial achievement disparities will be difficult, if not impossible. The principal leads the E-Team, is supervisor of the CARE Team, and is a member of the PASS Team.

The E-Teams are a continuous and growing force until the school culture is permanently and profoundly transformed. The ultimate goal is for every school in the district to live that vision of schooling presented earlier in this chapter. The various teams actualize the equity goal and parlay the initiatives into a current reality of academic success for all children.

As the site leader, the principal specifically translates and transfers the learning of the E-Team, CARE Team, and PASS Team members to the larger staff. The principal should do this work in partnership with teachers and community leaders, perhaps sharing a demonstration lesson or modeling an effective teacher–student–family conference. Teaching adults differs from teaching students, and thus, it is the principal's responsibility to develop the skills set necessary to effectively facilitate adult learning.

> **REFLECTION**
>
> What do you perceive are some inherent benefits of simultaneously focusing on leadership, learning and teaching, and community transformation? In what ways are principals in your system, individually or collectively, exhibiting effectiveness or ineffectiveness in terms of racial equity leadership?

Keeping the focus on student learning is the centerpiece of Systemic Racial Equity Transformation. Courageous Conversation is the strategy that enables educators from the institutional and established communities to focus their efforts on unifying community, developing leadership, and improving learning and teaching. As this framework is translated and transferred by site and district leaders—and particularly by principals—into everyday instructional practices by teachers, school systems will see the elimination of racial achievement disparities.

IMPLEMENTATION EXERCISE

SYSTEMIC RACIAL EQUITY TRANSFORMATION

Time required: 45 minutes

Materials required: For each participant, Courageous Conversation Journal and a copy of the worksheet that follows

1. Begin by sharing with the group the following quotation:

   Solving the problem of racism is America's unfinished agenda, and it must be regarded by educators as a moral imperative. (Gerald Pine and Asa Hilliard, 1990, p. 596)

   Pose the following question to the group:

   • To what degree are the equity efforts under way in this school system a demonstration of our "moral imperative"?

2. Lead the group through developing a *vision of equity* for the school.

   • First, divide the participants into small groups of four to five people.
   • Hand out the worksheet to each group.
   • Present the diagram for Systemic Racial Equity Transformation.
   • Have the group develop an equity goal for each of the three domains.

3. Bring the groups back together, and list each of the goals they created for the three domains. As a whole group, determine for each of the three domains which goal will stand as the equity goal for the school or school system.

4. After the meeting, prepare a polished copy of the agreed-upon goals for distribution so that all stakeholders groups who will benefit from these goals can have access to them.

PACIFIC EDUCATIONAL GROUP'S SYSTEMIC RACIAL EQUITY TRANSFORMATION FRAMEWORK

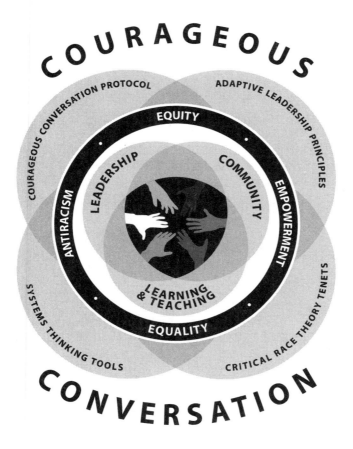

➢ Leadership

_____

_____

_____

_____

_____

➢ Learning and Teaching

_____

_____

_____

_____

➢ Community

_____

_____

_____

_____

UNSUK ZUCKER

My name is UnSuk. I was born and raised in Boise, Idaho. I am a proud Asian American woman. Boise and Asian Americans are not often associated with one another. And thus begins my journey of reclaiming who I am as well as who and what define me. As I share this story, I share pieces of me, pieces of that I am slowly regaining after years of giving them up. I have been told all of my life that there are pieces of me that this country doesn't want or need. As an Asian American woman, I have been taught that I must prove that I belong in this country. I need to assimilate; culturally amputating myself piece by piece. I learned to appease the White, dominant culture without even knowing I was doing so.

It was not until a district meeting one day, when I listened to a district administrator share his story of growing up as a Japanese American in Colorado, that someone was able to articulate what I had spent 32 years burying. I connected to his description of uncomfortably laughing at racially offensive jokes, in fear of being too "politically correct." I empathized with his overwhelming desire to be "accepted." It revealed what I had lost over the course of my life, of what I had been willing to give up.

I wanted to be "American," and I realize now, that to be "American" meant to be White—blonde hair and blue eyes—because that was the definition of "American beauty." I was often embarrassed by my parents' accents, by the food we ate, and by the customs we kept. I remember how excited I was the first time I had a friend over for dinner, asking my mother if she would make an extra special meal for my friend. Pride surged when my mom laid out a beautiful table with delicacies like dried squid flown straight from Korea. I couldn't wait for my friend to feel as special as I did to see such a rare treat. Becky came in, saw the table, and asked what was on the table. "Try it! It's so good!" Then I remember shrinking inside as I watched her nose wrinkle in disgust when I proudly told her that it was dried squid. "It smells weird. Your house smells weird. What else are we going to eat? Is it going to be gross like this squid?" From that day on, only Korean barbeque or fried rice (evidently, the only dishes deemed acceptable in my American culture) were served in front of friends. I became irritated that neighbors could smell the food coming from our home; couldn't my mother make something better, like tuna fish sandwiches? Absurdly, I traded the smell of kimchi for pungent tuna fish, because tuna fish was "normal" to my white counterparts, and "normal" was what I wanted to be more than anything else.

I spent a lot of time embarrassed that my parents had thick accents and then guilty when they expressed the struggles they had because of their lack of English language skills. Piece by piece, bit by bit, I gave myself, and who my family was, away. Signs of "acceptance" through statements such as "I forget that you're

(Continued)

RACIAL AUTOBIOGRAPHY

(Continued)

Asian" or "you're pretty White to me" I experienced as compliments. I had given so much of myself away, my Asian identity, that those around me no longer saw my differences, because I had buried them so deeply. They were no longer required to see me as the Asian girl that I was. I had, again, accommodated to and appeased the dominant group, making its members comfortable, denying the beauty of who I really was.

I realized, through this journey, what unimaginable power Whiteness holds. Whiteness decides what parts of me are accepted as "American" and what parts of me are disposable. "Wait, what's your name again? Un-what? I don't think I can say that, I'll just call you Sue. How's that? Isn't that much better?" "Sure, that's fine," I would say with a smile, hiding humiliation and pain as I, again, attempted to ensure the comfort of those around me. For many years I tried to tell people how to say my name, but I eventually gave up, growing tired of their confusion and judgment, and sometimes their disgusted faces, when I attempted to correct their pronunciation. I grew tired of answering repeated questions of whether I had ever thought about changing my name to an "American" one, a better one. Finally, I gave up on the Korean pronunciation of my name and began introducing myself according to English phonetic rules, not as my mother so beautifully calls me. I wonder whether or not my education, talents, and experience were actually enough to earn the job I have, or if I simply was given the position because I am Asian, again, my worth and value dismissed.

I come back to that district meeting where I heard the Japanese American man speak; I look around the room and notice a sea of tears, and I realize that I am not alone. I realize that Asian American students in our educational system, students of color in *my* classroom, are often isolated as well. I realize that I have given up too much, our kids have given up too much, and it is time to do something different.

My eyes are just as American as blue eyes, and my name is just as American as that of any CEO, president, or senator. What is taken from our students each day as they walk into our school system? I *need* and *deserve* every part of me, and our kids and educators of color *need* and *deserve* every part of them. Our educational system, our country, needs *every* part of us too.

My name is UnSuk, not Sue, not U-suck, not UnSuck, it's UnSuk. Will you stand with me to achieve racial justice and healing?

MALCOLM FIALHO

RACIAL AUTOBIOGRAPHY

I grew up in Bombay (now Mumbai) in a Goan community steeped in postcolonial "markers" that identified groups of people in terms of the kind of English they spoke (the Queen's English was the Holy Grail) and in their food, music, and other aspects of material culture. My family was Catholic and deeply influenced by the Western ideologies of Christianity. I vividly remember the family tuning into Radio Ceylon every Saturday evening, where the popular Western singers (Jim Reeves, Bee Gees, Olivia Newton John, Cliff Richard, etc.) delighted members of the Goan and Anglo-Indian community in the large metropolitan centers. We never listened to either popular or classical Indian music in our home or at community events.

Postcolonialism and "Indianness" were colliding against each other in every aspect of growing up in Bombay in the 1970s and early 1980s. The Goan (of Portuguese extraction) and Anglo-Indian (of British extraction) communities were constantly vying for supremacy at being like the Europeans, and there was a healthy rivalry between the two. But, these Christian (primarily Catholic) communities were united in keeping Indianness and Hinduism beyond the church fence. Despite the omnipresent tensions, there was a unique camaraderie amongst Hindus, Catholics, Muslims, Jains, Parsees, and Sikhs, and we all lived, worked, studied, and played together in multiethnic and multireligious neighborhoods. People from other religious faiths would join us in celebrating Christmas traditions (Goans always distributed sweets to members of their own community and to non-Catholics), and I recall actively participating in the festival of Holi by throwing color on my friends as well as in the festival of Lights, Deepavali. I also fondly recall enjoying a mutton biryani that my Muslim friends had ceremonially prepared for Eid. I recall a beautiful—and I don't believe I am romanticizing this— a *fine* balance between adopting a Goan-Catholic identity while actively embracing other faiths and ethnicities in my community.

The cultural immersion was marked extremely for about six weeks each year (a month in the summer and a fortnight around Christmas) when we travelled from Bombay to stay at the family home in Goa. My father was a senior executive in the Indian Railways, so the journey involved an exciting and luxurious first-class trip through the evocative Sahyadri ranges and then a descent across the plains to the Arabian Sea where Goa was situated. The visits involved the observance of many Catholic rituals and an opportunity to mix with other Goan families that had sought refuge from the rest of India. Goa was seen as the bastion of Indian Catholicism, and the Goans were determined to affirm that strong minority religious identity.

Looking back on the experience through the lens of a politicized racial equity practitioner, I can now see many interesting parallels between my situation and that of racial minorities living in modern Western liberal democracies, the only

(Continued)

(Continued)

exception being that, in my situation, the basis of systemic discrimination was largely religious as opposed to racial. While there was an unspoken, rudimentary form of multiculturalism and harmony fostered by the majority Hindu government, there is no doubt that Hindus enjoyed enormous power in all facets of Indian life. There was a mere smattering of Christians and Muslims (the largest two racial minorities) at senior levels in political, cultural, and economic spheres of activity. During the 1970s and 1980s, there was a mass exodus of Goans and Anglo-Indians to Western countries such as Australia, the United States, and Canada. While a better economic life was definitely a "push" factor for many, I suspect that issues around cultural identity and a sense of belonging were equally important, as many in these communities felt that they would be more at home in the West rather than in a predominantly Hindu India.

I migrated to Australia in the early 1980s with my parents to join my elder siblings who had already settled there in the mid- to late 1970s. I was totally unprepared for the extent of the culture shock, despite my Western upbringing. Perth was predominantly White in the mid-1980s when I arrived, and I recall being extremely self-conscious when boarding public transport and looking out into a sea of White faces in a train carriage. I commenced an undergraduate program in psychology at the University of Western Australia (UWA), and the majority of my friendship network comprised first- and second-generation students from a variety of Asian backgrounds. I had very few White friends in the early years in Perth, and, despite some contradictions, I felt more comfortable with my own kind.

The contradictions arose from being picked on—albeit in so called jest—by the Australian-born Asian immigrant students. They would often imitate the stronger accents of those recently arrived and make crass jokes around stereotypical Asian symbols, such as curry puffs, samosas, the Indian "nod," and Chinese eyes. I laughed at these racially based caricatures on the outside, but I felt very uncomfortable internally. This also manifested in a loss of confidence in my skills and abilities, and I began to remain silent during tutorials and workshops for fear of inciting ridicule around my British Indian accent. In hindsight, and with enhanced understanding of the nexus between Whiteness and internalized racism, I can make sense of, and have come to peace with, these experiences.

The other perplexing aspect of my student years during the late 1980s at UWA was the complete invisibility of race and racial minority phenomena in the curriculum. There were a few brief allusions—mostly stereotypic and romanticized—to aboriginal people and "native" ways in cross-cultural psychology, but certainly not even the early foundations of a "privilege" analysis in the social or clinical psychology units I had selected. I recall feeling invisible in both the curriculum and student experience, thus actively submerging my Indianness in an effort to assimilate.

I was lucky to obtain a position in a fast-track graduate management program with the commonwealth government in 1990, and since then I have worked primarily in the human rights and social justice space with a primary focus on racial equity. I have worked in this space across three sectors: government, community, and higher education. In the mid-1990s, I was the first visible member of a minority group, and first South Asian, to direct a migrant center in Perth's rapidly growing north metropolitan region.

I've had to make complexity my best friend in order to manage the race-based dissonance and tensions that have marked more than two decades of equity work. Critical Race Theory—my wise companion and teacher—just "gets" it so cogently. I've been elated by enormous racial equity progress in the higher education sector on some fronts, and then despondent at recidivism or stagnation on others. I began interrogating and unpacking the "bamboo ceiling" in the Western Australia government sector in the early 1990s, and I feel frustrated that, two decades later, the senior executive service remains predominantly White. I have enjoyed the company of a small, passionate group of indigenous and migrant activists, only to witness them burn out and move on to safer, neutral professional pastures. I have personally bumped up against and been bruised by various manifestations of Whiteness while undertaking racial equity work.

I choose to focus on the remarkable exponential growth and multisectoral systemic impact of Courageous Conversations about Race in Australia and New Zealand, the strong partnership my university has forged with the parent body, Pacific Educational Group, and my deep friendship with its president and founder, Glenn Singleton. It is these episodes of transformation and collaboration, spanning three countries, that give me renewed hope, vigor, and a sense of purpose to continue the conversation till I am hoarse. At times, however, I feel hopeless and dejected at the immense and enduring power and permanence of racism. In these moments, I wonder—am I wasting my time in dedicating my working life to eliminating the racially determined educational achievement and employment participation gap?

THIRTEEN

Courageous Conversation as a Strategy for Achieving Equity in Schools

The major challenge is to meet the need to generate new leadership. The paucity of courageous leaders . . . requires that we look beyond the same elites and voices that recycle the older frameworks. We need leaders— neither saints nor sparkling television personalities—who can situate themselves within a larger historical narrative of this country and our world, who can grasp the complex dynamics of our peoplehood and imagine a future grounded in the best of our past, yet who are attuned to the frightening obstacles that now perplex us. Our ideals of freedom, democracy, and equality must be invoked to invigorate all of us, especially the landless, propertyless, and luckless. Only a visionary leadership that can motivate "the better angels of our nature," as Lincoln said, and activate possibilities for a freer, more efficient, and stable America—only that leadership deserves cultivation and support.

—Cornel West (2001, p. 7)

When Cornel West wrote this, he was responding to national concerns about the lack of emerging leadership in the Black community. Today, however, his words ring true in education, where we have a pronounced need to develop powerful, dynamic, and engaged leaders who are willing to do what is necessary to build a racially equitable educational system where *all* students succeed. An effective force of racial equity leaders can foster real transformation in America's schools and districts.

This leadership needs to exercise *passion,* be engaged in the design and delivery of innovative *practice,* and demonstrate *persistence* toward achieving equity at all levels of the system—from the district office to the classroom and throughout the established community. In this final chapter, I explore what racial equity leadership looks and feels like at the personal, individual teacher, whole school, and systemic levels. Included is a case study of the systemic racial equity transformation work still under way in the St. Paul Public Schools located in St. Paul, Minnesota.

PERSONAL RACIAL EQUITY LEADERSHIP

Each of us as individuals can begin or continue along a personal journey toward racial equity leadership by recognizing that White educators, educators of color, and indigenous educators have equal amounts to offer to the conversation on race and to the work of educating all students. As we begin or continue in this critical effort, we must be introduced to or reignite our passion for this essential work. Key to this discovery is examining within ourselves our current level of appreciation and need for people of races different than our own. Sustenance and depth of understanding in this work occur only when we make ourselves available to people of diverse racial backgrounds and perspectives. People who challenge our tightly held beliefs and those who encourage us to be introspective, self-critical, and self-corrective are our truest allies along the journey. For me as a Black educator, this not only meant that I needed to examine my internalized racism, which still causes me to diminish myself and other Black people from time to time. My passion for achieving racial equity and eliminating racism in my world also requires that I continuously and consistently peer deeper into my own racial blind spots and surface and address how I contribute to circumstances that, for example, make indigenous people invisible.

When Harvard legal scholar Derrick Bell (1992), the father of Critical Race Theory, suggests that "the faces at the bottom of the well" are Black, he encourages us to understand that until we all locate our deep and soulful need to know, to understand, and to be in the company of Black people, we will not have fully challenged our own deepest level of internalized racism. In schools, this need for connecting with Black people translates to the need to connect with our Black male students, whom we categorically find at the bottom of most if not all achievement indices. I now understand Bell's suggestion not as focusing our attention on the plight of African American students only, but as an admonishment that we pay attention to our darkest-skinned students, whether they be Latino, Hmong, Indigenous, or Somali. Once we discover and act on our personal and professional connection to Black people in our daily lives, then members of the entire racial continuum of color populations—Brown, Asian, Indigenous, and multiracial as well as Black—gains presence, position, and power in our schools.

Graig Meyer, a district equity coach in the Chapel Hill–Carrboro School District in Chapel Hill, North Carolina, offers us the following reflection on his personal anti-racist work as a White male. I have chosen to include his voice over many other powerful voices of color and White voices specifically because White males not only continue to wield tremendous power in school districts but are also the most difficult group to engage as racial equity leaders.

> The truly difficult work is looking deep within myself to recognize where my own reservoirs of Whiteness reside and what value or burdens they present to me. Every time I review Peggy McIntosh's inventory of White privilege I learn something more about myself, and—through attentiveness to my own experience—I think I could add a few more forms of racial privilege to her list. Frequently, I find myself examining my blind spots when a colleague of color expresses very different feelings about some experience we shared. This is fairly painless when it simply requires hearing about how they read between the lines of a presentation or caught a racist remark that sailed over my head. When the dissonance in our experience was in some way the result of my Whiteness, it's a little more painful but also more revealing.
>
> My White guilt tends to creep up most when I'm forced to reflect on the power I wield. For instance, I will spend weeks mentally reviewing an incident when one of my staff members bears the brunt of my ignorance or proclivity for dominance. I want them to trust me, I want them to like me, and I anger myself when I learn that I may have done something that makes it more difficult for them to do either.
>
> Perhaps even more important to our work are times when my power allows me to make decisions that negatively impact students of color. Although I often try to seek counsel of colleagues of color, it is inevitable that times arise where it's only after the fact that one of them points out some flaw in my reasoning. The flaws are often the result of my ingrained Whiteness and my own blindness to its perpetual presence.
>
> I suppose it's cliché to say that the work is never done or that none of us ever fully "get it." But I can't help feeling a strong desire to master this work, to learn all there is to know, and to do enough to become the "good White guy." Ultimately, it's probably the deepest vestige of my own White supremacy that feeds this need to know it all, to be right, and to be in charge. Paradoxically, the deeper I delve into this process, the more I feel called to lead other colleagues through the journey. My own capacity for leadership perpetuates the Whiteness within me, beckoning a return trip to look in the mirror. Perhaps I can't fully suppress all the Whiteness within me, and maybe that's for the better. The process is the task, the journey has no end, and I will always be White. (personal communication, March 2005)

Persistent in developing consciousness related to his own Whiteness, Graig tirelessly works to overcome the inherent and known challenges he faces in this work as a racial equity leader. He is clear about the difficulty he experiences when it comes to listening to people of color. Thus, he can remain aware of his dominant viewpoint and actions in a way that challenges his White racial tendencies to define, take charge of, and master anti-racist equity leadership. This self-examination is at the heart of Graig's effectiveness in his school district.

INDIVIDUAL TEACHER RACIAL EQUITY LEADERSHIP

Just as individuals like Graig can dismantle racism through developing a respect and personal need for people of all races whom they meet, every teacher needs to discover and communicate a personal need for and understanding of students and families of color and indigenous students and families. Until teachers intentionally and consistently create classrooms that embrace racial diversity and place the needs of students of color and indigenous students on a level equal to that of White students, they will perpetuate racism on a daily basis and make it more deeply systemic.

Beyond developing a fundamental understanding of race, teachers must establish high expectations and implement effective instructional practices to eliminate racial achievement disparities. Teachers often claim to have high-level expectations for students of color, but then they demonstrate little surprise when their students perform poorly. This lack of disappointment reveals the true level of expectation that a teacher holds. To vocalize belief in the student's abilities but not act on or support those beliefs is not only hypocritical but also destructive to students.

When issues of race are thoughtfully addressed at the classroom level, teachers feel greater efficacy in terms of their ability to exact changes in their practice. This in turn reduces their anxiety related to known and unknown personal or professional deficiencies. Examining race openly and honestly encourages teachers to stop employing harmful practices and to replenish their toolbox with racially equitable, culturally responsive instructional strategies that support the success of *all* children.

Teachers who succeed with children of color and indigenous children do not describe their work as more difficult. Also, these teachers typically do not orchestrate quality student learning through the imposition of endless rules and regulations. They expertly focus on creating innovative ways to engage students in learning rather than seeking ways to punish them for not learning. Racial equity teachers clearly define what all students must know and be able to do; they develop multiple ways of assessing which students know it and are able to do it; and they have a repertoire of strategies to use when they discover that some students have not yet mastered the essential knowledge and skills. Ultimately, these racial equity teachers take responsibility not only for what is taught but also for what is learned by every child, every day.

> **REFLECTION**
>
> Have you known a teacher who succeeds with children of color and/or indigenous children but would not describe his or her work as difficult? What was it about this educator's practice that allowed him or her to succeed without putting forth more effort or experiencing added stress?

WHOLE SCHOOL RACIAL EQUITY LEADERSHIP

Every student who graduates not fully educated is another student whom educators have willingly allowed to exit the system unprepared to face the exciting, yet demanding challenges of our rapidly changing world. Students' lack of preparation and readiness comes at a great cost to society and to the reputation of the US education system. But mostly, their lack of requisite knowledge, skills, and capacities will cost the students future access to opportunities for success. The challenge for schools has long been to more effectively educate White, Anglo, middle-class students while simultaneously providing accelerated support for students who share few or none of those characteristics. As whole schools embrace the requirement of achieving racial equity, educators will need to examine how the institution increasingly and almost naturally became an inappropriate and harmful environment for the growing number of students of color and indigenous students, as well as for students from low-income and or English language-learning backgrounds.

According to Mary Montel Bacon (2005), what we have to work toward is making difference rather than likeness the norm in our personal lives, at school, and in our larger community. Individuals are inherently different, not just racially but in a variety of ways, including styles of communication, expressions of emotion, political opinions, religious thoughts, values, and traditions. When likeness is the norm, then White middle-class values will probably be the standard that is imposed on the racial others, so we are prevented from being present and empowered as who we are. When Whiteness is the standard, all individuals are invited to participate to the degree that they will bend and conform to the experience of the racially dominant population.

By engaging in racial equity leadership, educators learn how to embrace differences and prepare all of our children to face a future of limitless opportunities. The goal of whole school racial equity leadership is not to gain accolades, recognition, or awards but rather to correct the current system of institutional White racial advantage, which should never have existed in the first place. Establishing leadership for racial equity throughout the whole school calls for a courageous superintendent who nurtures courageous principals, who in turn foster participation of all teachers, families, and students in the learning community.

Achieving equity requires that White educators engage as racial equity leaders to the same degree as educators of color and indigenous educators—or perhaps even more. As they increase their recognition of the reality and devastating impact of institutionalized White supremacy, White educators need to lower their personal defenses; this enables them to acquire additional skills and become more intentional and explicit in their racial equity leadership development and actions. The focus of racial equity means dismantling White privilege by creating circumstances in which White people engage with people of color and indigenous people on a level playing field of access and opportunity that both desire.

Some White educators see themselves as "caretakers" for people of color and indigenous people, a perspective that emerges from a need to serve the "downtrodden" functioning beneath them. When this occurs, White educators understand their own *love and caring* for people of color and indigenous people far more than they actually understand people of color or truly see and value indigenous people. In short, some White school leaders initially will try to "take care of" people of color and "their race problems" in "the White way."

White educators who are focused on racial equity throughout a school and system of schools must embrace their leadership role as a way of *being* rather than a way of *doing*. Confronting racial inequities is an issue of deep personal and professional responsibility. Whenever White school leaders allow racial equity work to move beyond continuous personal development and into the realm of self-importance, judgmentalism, or intellectualism, they will have abstracted and objectified the issue of racism and the difficult plight of their colleagues, students, and families of color. Such behaviors serve only to divide a school rather than unite it around a moral purpose that is educationally just.

REFLECTION

When we state that equity leadership is about *being* rather than *doing*, what response or reaction does this statement conjure up for you? Are you familiar with White educators who present themselves to children, families, and educators of color as their "caretaker"? In what ways might this mind-set and related behaviors demonstrate a potential lack of altruism that should arise from our pursuit of equity? How might such educators present problems for their colleagues and a schoolwide quest for equity?

SYSTEMIC RACIAL EQUITY LEADERSHIP

It is clear why racial equity leadership must be present at the individual and school levels, but we must not mistake personal anti-racism for systemic racial equity transformation. Instructional and operational staff members, individually, as well as whole schools of educators, collectively, must compose an entire community of courageous, passionate, and mutually supportive leaders in the district for lasting change at the system level to occur.

Successful equity work systemwide demands racial equity leaders at the highest levels who are willing to speak up, be honest, and challenge the privileges afforded to White people at the expense of people of color and indigenous people. In doing so, such leaders will recognize and examine the system of unaddressed educational inequities and vestiges of past practices as well as contemporary constructs of institutional racism.

The urgent requirement for systemic racial equity transformation leaves no time for pointing out other people's racism. Instead, the process for sustainable change focuses educators, first and foremost, on uncovering and dismantling their own racism. After educators begin engaging in this work personally, they can collectively redefine and invent instructional practices that accelerate higher achievement of underserved student populations. Those with significant institutional power have the potential to challenge racism and inequity rather than merely identifying it and talking about it.

ST. PAUL PUBLIC SCHOOLS: A CASE STUDY

With effective racial equity leadership, school systems can accomplish Systemic Racial Equity Transformation. As described in the previous chapter and illustrated in Figure 13.1, Courageous Conversation serves as the bounding strategy that brings depth and breadth to the three domains of transformation: leadership, learning and teaching, and community. Through their emerging proficiency applying the Courageous Conversation protocol, educators throughout the system can embrace a set of core and common principles that guide them in examining and transforming each of these domains and thus ushering in improved achievement for all students.

Focusing on Equity in St. Paul Public Schools

Racial equity transformation has been embraced at all levels in the St. Paul Public Schools (SPPS) in St. Paul, Minnesota. Now in its fourth year of focused work, the district has seen growth in student engagement and achievement as a result of using the Courageous Conversations About Race Protocol and Framework in the three domains of systemic racial equity transformation (leadership, learning and teaching, and community empowerment and family engagement). The SPPS board of education began its engagement with systemic racial equity transformation in the summer of 2011, attending a Beyond Diversity workshop conducted by Pacific Educational Group (PEG) with a group of staff and community partners. The school board's work continues through PEG-designed professional learning seminars, training, and coaching specifically tailored to address challenges of governance. The focus on racial equity in St. Paul was codified with the board of education adopting of the district's Racial Equity Policy on July 16, 2013.

Superintendent Valeria Silva began leading SPPS in 2010, following more than two decades serving as a teacher, principal, and administrator. In 2009, the school district was beginning the second year of culturally responsive training for all staff based on the Intercultural Development Inventory (http://idiinventory.com). This work entailed 12 hours of training and was focused on assessing culture, not race. As Silva began to draft SPPS's strategic plan using census block data, two factors become evident: The demographics of the City of St. Paul and of the student population had dramatically shifted over the previous decade, and student achievement in the school system was predictable by race.

While there was awareness that the work being done was culture-centered and included race as a component, the approach was very theoretical and did not address application or accountability. SPPS wanted and needed to deepen its understanding of the data. Silva wanted to have a clearer sense of how the change in demographics and racial predictability of student achievement were connected. Why was African American student performance significantly lower than White student performance? Why was this disparity also evident in the performance of other students of color and Native American students? Last, why did these racial disparities persist within and across economic strata? Superintendent Silva needed to better understand the causes of the disparity, not just recognize its presence.

SPPS leadership became familiar with the engagement and progress experienced by neighboring school districts (Hopkins Public Schools, Edina Public Schools, and Eden Prairie Schools) in the Twin Cities region as a result of their partnership with Pacific Educational Group. A former administrator of Hopkins Public Schools was now employed in SPPS and discussed the work of PEG with Superintendent Silva. In August of 2010, the former Hopkins superintendent, members of the Eden Prairie Schools leadership team, Silva, and her SPPS cabinet members and equity coordinator met with me. The purpose of the meeting was to review and discuss the racial disparity reflected in the data from St. Paul, explore its causes, and propose solutions to the challenge.

Through this initial introduction to the Courageous Conversation protocol, and later through the PEG Systemic Racial Equity Transformation Framework (Figure 13.1), the SPPS leadership team discovered that in order to seriously and critically examine the racial disparities evident in data, it was imperative they focus on race. Thus would begin a personal and professional journey for each member of the group as they sought to understand more deeply how race influenced their organization and its systems at the district, school, and community levels.

Led by Silva, in December 2010, SPPS initiated its efforts toward systemic racial equity transformation by focusing on school and district leadership. This

Figure 13.1 Pacific Educational Group's Systemic Racial Equity Transformation Framework

began with a series of Beyond Diversity seminars, PEG's foundational introduction to Courageous Conversation, for the superintendent along with all the members of the cabinet, department directors, and school principals. The experience proved to be personally transforming for Silva, as she shared with her staff:

> Beginning with an open mind, I began to learn the CCAR protocol. After some time reflecting on my introduction, it dawned on me that I didn't know myself racially, and because of this, I wouldn't be able to lead others in engaging in this work. The training helped me realize my own biases and weaknesses: How, living in this country, I didn't see myself as a person of color, especially as coming to the US from Chile. It was turbulent for me. How my life and my actions were steeped in whiteness. How proud am I to be Latina. How blind I was about racial equity and issues related to educating students of color, which I believed I already understood.

Current Demographics

SPPS is one of Minnesota's largest school districts; it has more than 39,000 students. The system boasts of a highly diverse student population enrolled in 85 schools and programs. Seventy-six percent of SPPS students are Black, Asian, Latino, or American Indian. Highly trained and deeply dedicated staff, cutting-edge academic programs, and strong community support are among the district's hallmarks.

- Students speak more than 125 languages and dialects.
- Approximately 33% of students are English language learners.
- Approximately 4,000 students are new to SPPS each year, 2,000 at the secondary level.
- 17% of students require special education services.
- 73% of students are eligible for free or reduced-price lunch.

Additional demographic data are shown in Table 13.1. Data on academic performance are displayed in Figure 13.2.

Table 13.1   St. Paul Public Schools: Current Demographics

	Number	*Percentage*
Student Population		
Total elementary	19,299	51.03
Total secondary school	18,526	48.97
Total enrollment	37,825	
Student Population by Race		
Hispanic American	5,296	13.84
White American	8,684	22.96
African American	11,398	30.21
Asian American	11,788	31.24
American Indian/Alaskan	658	1.80
Total student of color population	29,140	77.04
Total student population	37,825	
English Language Learners		
Total of English language learners	12,482	33.00

	Number	Percentage
Students Receiving Free or Reduced-Price Meals		
Total free or reduced-price meals	27,612	73.00
Funding per Pupil		
St. Paul	$13,672	
State average	$10,685	

Source: Information obtained from district website at www.datacenter.spps.org/Student_Enrollment.html

District-Level Equity Transformation

Superintendent Silva knew that in order to lead systemic change, the highest level of decision makers in the district would need to engage in and model racial equity transformation that began with them developing proficiency with the Courageous Conversation Protocol. She led from this belief and established the District Equity Leadership Team that, initially, would develop a plan for systemic transformation that included professional learning for all the system's administrators, faculty, and staff. Silva's plan for development also included the board of education, the St. Paul Federation of Teachers, and key community partners. As a result, the school board, with broad community support, adopted the St. Paul Racial Equity Policy.

Following the Beyond Diversity workshop with district leaders, St. Paul continued their racial equity development with a series of leadership seminars. These seminars were tailored to guide and support leaders in leading equity and anti-racist development in school systems and to begin to move the personally developed racial equity learning and understandings into professional and organizational contexts. Subsequently, the executive directors, program administrators, and building principals began to craft visions for racial equity in their own schools and areas of focus while developing the knowledge, will, skill, and capacity to plan for and implement their visions.

SPPS's earlier review of data revealed some troubling trends related to students with special needs. Improved effectiveness with the Courageous Conversation Protocol enabled leaders to have more meaningful and impactful dialogue about the racial challenges before them. There was disproportionate representation of African American students in special education, a high overall system rate of special education identification at 18% (compared to a state and national rate of 13%), and an alarming disparity in academic achievement in special education (particularly for African American males). In the fall of 2011, at the district's request, Council of the Great City Schools (CGCS), audited the system's special education services to provide recommendations that would help provide effective and high-quality instruction to students with disabilities.

Figure 13.2 Student Performance

Graduation rates up across the board

From 2009 to 2012 (most recent data available), the overall SPPS four-year graduation rate increased by 7 percentage points (+7), from 59% to 66%, and racial disparities have narrowed in this area.

2012 four-year graduation rate by race

53%
(+22)
American Indian

59%
(+15)
Latino

70%
(+7)
Asian American

57%
(+5)
African American

77%
(+4)
Caucasian

ACT participation and scores up

- The percentage of 12th grade SPPS students taking the ACT increased from 57% in 2010 to 63% in 2013.
- From 2010-11 to 2012-13, the percentage of ACT-takers scoring 21 or higher increased from 34% to 37%.

MCA Reading scores up

5 percentage points from 2009-10 to 2011-12.

MCA Math scores up

3 percentage points from 2010-11 to 2012-13.

Multiple Measurement Ratings (MMR)*

- Out of the 44 SPPS schools rated under the statewide MMR in 2012 and 2013, 10 (23%) schools improved their designations this year
- Monroe, Harding and Washington schools are now MMR "Celebration Schools"

- Of the 10 schools going up a designation, Humboldt and Phalen Lake jumped up two levels
- Only two schools went down in their MMR designations

* The MMR is based on MCA proficiency and growth results, with graduation rates also included for high schools.

 The number of AVID high school students getting ready for graduation and college has risen from 1,042 to 1,384.

Source: St. Paul Public Schools, 2014. Used with permission.

What the Council found was that SPPS had a significant, disproportionate representation of African American students in special education and that 67% of students identified as having an emotional behavior disorder (EBD) were

African American. In addition, 80% of the EBD students served in restrictive setting programs were African American. African American students, however, composed only 30% of the overall student population in SPPS. CGCS also found that the special education identification rate was trending upward, and while schools nationwide had reduced the number of students diagnosed with an EBD to 6% of all the students in special education, SPPS's comparable number had increased to 13%.

One of the recommendations from the report was for SPPS leadership to investigate Courageous Conversation as a way to understand and interrupt the processes by which a disproportionate number of African American students were disciplined and/or were identified for special education. Three key concerns were identified in the report: the high proportion of African American students (especially males) identified as having an EBD, the placement of students in restrictive settings (i.e., separate classes and schools), and the disproportionate number of African American students suspended for more than 10 days in a school year. In order to facilitate integration of these issues into SPPS's work around cultural competency, the report recommended that the district explore systemic engagement with PEG to cover these topics.

Using the Courageous Conversation protocol and framework (refer back to Figure 13.1) to review and discuss the Council of the Great City Schools report at the SPPS cabinet level, it was apparent that the process of identifying and addressing major concerns in how special education was being programmed would support overall positive outcomes in SPPS. Clearly changes had to be made not only in special education but also in the general education program. The district leadership's use of Courageous Conversation had helped them to unveil how special education increasingly was becoming a holding space for African American students who were not successfully served in general education classrooms.

This understanding is highlighted in the reflection of Elizabeth Keenan, the district's special education director:

> As the new Assistant Superintendent for the Offices of Specialized Services, I came into the district in August of 2011 and the Council of Great City Schools came into the district to do their review of special education services in SPPS in September of 2011. I was right away confronted by the inequities that were playing out in the area of special education. As a white woman in charge of the area of special education, I needed a foundation in order to look at a systemic practice of racially isolating students under the umbrella or language of special education. Special education language and bureaucracy easily masked a broader understanding of how race was impacting special education. The problem was that once students were in special education, the special education department was building deep isolated programs and was justifying them because the students "needed" that type of specially isolated programming.

The Courageous Conversation protocol and framework provided the foundation and lens to examine the beliefs underlying policy upon which longstanding programs and practices were constructed. While initiating systemwide transformation of beliefs and behaviors needed to be authorized and executed by executive leadership, it could not be conducted solely through the eyes and experiences of SPPS's administration. Such an effort required seeking out, inviting, and hearing the voices and perspectives of students, parents, and members of the communities of color and indigenous communities most critically impacted. Through a conscious and concerted effort to do just that and respond equitably, in the fall of 2013, SPPS eliminated separate learning centers for EBD students as one of several examples of systems level or districtwide racial equity transformation.

School-Level Equity Transformation

Engaging, sustaining, and deepening dialogue about race and its influence on schooling at the overall district level is the essential catalyst for systemic racial equity transformation. But, for real impact to occur, the Courageous Conversation must move quickly to the school level. In line with development of district-level leadership during their first year of racial equity training, SPPS's District Equity Leadership Team (DELT) in turn charged the principals with selecting school-based leadership teams to engage and operationalize the vision at their schools. These Equity Teams (E-Teams), led by the principal, are a primary and essential component of building a school community focused on racial equity transformation.

In consideration of the high-level resources, scope, and magnitude of their charge, DELT invited principals to apply to participate in an action-research/development initiative designed to deepen and accelerate racial equity transformation outcomes in identified schools. PEG's *Beacon School* concept created a space for willing principals and their E-Teams, through increased training and coaching, to accelerate the racial equity transformation process and capitalize on their expressed desire to see greater and more immediate equity impact in their schools.

Seven *Beacon Schools* led SPPS's early work at the school sites in September of 2011. Five principals of color and two by white principals led these seven schools. Of the seven school sites, three were K–8 schools, three were K–6 schools, and one was an alternative high school. One school had a new principal who had transferred from a previous school. These schools served as prototypes to help other educators understand—in a tangible way—how progress toward achieving equity outcomes can be accelerated through focused leadership, learning, and coaching support.

The reflection of Dr. Celeste Carty, principal of Crossroads Montessori and Science Elementary offers a glimpse of the opportunity of being a Beacon School:

We were able to begin to start training, to have those conversations about race, those courageous conversations about race and how that impacts our kids of color, especially our African American kids of color, in which we did have a definite disparity between our Caucasian students and our African American students. And so, we had always been talking about it, but the solutions and those conversations of really talking as it related to institutional racism were not happening, and we needed the tools in order to have those conversations . . . in order to open up the dialogue between all staff and eventually with parents, to better educate our students of color.

Leadership

With Beacon Schools blazing the path yet at times stumbling forward, SPPS leadership responding to the requests of these frontrunners for additional ongoing in-district assistance, and the need to continue to build the school system's capacity to support the structured broadening of the racial equity transformation effort it envisioned, SPPS established the district Office of Equity. The explicit goal of this office is to support the district schools' efforts to eliminate racial disproportionality and predictability of low achievement by accelerating the achievement of our lowest-performing students and increasing achievement for all students.

All SPPS schools have established site-based E-Teams, which are implementing racial equity development and training at each of the school sites. All schools are also engaged in developing culturally relevant pedagogy through districtwide professional development and site coaching.

Since SPPS began its efforts, over 1,200 employees, including some in every SPPS school, have received training in racial equity transformation. Suspensions have decreased by 38% from 2011 to 2013. SPPS continues to work toward racial and economic diversity in each school, and 82% of low-income students have been placed in schools with higher-income student populations to create mixed-income environments.

Learning and Teaching

In 2012–13, SPPS targeted eight schools that engaged teachers who demonstrated readiness to explore equity transformation at a deeper level in Collaborative Action Research for Equity (CARE). CARE Teams consist of four to six equity teacher leaders and are led by the school principal. They design, deliver, and disseminate equitable pedagogical practices that are explicitly and intentionally planned to improve engagement and achievement for underserved students of color. The overarching goal of the CARE Teams is to conduct classroom action research to discover, develop, document, deliver, and disseminate culturally relevant learning and teaching practices. Each school team is engaged in seminars and coaching focused on building racial/cultural proficiency, using action research to document culturally relevant pedagogy, and developing and sharing culturally relevant instructional practices. Target CARE participants are principals and classroom teachers.

Key findings from an early evaluation of the CARE work in eight schools address the two evaluation questions posed.

1. What systemic practices have been interrupted by this work?
2. What impact does CARE have on
   a. Instruction
   b. Focal students (African American, Latino, and American Indian)
   c. All students
   d. Cultural consciousness
   e. Cultural relevance of teaching practices

Key Findings

1. What systemic practices have been interrupted by this work?

When asked what changes they had seen at the building or leadership level since the beginning of the CARE work, staff talked about changes to their teaching practices, adaptive changes, and increased awareness of race.

Teaching Practices: Behavioral Issues

"Even if a teacher is having an issue with a child, they are looking at it with an equity lens."

"Engagement vs. compliance: I back off from criss-cross apple sauce and raising your hands. I let them know when it's appropriate to raise hands and when it's fine to just call out and respond."

Adaptive Changes

Staffs are having Courageous Conversations regarding adaptive changes.

"We as a school decided to make an adaptive change to how we do dismissal. We use to have a zero-noise policy at the end of the day. It was exhausting. Principal brought it to the CARE team and to the school and said hey how about if we make an adaptive change. We can still have level 1 and 2 voices without screaming. Some teachers found it hard to let go, fear of control but it has gone really well. A lot less stressful for teachers and still so much calmer. There is no chaos."

Conversations on Race

"Before, if you were talking in PLC and it's about race, it didn't go anywhere."

"Four years ago not much talk about race, now we talk about it."

"We talk about race every day."

2. What impact has CARE had on instruction, focal students, all students, and cultural consciousness and relevance?

Teachers report the key components of CARE that have been implemented at the school are finding "below-the-line" information on their students, building relationships with focal students, and preparing lessons that are culturally relevant.

> "Lessons are designed for the focal student, but the lesson is supposed to benefit the rest of the students."

Instruction

Teachers report they are more conscious of the cultures of students in their classrooms and of how they can incorporate lessons and literature that connects with students. They are trying to recognize and treat each child as an individual while also being knowledgeable about and respectful of the

> "The kids that need structure, they are at their desks, but the kids that don't are walking."

child's collective racial culture. They are also pausing to dig deeper into the reasons behind students' behavior. When a student acts out, they don't automatically send the student out and instead try to understand why the student is acting that way. According to one teacher, "Behavior comes up, teachers are now spending time figuring out what the child needs and how to build skills in that child rather than be punitive and have no discussion. . . . Teachers are talking more about diagnosing the problem." They are also adjusting their teaching practices to make room for students who need a different learning environment.

Focal Students

All staff reported that they noticed improvement in students' self-esteem, confidence, engagement, behavior, and academic performance since the beginning of the CARE work. They attribute much of the change to the relationships they developed with the students. By learning more about the below-the-line information, they were able to make connections with students. Some staff have even taken it a step further by showing an interest in students outside of the classroom and by attending baseball games and other extracurricular activities. One stated, "Building that relationship outside of school. Once they see that someone cares about them, when they come in my room they are excited. Their facial expressions are different. . . . Building relationships increases student engagement." Students then felt a sense of belonging, that they were of value and were worthy.

All Students in the Classroom

Staff reported that the strategies and lessons they incorporated into their instruction helped not only the focal students but the rest of the students as well. When they created a space that was more inclusive of each child's race and culture, they noticed positive changes in academics, behavior, maturity, and confidence. Students felt liberated to

> "Giving them voice and the words and the ability to do those things that affect the academics."

be themselves, and there seemed to be a decrease in the number of behavior issues and an increase in empathy in the classroom. Staff also indicated that the depth of the students' conversations had increased.

When asked how they knew students were doing well in their classes, one teacher responded, "I have 29 students, and only two are not reading at grade level." Another example given was the teachers' new practice of having students track their own behavior, including how many times each student needed to "take a break." After allowing students to track their behavior and giving them tools to deal with their behavior, the teachers had seen a decrease in negative behaviors.

Racial Consciousness and Cultural Relevance of Instruction

All staff reported seeking out culturally relevant resources and incorporating them into their classrooms. Some examples included using the chants and commands of the African American stepping tradition, using music during transitions, and incorporating culturally relevant books and authors into lessons. They also spent a lot of time building the students' self-esteem by doing activities grounded in the students' racial culture and incorporating the students' interests into their lessons. An example was that if a student was interested in Yogi Cards or basketball, a teacher would use a word problem that included the student's interest. However, staff still struggled with finding culturally relevant resources. Either they did not know where to find the resources, or resources were limited.

Feedback from staff regarding the CARE work:

"Excited the district is on this journey. We are staying the course, it has caused discomfort and made people angry, but it is comforting to know that we are not going to throw it away."

"Great work and it better not go away; I believe in it as a parent and as a staff member. It is important."

Community and Family Empowerment

Systemic racial equity transformation requires establishing effective and supportive relationships with families and others throughout the community, as well as acknowledging that the school (administrators, teachers, and students) is a community in and of itself. SPPS has yet to formally engage in PEG's programming to build Partnerships for Academically Successful Students (PASS), but E-Teams have actively sought the support of homes, churches, community organizations, and neighborhoods in sustaining and deepening their commitment to the pursuit of transformation for racial equity.

A remarkable example of this partnering was on display during a regular meeting of the SPPS school board of directors in May 2014. Because of the schools' learning, practicing, and applying the Courageous Conversation protocol to engage, sustain, and deepen dialogue about race with staff, students, and parents, an amazing demonstration of support and connectedness was evident in the voices of parents, students, and board members at the meeting.

Leadership for Racial Equity

Effective leadership for racial equity goes beyond working to address obvious examples of institutional racism and inequities. This work is necessarily personal and far reaching. Marching toward racial equity emerges as a life purpose for many educators, as they focus on eradicating the racial caste system that exists in their classrooms, schools, and larger community. It appears insufficient, however, just to believe in and support racial equity on a personal level. Systemic transformation requires that individual efforts actually translate into improvements in pedagogies that positively impact colleagues' work and improve students' learning. Success is measured one system at a time.

To pursue equity for children everywhere in St. Paul, school district leaders are working closely with City of St. Paul and Ramsey County leaders on issues of race. Based upon the work and relationship building necessary in developing the district's strategic plan, "Strong Schools, Strong Communities"; and upon her growing proficiency with the Courageous Conversation protocol and framework; Superintendent Silva engaged city and county officials around the governmental entities' need to collaborate and to examine more closely, through a lens of race, pressing issues being faced by each. These government leaders could well benefit from the skill and capacity the school system was developing, and I was approached to facilitate a dialogue with key leadership figures about how an examination of race might support their planning and development. After engaging in an introductory seminar facilitated by PEG, and working in partnership with SPPS and Ramsey County government leadership, Chris Coleman, mayor of the City of St. Paul, shared in an interview with the School Improvement Network,

> I have a great faith in the St. Paul Public School system, and I have a great faith in the City of St. Paul, but the statistics don't lie . . . and we have to ask ourselves what needs to change in order to ensure that all of our children have the resources they need to be successful. . . . It's one thing to be able to verbalize that racism exists in society; it's another thing to understand [how] you fit into that picture. The persistence of this approach and the real, deep dive that we take, that is not a one and done . . . and it's kind of a total consciousness changing about how we approach these issues.

SPPS school board members are also actively engaged in thinking about their governance role through the lens of racial equity. Reflecting on their personal equity learning experiences over the first 18 months of this engagement, board members noted that in order for equity work to be effective, it must go deep, and to go deep, it takes time to build knowledge and trust. Board chair Judy Moran, in responding to the uneasiness of factions of the St. Paul community and pockets of resistance from some faculty and staff seeking to halt it's progress, said, "This is school reform and involves personal behavior and beliefs; it takes time and effort to implement."

In a statement from the St. Paul Federation of Teachers (May 20, 2014), union president Mary Cathryn Ricker pledges,

We will only succeed in building more racially equitable schools when we join together as educators, parents and community members, share our experiences and build a consensus that all students have a right to

- schools free from institutional racism,
- receive the support they deserve based on their individual needs,
- equitable access to the resources needed for their education,
- a safe and healthy school climate for learning, and
- transparent decisions about their schools and education.

Our union is committed to seeking multiple perspectives and constructing solutions together.

SPPS, due to its systemic approach fueled by passion, practice, and persistence is advancing toward equity. Increasingly recognized as a national leader in addressing racial equity and finding meaningful solutions that reduce racial disparity, SPPS's highly trained and developed leaders at all levels of the district and throughout the broader community represent a successful demonstration of Systemic Racial Equity Transformation.

Video

2013 National Summit for Courageous Conversation
www.corwin.com/ CCAR

REFLECTION

Based on this case study of SPPS's efforts in equity transformation, what have you learned that you can implement in your own school or school system? Where should you begin? Who else should you engage in this work around equity?

To not be involved and engaged in racial equity work is to perpetuate systemic racism. There is no nonracist place—you are either leading for racial equity or perpetuating the racism that already exists. All potential racial equity leaders must find within themselves how racism is affecting them, personally, on a daily basis. They must then create their own personal and internal strategy that provides instruction on how to address their own individual racism. Having satisfied these prerequisites, they can engage with colleagues in discovering strategies to examine and eradicate inequities and racism at the classroom, school, district, and institutional levels.

Finding passion for equity, developing equitable classroom practices, and being persistent in this work are the key components of and guiding strategy for racial equity leaders. I wrote this book to provide you with the insight and tools you need to eliminate racial achievement disparities. Remain true to yourself in this work, fight for the sake of your students, and use an equity lens to determine appropriateness in all you do and become. I wish you the best of luck. Stay courageous and remain hopeful that your racial equity leadership is the next essential step in our journey to the possibility proclaimed by W. E. B. DuBois (1949/1970): *the right to learn.* Our children deserve nothing less!

GLENN SINGLETON

Since my move to the West, I can name thousands of times in which race has dramatically impacted the outcome of a situation. From attending Stanford University Graduate School of Education, to purchasing my first house, to buying cars, to being seated in restaurants, to walking down my fancy neighborhood streets and having some teenager call me a "nigger" out the window of a passing car, demoralizing experiences have chipped away at my racial naivety and belief that once I earned degrees and entered the middle class, I would transcend race and racism. Rapidly, I was awakening. Race in California seems to be nuanced in ways different than back East. Since they live in a state known as the place of diversity, Californians can be quite smug about matters racial. To suggest that one does not view the Golden State as socially progressive when it comes to these matters, but rather that one sees many residents as a bit delusional, can cause a deafening silence and a "polite" dismissal. Sometimes, I wish White, Brown, and even some Black Californians would just tell me that my Black skin creates discomfort for them, rather than have me "accidentally" arrive at this conclusion through some covert maze of alienation and behind-the-scenes marginalization. Growing up in Baltimore, I am used to racist people just expressing their racism openly, so I know exactly where we stand.

Today, some 24 years since I relocated here, when driving through the intensely segregated San Francisco neighborhoods, I witness the massive "forced evacuation" of Black and Brown people from the very neighborhoods where West Coast jazz was founded. White gentrification is alive and well, perhaps outpacing gentrification in places like Baltimore, Philadelphia, and Harlem. Each day, more than a dozen Google, Facebook, LinkedIn, and Apple luxury coaches transport hundreds of White and Asian millennials from my neighborhood to and from work. Statistics suggests that in these Silicon Valley high-tech companies, less than 5% of the middle- and executive-level employees are Black, Brown, or Indigenous. Based on the demographics of those being bused to work each day, this precious cargo for whom the city commences construction on a new "housing project" each month, the next generation of high-tech executives will be even less colorful.

I never envisioned myself tackling racism on a local or national, much less a global, scale. Certainly I never pictured myself developing a protocol so people

RACIAL AUTOBIOGRAPHY PART II

(Continued)

(Continued)

could effectively break their racial silence and develop consciousness. But the daily confrontation with a United States of America unwilling to respect my education, insights, experiences, and professional accomplishment led me into a struggle that I noticed was not mine alone. As White Ivy League graduates named their success, the price for advancement of people of color and indigenous people seemed to be attached to a requirement that we embrace Whiteness and live behind a mask. I saw no difference between this prescribed pathway and that of my ancestors who were subjugated as slaves on plantations at the turn of the 18th century or as domestics working in mansions at the turns of the 20th and 21st centuries. I began to recognize that education was the key to our collective liberation, and higher education was our entrée into the middle class only if we could effectively navigate racism. But navigating racism needed to be different than what I had learned to do at Park, Penn, and Stanford.

The blessing of witnessing a Black president in the White House quite publicly navigating racism, consistently surrounding myself with positive role models of color, holding myself responsible for studying and understanding the history of racial injustice, and maintaining my faith in the higher power equips me to live—mind, body, and soul—as a color-conscious man. Never again will I be blind to or silent about racism, and always will I call out White supremacy when I recognize it, because I truly do not feel that we are, as a human family, at risk of developing too much racial consciousness. Having said that, I recognize that even friends grow tired of me challenging racism with all deliberate speed, and they can be quick to accuse me of "playing the race card" in my personal and professional transactions. When hearing their assertion, I just smile and I embrace their discomfort, or perhaps naivety, as an invitation to have yet another Courageous Conversation About Race.

FINAL JOURNAL REFLECTION

Commit to paper your personal thoughts about the journey you have made as you read this book. Where did you begin in your understanding of race? Where are you now? How will your increased will, skill, knowledge, and capacity to examine race impact your personal and professional experiences? How will you continue your learning? What new commitments can you make to engage in racial equity work?

References and Selected Bibliography

Adelman, L. (2003). *Race—the power of an illusion* [Video]. San Francisco, CA: Newsreel/PBS.

Arciniega, T. A. (1977). The challenge of multicultural education for teacher educators. *Journal of Research and Development in Education, 11*(1), 52–69.

Aronson, J. (2004). The threat of stereotype. *Educational Leadership, 62*(3), 14–20.

Aronson, J., & Dee, T. (2011). Stereotype threat in the real world. In T. Schmader & M. Inzlicht (Eds.), *Stereotype threat: Theory, process, and application* (264–279). Oxford, United Kingdom: Oxford University Press.

Bacon, M. M., & TechStream. (2005). *Working with students from the culture of poverty.* Sandy, Utah: LPD Video Journal of Education & TechStream.

Barnes, J. E. (2004, March 22). Unequal education. *U.S. News & World Report,* 66–75.

Barth, S. R. (2004). *Learning by heart.* San Francisco, CA: Jossey-Bass.

Barth, R. S. (2006). Improving relationships within the schoolhouse. *Educational Leadership, 63*(6), 29–33.

Bell, D. A. (1992). *Faces at the bottom of the well: The permanence of racism.* New York, NY: Basic Books.

Bell, D. A. (2008). *Race, racism and American law* (6th ed.) New York, NY: Aspen.

Chapel Hill–Carrboro School District. (2004, July 19). *Chapel Hill–Carrboro School District achieves Adequate Yearly Progress (AYP) on national goals* (news release). Retrieved June 4, 2005, from http://www.chccs.k12.nc.us/news/news1.asp?ID=377

Chapel Hill–Carrboro School District. (2005). *District report card on African American and Latino student progress.* Chapel Hill, NC: Author.

College Board. (2010–2011). *College-bound seniors 2010 and 2011, total group profile report.* Retrieved from http://www.collegeboard.org

Corbett, H. D., Williams, B., Corbett, D., & Wilson, B. (2002). *Effort and excellence in urban classrooms: Expecting, and getting, success with all students.* New York, NY: Teachers College Press.

Darling-Hammond, L. (1997). *The right to learn.* San Francisco, CA: Jossey-Bass.

Darling-Hammond, L. (2010). Restoring our schools: Forget quick fixes. To compete internationally we need to improve the whole system. *The Nation, 290*(23), 1–2.

DeCuir, J. T., & Dixson, A. D. (2004). "So when it comes out, they aren't that surprised that it is there": Using critical race theory as a tool of analysis of race and racism in education. *Educational Researcher, 33*(5), 26–31.

Delgado, R., & Stefancic, J. (2012). *Critical race theory: An introduction* (2nd ed.). New York: New York University Press.

Delpit, L. (1995a). *Other people's children: Cultural conflict in the classroom.* New York, NY: The New Press.

Delpit, L. (1995b). The silenced dialogue. In L. Delpit, *Other people's children: Cultural conflict in the classroom* (pp. 21–47). New York, NY: The New Press. (Original work published 1988)

Delpit, L. (2011). *Multiplication is for White people: Raising expectations for other people's children.* New York, NY: The New Press.

Dixson, A. (2014). *Researching race in education: Policy, practice and qualitative research.* Education Policy in Practice: Critical Cultural Studies series. Charlotte, NC: Information Age.

DuBois, W. E. B. (1970). The freedom to learn. In P. S. Foner (Ed.), *W. E. B. DuBois speaks* (pp. 230–231). New York, NY: Pathfinder. (Original work published 1949)

DuBois, W. E. B. (1996). *The souls of black folk.* New York, NY: Random House. (Original work published 1903)

Editorial Projects in Education Research Center. (2011, July 7). Issues A-Z: Achievement gap. *Education Week.* Retrieved from http://www.edweek.org/ew/issues/achievement-gap/

The Education Trust. (2009). *Getting results by focusing on teaching and learning: Lessons from schools and districts on the performance frontier.* Retrieved August 26, 2014 from http://www.edtrust.org/dc/presentation/getting-results-by-focusing-on-teaching-and-learning-lessons-from-schools-and-distri

The Education Trust. (2013a). *The state of education for native students* [Slide presentation.] Washington, DC: Author.

The Education Trust. (2013b). *Uneven at the start: Differences in state track records foreshadow challenges and opportunities for Common Core.* Washington, DC: Author.

Grigg, W., Moran, R., & Kuang, M. (2010). *National Indian Education Study, Part I: Performance of American Indian and Alaska Native students at grades 4 and 8 on NAEP 2009 reading and mathematics assessments.* NCES 2010–462. Washington, DC: National Center for Education Statistics, Institute of Education Sciences, U.S. Department of Education.

Hale, J. E. (2004). How schools shortchange African American students. *Educational Leadership, 62*(3), 34–37.

Helms, J. E. (Ed.). (1990). *Black and White racial identity: Theory, research, and practice.* Westport, CT: Greenwood.

Helms, J. E. (2008). *A race is a nice thing to have: A guide to being a white person or understanding the white persons in your life* (2nd Ed.). Hanover, MA: Microtraining Associates.

Helms, J. E., & Ford, D. Y. (2012, Summer). Testing and assessing African Americans: "Unbiased" tests are still unfair. *The Journal of Negro Education, 81,* 186–189.

Henze, R., Katz, A., Norte, E., Sather, S., & Walker, E. (2002). *Leading for diversity: How school leaders promote interethnic relations.* Thousand Oaks, CA: Corwin.

Herrnstein, R., & Murray, C. (1994). *The bell curve: Intelligence and class structure in American life.* New York, NY: Free Press.

Hilliard, A. (1995). Do we have the will to educate all children? In *The maroon within us: Selected essays on African American community socialization* (pp. 194–206) Baltimore, MD: Black Classic Press.

Hilliard, A. G., III. (2001). To be an African teacher. *Psych Discourse, 32(8),* 4–7.

Hilliard, A. G., III (Ed.). (2012). *The teachings of Ptahhotep: The oldest book in the world.* Grand Forks, ND: Blackwood Press.

Hoffman, F. L. (2004). *Race traits and tendencies of the American Negro.* Buffalo, NY: William S. Hein. (Original work published 1896)

Jefferson, T. (1996). *Notes on the State of Virginia.* (W. Peden, Ed.). Chapel Hill: University of North Carolina Press. (Original work published 1781)

Johnson, R. (2002). *Using data to close the achievement gap.* Thousand Oaks, CA: Corwin.

Katz, J. H. (2003). *White awareness.* Norman: University of Oklahoma Press.

KidsCount. (2014). *Child population by race.* Retrieved August 24, 2014, from http://datacenter.kidscount.org/data/tables/103-child-population-by-race?loc=1&loct=2#detailed/2/2–52/false/36,868,867,133,38/66,67,68,69,70,71,12,72/423,424

King, L. M. (2001). *Closing the achievement gap: A vision for students in a world of diversity.* Lemon Grove, CA: Lemon Grove School District.

King, M. L., Jr. (1968, March 14). *The other America.* Speech. Grosse Pointe High School, MI. Retrieved from http://www.gphistorical.org/mlk/mlkspeech/

Kivel, P. (2002). *Uprooting racism: How White people can work for racial justice.* Philadelphia, PA: New Society.

Ladson-Billings, G. J., & Tate, W. F. (1994). Toward a theory of critical race theory in education. *Teachers College Record, 97,* 47–68.

Ladson-Billings, G. (2006, October). From the achievement gap to the education debt: Understanding achievement in U.S. schools. *Educational Researcher, 35(7),* 3–12.

Landsman, J. (2004). Confronting the racism of low expectations. *Educational Leadership, 62(3),* 28–33.

Lindsey, R. B., Nuri Robins, K., & Terrell, R. D. (2003). *Cultural proficiency: A manual for school leaders.* Thousand Oaks, CA: Corwin.

Marzano, R. J., Pickering, D., & Pollock, J. E. (2001). *Classroom instruction that works: Research-based strategies for increasing student achievement.* Alexandria, VA: Association for Staff and Curriculum Development.

McIntosh, P. (1988). *White privilege and male privilege: A personal account of coming to see correspondences through work in women's studies.* Working Paper No. 189. Wellesley, MA: Wellesley College Center for Research on Women.

McIntosh, P. (1989, July/August). White privilege: Unpacking the invisible knapsack. *Peace and Freedom,* 10–12.

Nakao, A. (1998, June 7). How race colors learning. *San Francisco Examiner.* http://www.sfgate.com/news/article/How-race-colors-learning-3085279.php

National Center for Education Statistics. (2013). *The nation's report card: A first look: 2013 mathematics and reading.* NCES 2014–451. Washington, DC: Institute of Education Sciences, U.S. Department of Education. Retrieved from http://www.nationsreportcard.gov/reading_math_2013/#/gains-by-group

Pine, G., & Hilliard, A. (1990). Rx for racism: Imperatives for America's schools. *Phi Delta Kappan, 71(8),* 593–600.

Regan, S. (2012, January 30). Julie Landsman on race, white privilege and the achievement gap. *Twin Cities Dailey Planet.* Retrieved from http://www.tcdailyplanet.net

St. Paul Public Schools. (2014, January). *Strong schools, strong communities: Report to the community.* Retrieved from http://www.spps.org/uploads/2014_spps_report_to_community.pdf

San Diego Union Tribune. (2003, February 27). East county opinion: Two East County school districts are setting the pace. *The San Diego Union Tribune,* p. B15. Retrieved from http://legacy.utsandiego.com/news/op-ed/editorial1/20030227-9999_mz2ed-27top.html

Singham, M. (1998). The canary in the mine: The achievement gap between Black and White students. *Phi Delta Kappan, 80*(1), 9–15.

Singleton, G. (1997). *White is a color!* San Francisco, CA: Pacific Educational Group.

Singleton, G. (2002). *Closing the achievement gap* [Video]. *Video Journal of Education, 12*(1). Retrieved August 19, 2014, from http://www.teachertube.com/video/closing-the-achievement-gap-75655

Singleton, G. (2012). *More courageous conversations about race.* Thousand Oaks, CA: Corwin.

Sparks, D. (2004). How to have conversations about race, an interview with Beverly Daniel Tatum. *Journal of Staff Development, 25*(4), 48–52.

Steele, C. M. (2011). *Whistling Vivaldi: How stereotypes affect us and what we can do.* Issues of Our Time. New York, NY: W. W. Norton.

Tatum, B. D. (1997). *"Why are all the Black kids sitting together in the cafeteria?" and other conversations about race.* New York, NY: HarperCollins.

Tatum, B. D. (2007). *Can we talk about race? And other conversations in an era of school resegregation.* Boston, MA: Beacon Press.

Trumbull, E., Rothstein-Fisch, C., Greenfield, P. M., & Quiroz, B. (2000). *A practical framework for understanding cultural differences: Bridging cultures in our schools: New approaches that work.* Berkeley, CA: WestEd.

The unfriendly border. (2005, August 25). *The Economist.* Retrieved from http://www.economist.com/node/4321929

Weissglass, J. (2001). Racism and the achievement gap. *Education Week, 20*(43), 49–50, 72.

West, C. (2001). *Race matters.* Boston, MA: Beacon Press.

Wheatley, M. (2002). *Turning to one another: Simple conversations to restore hope to the future.* San Francisco, CA: Berrett-Koehler.

Wiggins, G., & McTighe, J. (1998). *Understanding by design.* Alexandria, VA: Association for Supervision and Curriculum Development.

Williams, B. (2003). *Closing the achievement gap. A vision for changing beliefs and practices.* Alexandria, VA: Association for Supervision and Curriculum Development.

Williams, B. (2007). Closing the achievement gaps: What's missing from the current debates. *Partnerships in Education, 1*(1), 12–14.

Williams, L. (2000). *It's the little things: The everyday interactions that get under the skin of Blacks and Whites.* New York, NY: Harcourt.

Wise, T. (2000). *Membership has its privileges: Thoughts on acknowledging and challenging whiteness.* Retrieved from http://www.zmag.org/sustainers/content/2000-06/22wise.htm

Wise, T. (2002). White like me: Race and identity through majority eyes. In B. Singley (Ed.), *When race becomes real: Black and White writers confront their personal histories* (pp. 225–240). Chicago, IL: Lawrence Hill Books.

Woods, T. (1997). *Tiger Woods on Tiger Woods.* http://www.tigerwoods.com

WRAL. (2003). *Some parents upset over proposed merger plans.* Retrieved October 13, 2003, from http://www.wral.com/education/2551687/detail.html

Index